CONTRA TERROR IN NICARAGUA

Contra Terror in Nicaragua

Report of a Fact-finding Mission:
September 1984—January 1985

by Reed Brody

South End Press   Boston, MA

Dedication

To Mompi and Prettynka
and to the memory of my mother and my uncle Cy.

Library of Congress Cataloging-in-Publication Data

Brody, Reed, 1953—
    Contra terror in Nicaragua.

    1. Nicaragua—Politics and government—1979.
2. Counterrevolutions—Nicaragua. 3. Terrorism—
Nicaragua. 4. Interviews—Nicaragua. I. Title.
F1528.B76 1985   972.85′053   85-18404
ISBN 0-89608-313-6
ISBN 0-89608-312-8 (pbk.)

Typeset, design, and layout by the South End Press collective.
Cover painting: *White Squad VIII* by Leon Golub, courtesy of
    Barbara Gladstone Gallery, NY.
Photo by David Reynolds
Cover by Todd Jailer & Lydia Sargent

Table of Contents

Acknowledgments

This report is long overdue. Since 1981, the contras have used American advice and dollars to terrorize the civilian population of Nicaragua and hardly a word about it was printed in the United States.

Some groups have tried to alert us. In a 1982 lawsuit, the Center for Constitutional Rights described numerous cases of atrocities against Nicaraguan civilians. Since 1983, Witness for Peace, a non-violent faith-based group which maintains a permanent presence in the conflict zones of Nicaragua, has documented and published accounts of countless attacks. In April and again in June 1984, Americas Watch reported that "the FDN has engaged repeatedly in killings, torture and murder of unarmed civilians." Nevertheless, the silence surrounding this systematic brutality remained such that as late as February 1985, the President of the United States felt confident enough to call its perpetrators "the moral equals of our Founding Fathers."

Part of the credit for this report's success in influencing public debate must therefore go to Sister Lisa Fitzgerald and Paul Reichler who helped me devise the methodology we used. They realized that if our investigation substantiated the findings of these other groups, the Administration would inevitably charge that our report was "Sandinista propaganda." The charge did come when the report was released, but it was hollow: each account in the report is based on the sworn affidavits of eyewitnesses who were selected and interviewed with no Nicaraguan government interference, and whose names and addresses were listed to facilitate verification. The report's accuracy was verified by several independent groups (see Appendix 1).

Team member Sister Sandra Price courageously documented some of the attacks in her remote Siuna region. On April 19, 1985, after the report had been released and widely distributed, Sister Sandra and Father Enrique Blandon, whose testimony also appears in the report, were forcibly detained by an FDN task force while making a pastoral visit. Sister Sandra reports that her captors said "they were angry because we had been saying that the contras killed campesinos, women and children." After being held for two days they were released, but Father Blandon was warned that next time he would be killed.

1

Many other people made this report possible: the long-term team of Witness for Peace in Nicaragua, especially Peter Olsen, Sister Jean Abbott and Mary Dutcher, who provided me with hospitality and help in finding witnesses; team member Jim Bordelon; Sister Margarita Navarro, Sister Andrea Balconis and Rosario Quant who transcribed and typed many of the affidavits in Managua; Judy Appelbaum, Father Evaristo Bertrand, Dick Bolles, Borinquen Camacho, Betsy Cohn, Byron Corrales, Karen Ellingston, David Fenton, Father James Feltz, Benny McCabe, Reggie Norton, Father Enrique Oggier, Sister Rachel Pinal, Judy Rabinowitz, Michael Ratner, Gretchen Sleicher and Beth Stephens. I would also like to thank the South End Press collective who helped to turn this report into a book, and who shared my sense of urgency about getting this information out to as many people as possible, as quickly as possible.

I want to give special thanks to two people: Father Alfredo Gundrum, who has stood shoulder to shoulder with the Nicaraguan people for 16 years and who opened my eyes to their hopes and sufferings; and Sister Mary Hartman, whose gracious assistance and moral support during my four months in Nicaragua made my burden a little lighter.

Most of all, however, this report belongs to the Nicaraguans whose stories it documents. People who have seen loved ones murdered before their eyes, who have been kidnapped, who have been beaten, who have been raped. People, too, of great courage. Humble, peace-loving people who had sacrificed in the insurrection against Somoza and who were not cowed into submission by the terror now being visited on them. I felt both a great privilege and a deep responsibility at being the communicator for their sufferings.

The people who were interviewed for this report come from all walks of Nicaraguan life: peasants, workers, churchpeople, merchants, professionals. Some were victimized because they are committed Sandinistas; most just happened to be in the wrong place at the wrong time. It was unpleasant for these people to relive their tragedies, often excruciating for them to supply the gory details. Providing me with their names and addresses also exposed them to the very real risk of retaliation by the contras. Few, however, declined my invitation to tell their tale: almost everyone believed that if the horrible truth were told to the American people, we would not allow the brutality committed in our name to continue. That became my hope, too, and it is the goal of this report.

Reed Kalman Brody
June, 1985

Introduction

by Reggie Norton

In June 1985, as Congress debated whether to supply so-called "humanitarian aid" to the contras, House Majority Leader Jim Wright warned that approval would mean "For the first time we're going to be saying that we are accessories to overthrowing the government of Nicaragua."[1] Both the House and the Senate voted in support of contra aid packages, handing President Reagan the equivalent of the Gulf of Tonkin Resolution which gave President Johnson a green light to escalate U.S. intervention in Vietnam.[2]

It is a moral obligation that U.S. citizens understand who the contras are and what they are doing. The first step is perhaps the most difficult: to be skeptical about what the U.S. government is saying about Nicaragua and the contras, and be open to other sources of information. When former Senator J. William Fulbright was asked by the *New York Times* to comment on the lessons of Vietnam, he replied: "Not to trust Government statements." Speaking of officials' statements on Vietnam and Central America, Fulbright added, "They fit the facts to fit the policy. We made a great mistake in Vietnam and are making another one in Central America."[3] Fulbright opposed escalating U.S. military involvement in Vietnam as chairman of the Foreign Relations Committee. We would do well to heed his words now. Already, the Nicaraguans (with a population of three-and-a-half million) have suffered almost ten times as many deaths, proportionately, as the U.S. suffered during the Vietnam war. The Brody report provides some measure of the wanton cruelty of those deaths and challenges us to condemn, rather than support, the killers.

According to the President, "The Nicaraguan people are trapped in a totalitarian dungeon." The Sandinistas, he says, have "rendered the democratic freedoms of speech, press and assembly punishable by officially sanctioned harassment, and imprisonment or death," are attacking their neighbors, smuggling drugs into the U.S., persecuting Catholics and Jews, and committing a "campaign of virtual genocide against the Miskito Indians." In the highly charged atmosphere following the hijacking of

---

Reggie Norton is a Senior Associate of the Washington Office on Latin America.

a TWA plane to Beirut, he accused Nicaragua of being part of a "confederation of terrorist states" (along with Iran, Libya, North Korea, and Cuba) that had committed "outright acts of war" against the United States. These "outlaw states," said Reagan, were "run by the strangest collection of misfits, Looney Tunes and squalid criminals since the advent of the Third Reich." In short, no epithet, however lurid or fantastic, has been spared in an effort to convince the American public to support the campaign against Nicaragua.

The contras, on the other hand, are lauded as "freedom fighters." Many of the contras, says President Reagan, "are anti-Somoza heroes" who "have been denied any part in the new government because they truly wanted democracy and still do." President Reagan has saluted the contras as the "moral equal of our Founding Fathers." Such an equation is a grave insult to the people of the United States. If anything, the contras may be equated to the Tory forces which sided with the British Crown in opposing the American Revolution. Indeed, the contras are far more vicious. The chief of military operations for Misura, one of the contra forces supported by the U.S. government, actually told a reporter:

> "I love killing; I have been killing for the past seven years. There's nothing I like better. If I could, I'd kill several people a day."[4]

The Brody report is a particularly valuable document because it reveals the reality of contra activities in Nicaragua. Other reports have exposed the distortions underlying many of the President's charges against Nicaragua. The July 1985 report by the internationally-respected human rights organization America's Watch, *Human Rights in Nicaragua: Reagan, Rhetoric and Reality*, finds the Reagan Administration approach to Nicaraguan human rights to be "deceptive and harmful." The report states:

> The Administration's accusations against Nicaragua rest upon a core of fact; the Sandinistas have committed serious abuses, especially in 1981 and 1982, including arbitrary arrests and the summary relocation of thousands of Miskito Indians. Around the core of fact, however, U.S. officials have built an edifice of innuendo and exaggeration. The misuse of human rights data has become pervasive...When inconvenient, findings of the U.S. Embassy in Managua have been ignored; the same is true of data gathered by independent sources.
>
> In Nicaragua there is no systematic practice of forced disappearances, extrajudicial killings or torture— as has been the case with the "friendly" armed forces of El Salvador. While prior censorship has been imposed by emergency legislation, debate on major social and political questions is robust, outspoken, even often

strident. The November 1984 elections, though deficient, were a democratic advance over the past five decades of Nicaraguan history and compare favorably with those of El Salvador and Guatemala and do not suffer significantly by comparison with those of Honduras, Mexico or Panama. The Sandinista party obtained a popular mandate, while the opposition parties that chose to participate secured some 30 percent of the seats in the Constituent Assembly. Nor has the Government practiced elimination of cultural or ethnic groups, as the Administration frequently claims; indeed in this respect, as in most others, Nicaragua's record is by no means so bad as that of Guatemala, whose government the Administration consistently defends. Moreover, some notable reductions in abuses have occurred in Nicaragua since 1982, despite the pressure caused by escalating external attacks...

[The] description of a totalitarian state bears no resemblance to Nicaragua in 1985.

Why Believe This Report

When Reed Brody first approached the Washington Office on Latin America (WOLA)—a private church-supported, human-rights organization—to help publicize his original report we showed immediate interest. Brody is a former Assistant Attorney General of the State of New York. His documentation of contra atrocities appeared more meticulous than any produced to date and carried several important indices of credibility. The report contained 145 sworn affidavits, some of which described incidents with which I was already familiar from U.S. religious persons working in Nicaragua. Each statement in the report was supported by at least one, and often several, sworn affidavits from witnesses whose names and addresses were provided for verification purposes. However, because Brody had approached WOLA through an introduction provided by Paul Reichler, a Washington lawyer who represents the Nicaraguan government, we decided that before publicizing the report WOLA would independently verify its findings.

WOLA carried out a joint investigation with the International Human Rights Law Group in February 1985. Attorney Donald Fox, a member of the executive committee of the American Association for the International Commission of Jurists, and Professor Michael Glennon, of the University of Cincinnati Law School and former legal counsel to the Senate Foreign Relations Committee, conducted the investigation; neither Fox nor Glennon were previously associated with WOLA or the International Human Rights Law Group. Kathleen Bertelsen, aide to Representative Sam Gejdenson (D-Connecticut), participated as an investigation observer.

In a meeting with officials at the State Department, who insisted upon anonymity, Fox and Glennon were told that the contras had two objectives: "debilitation of the Nicaraguan economy" and "killing Nicaraguan soldiers." The April 1985 report by Fox and Glennon found contra targets to be much less limited, and corroborated Brody's findings:

*The preponderance of the evidence indicates that the contras are committing serious abuses against civilians. They include torture, rape, kidnapping, mutilation, and murder.

*The incidents appear to involve intentional attacks on unarmed civilians, persons who are protected under international law. Many involved large numbers of contras, reasonably indicating the presence of commanding officers, and thus negating the idea that abuses are committed only by "renegade" contras.

*The ten affidavits in Mr. Brody's report which were investigated at random proved materially accurate. Based on this sampling, and other samplings performed by private organizations and news media (discussed below-ed.), the probability is that the other affidavits are genuine.

On March 7, 1985, the *New York Times* ran a front-page story reporting on four incidents chosen at random from the Brody report. Two that correspondent Larry Rohter had corroborated were also corroborated by CBS News. Americas Watch spotchecked Brody's findings, confirming them as background to their March 1985 report *Violations of the Laws of War by Both Sides in Nicaragua*, which found that:

> Contra forces have systematically violated the applicable laws of war throughout the conflict. They have attacked civilians indiscriminately; they have tortured and mutilated prisoners; they have murdered those placed *hors de combat* by their wounds; they have taken hostages; and they have committed outrages against personal dignity.

The Americas Watch report found that on the Nicaraguan government side there had also been abuses, but there was a sharp decline in violations of the laws of war following 1982.

A senior State Department official responded to the Americas Watch charges about the contras by saying, "It seems to be what you would expect to have in a war." Another administration official commented, "What we see is that the Sandinista casualties are usually legitimate battle victims," adding, "The contras have a tendency to kidnap young girls."[5]

In an April follow-up report, Americas Watch reconfirmed its earlier findings and concluded that "the contras—particularly the largest of the contra forces, the Fuerza Democratica Nicaraguense (FDN)—practice terror as a deliberate policy." After reviewing the Brody affidavits and being briefed on the WOLA-sponsored investigation by aide Kathleen Bertelsen, Representative Gejdenson issued a statement condemning the contras as a "band of roving terrorists":

> What economic objective or military gain is there to be had in killing a five year old child, or in raping a grandmother? What military objective can be found in slaughtering a young bride in front of her parents, or in burning the home of a coffee picker, or in slitting the throat of an old man? The only achievement is that of imposing a climate of total fear. And therein lies the contra's objective: to blanket the population in fear.
>
> The most disturbing thing in all of this is that these acts of brutality cannot be simply attributed to the errant behavior of a few renegade contras. It appears to be the conscious policy of the contra leadership and it permeates the whole force. Disregard for internationally accepted standards of conduct regarding the treatment of civilians in conflict appears to be systematic.
>
> There are, to be sure, legitimate criticisms of the Sandinista government to be made, but we also have to ask, if the contras win, what kind of government would they put in place? What respect would there be for the rule of law imposed by men who savagely murder any who refuse to join them? What freedom of speech, religion, or press would there be under men who silence people by slashing their throats?
>
> As Americans we cannot countenance complicity in systematic brutality. If further review substantiates the material in this report, the President's request for more covert aid cannot be approved without making us knowing accomplices to the contras' crimes.

Fox and Glennon found that most Nicaraguans they met did not believe that U.S. citizens really knew what the contras were doing. If the people of the United States had a real say over U.S. policy, thought Nicaraguans, they would be on their side, recognize their desperate poverty, and understand that Nicaraguans "just want to live in peace." They would not, to use Gejdenson's words, be knowing accomplices to the contras' crimes.

"Intentional Ignorance"

In their talks with State Department officials, Fox and Glennon were told that these officials were not appraised of the validity of Brody's allegations about contra atrocities because they did not know what was going on in the field. U.S. intelligence had not been "tasked" to report on this. A high-ranking State Department official described the situation as "intentional ignorance."

In fact, the U.S. government is less intentionally ignorant than intentionally complicit. The CIA prepared a handbook for contra forces, *Psychological Operations in Guerrilla Warfare*, which called for the "Selective Use of Violence for Propagandistic Effects." The infamous CIA manual advised, "It is possible to neutralize carefully selected and planned targets such as [judges], police and State Security officials, CDS chiefs, etc." Neutralize is common CIA/military parlance for assassinate. Those targeted explicitly include civilian judges, community leaders, and government officials. After copies of this manual were circulated in the United States, it was rightly condemned by Congress. Yet, the atrocities continue, wrapped in a new cocoon of intentional ignorance. Indeed, intentional ignorance is an essential part of the strategy for selling the contra war to the U.S. public.

The administration's "public response to the gathering of information about abuses by the contras," observes Americas Watch, "has been to try to discredit those who publicize such information."[6] One State Department official characterized the reports documenting contra abuses as "a concerted propaganda campaign by the Sandinista government." The Reagan administration reacted aggressively to the release of the Brody report on March 7, 1985 by WOLA and the International Human Rights Law Group. Elliott Abrams, then Assistant Secretary of State for Human Rights and Humanitarian Affairs, and now Assistant Secretary of State for Inter-American Affairs, dismissed the report as "bought and paid for by the Sandinistas." President Reagan blasted the report in an April 15 address to the Nicaraguan Refugee Fund, shortly before a round of congressional votes on contra aid which Reagan was to lose (albeit temporarily):

> Just a few weeks ago, the whole world was treated to a so-called "independent investigation" of charges that the freedom fighters have committed atrocities. It spoke of these so-called "atrocities" in a rather riveting manner. And the report received great attention on television and in leading newspapers and publications. The report ignored communist brutality, the murder of the Indians and the arrest, torture and murder of political dissidents. But we really shouldn't be surprised by that, because, as our State Department discovered and Time Magazine reported, this so-called independent investigation was the work of one of dictator Ortega's supporters, a sympathizer who has openly embraced Sandinismo and who was shepherded through Nicaragua by Sandinista operatives.

Uninterested in investigating the substance of Brody's allegations, and risk discrediting its own case, the Reagan Administration attempted to smear Brody. *New York Times* columnist Anthony Lewis accused Reagan of Orwellian language and McCarthyite tactics. "Anyone who disagrees with his version of the Truth is an agent of the enemy," wrote Lewis on April 18, 1985. Lewis continued, "And so we see the President of the United States charging that honorable lawyers and human rights specialists who meticulously traced terrorist actions by the contras were 'bought and paid for by the Sandinistas.' It could have been said by Joe McCarthy."

The facts behind the Brody report, as explained in the original introduction and reproduced in this version, dispute the Reagan Administration's claims that Brody is an agent of Sandinista "disinformation." Brody used his own savings to finance the trip, and, for example, on the few occasions where he relied on the Nicaraguan government for transportation, he was taken to a location which he had selected and was not accompanied when he sought out witnesses.

Perhaps the seamiest episode in the administration's campaign against Brody occured when a press conference was staged to present one Bayardo de Jesus Payan. Payan, who had worked as an accountant for the Nicaraguan government, alleged that Brody's affidavits came from "manipulated peasants" whose accounts were altered to exclude positive statements they had supposedly made about the contras. Payan also alleged that Brody had received funding from the Nicaraguan government and that Brody "had asked Nicaraguans to vote for Sandinista leader Daniel Ortega in the November elections at the same time he interviewed them" about contra attacks. Only after Payan's charges were picked up by *Time* Magazine and the *Washington Times* (a paper owned by the church of Revered Sun Myung Moon, which has raised funds for the contras), and referred to by President Reagan, did the truth emerge at hearings before the House Foreign Affairs Committee Western Hemisphere Subcommittee.

At the April hearings, Payan admitted that his half-brother was the contra commander Luis Moreno Payan, better known as "Mike Lima," now in charge of operations (G-3) for the FDN general staff and formerly head of the Diriangen regional command which was implicated in various atrocities, including the October 18, 1983 attack on Pantasma in which 40 civilians were murdered. Under Somoza, Mike Lima had been a member of the National Guard's elite special forces (EEBI). Information received by our office indicates the likelihood that Mike Lima arranged for Payan to leave Nicaragua and come to the United States. More to the point, Payan was forced to admit when questioned at the hearings that, not having accompanied Brody during the interviews, he had no information on them; that he had not read the

Brody report; and that he was not in a position to say if the accounts were accurate.[7]

On May 21, a month after Reed Brody and others testified to Congress about contra atrocities, President Reagan gave this Boy Scout portrait of the contras in a speech to the Council of the Americas:

> I might point out something here that's rather of interest. Our [National Security Adviser] Bud McFarlane was in Central America not too long ago and he was talking to the contra leaders there. And he asked them—he said— apropos of what the guerrillas are doing in El Salvador and the attacks they're making on these vital structures—he said, "Why—if you're trying to put pressure on your government here—why don't you attack some of these vital strategic targets?" And to show you the difference between the contras and the guerrillas, the contras said, "No, that would hurt the people and we're of the people. We're not going to do that." I think they deserve our support.

Of course, the President neglected to mention that the CIA had prepared an illustrated manual for Nicaraguans, entitled *The Freedom Fighter's Manual* (referred to in the Ocotal chapter in the Brody report), which encouraged nearly forty methods of economic sabotage with the goal of "paralyzing the military-industrial complex of the traitorous Marxist state." Since 1980, the contras have blown up key bridges and attacked industrial plants, fishing boats, agricultural cooperatives and private farms, health clinics and hospitals, schools, childcare centers, and food storage facilities. In 1983 CIA-directed commandos rocketed oil storage tanks in the port of Corinto, destroying fuel, medicine and other supplies, and forcing the evacuation of over 25,000 residents. Setting dangerous precedents for terrorist action, CIA-supplied aircraft bombed Nicaragua's international airport in Managua in 1983 and CIA operatives mined Nicaraguan harbors in 1984.

"Of the People?"

The main contra force, the FDN, grew out of the September 15th Legion which was established by Somoza's National Guardsmen who had fled into neighboring Honduras, El Salvador, and Guatemala as the Sandinistas took power in July 1979. A July 1982 Defense Intelligence Agency Weekly Summary described the September 15th Legion as "a terrorist group." Some 50,000 Nicaraguans had died in the revolution to rout the National Guard and overthrow the 44-year Somoza family dictatorship. National Guardsmen were responsible for the rape, torture, and wounding of thousands of other Nicaraguan women, men, and children. In

June 1979 the U.S. public had received an eye-opening dose of Somocista brutality when National Guardsmen murdered ABC news reporter Bill Stewart in view of a television camera (in a film about the Nicaraguan revolution, "Under Fire," Gene Hackman plays a character whose execution by National Guardsmen recalls the Stewart murder).

The Sandinistas outlawed the death penalty upon taking power and established a maximum prison term of 30 years. Many National Guardsmen were pardoned, and most who were sentenced in special tribunals received light prison sentences. While many ex-guardsmen integrated themselves into the new Nicaragua, many others began mounting raids from across the Honduran border. Among the early victims of contra terror were seven literacy teachers—volunteers in the 1980 National Literacy Crusade which reduced Nicaraguan illiteracy from 50 to 12 percent.

Reagan officials showed early sympathy for the contra cause. During the 1980 Presidential campaign, Reagan and his advisers blasted the Carter Administration for failing to save the Somoza dictatorship and showed total hostility to the new Nicaraguan government, although such U.S.-oriented figures as Arturo Cruz were given high posts (Cruz served as a member of the Junta of National Reconstruction, president of Nicaragua's national bank, and Ambassador to the United States). The 1980 Republican Platform asserted:

> We deplore the Marxist Sandinista takeover of Nicaragua and the attempts to destabilize El Salvador, Guatemala, and Honduras...We oppose the Carter administration aid program for the government of Nicaragua. However, we will support the efforts of the Nicaraguan people to establish a free and independent government... We will return to the fundamental principle of treating a friend as a friend and self-proclaimed enemies as enemies, without apology.

The Sandinistas became branded enemies not through self-proclamation, but rather through the machinations of a self-fulfilling prophecy which the United States is attempting to impose upon Nicaragua. In March 1984 a "U.S. diplomat in Honduras" described the contra role this way:

> The contras are strictly an instrument of pressure. Some people around here and in Washington really thought— and still do, I guess—that they could incite an insurrection and overthrow the Sandinistas. I always thought that was a lot of crap. But in any event, the theory was that we couldn't lose. If they took Managua, wonderful. If not, the idea was that the Sandinistas would react one of two ways. Either they'd liberalize and stop exporting revolution [sic], which is fine and dandy, or they'd tighten up, alienate their own people, their international

support and their backers in the United States, in the long run making themselves much more vulnerable. In a way, that one was even better—or so the idea went.[8]

By 1980, Nicaraguan exiles were being trained at camps run by Cuban exiles in Florida (in 1960, the U.S. had used Nicaragua as a staging area for the unsuccessful Bay of Pigs invasion). Although the contra camps received increasing attention in the press in 1981 and the Nicaraguans spoke openly of their goal of overthrowing the Sandinistas, no action was ever taken by the U.S. Department of Justice to enforce the Neutrality Act. In December 1981, President Reagan signed a secret directive authorizing an expenditure of $19 million to conduct paramilitary operations against Nicaragua. Reagan Administration officials claimed before congressional intelligence committees that the purpose of contra aid was interdicting arms allegedly being supplied to the Salvadoran revolutionaries by the Nicaraguan government. However, in the words of former Ambassador to El Salvador Deane Hinton, "not one pistola" has been interdicted. David MacMichael, a CIA intelligence analyst from 1981 to 1983, charged in June 1984 that the CIA had "systematically misrepresented" Nicaraguan aid to the Salvadoran rebels. Since April 1981, he said, there had been no verified reports of arms shipments from Nicaragua to El Salvador.[9]

The Reagan administration thwarted public opinion, Congress, and the World Court as it spent more than $100 million in four years of financing the contras and carried out the mining of Nicaraguan harbors and other acts of war. In 1982 the House of Representatives had passed the Boland amendment, forbidding activities aimed at overthrowing the government of Nicaragua or provoking a military exchange between Nicaragua and Honduras. On May 10, 1984, the International Court of Justice (World Court) ruled unanimously that the U.S. should immediately halt any attempts to mine or blockade Niaraguan ports, and 14 to one that Nicaragua's political independence "Should be fully respected and should not be jeopardized by any military or paramilitary activities." The Court included judges from U.S. allies, including Great Britain, France, Italy, Japan, and West Germany. The Reagan Administration declared it would not accept World Court decisions regarding Central America for two years.

Over time, the arms interdiction rationale was forgotten as the Reagan administration challenged Congress and the public to rally behind the so-called democratic "freedom fighters." At a press conference on February 21, 1985 Reagan responded to a question about whether his goal was to remove the Nicaraguan government this way: "remove it in the sense of its present structure, in which it is a communist, totalitarian state and it is not a government chosen by the people." Asked if this was not tantamount to seeking its overthrow, Reagan responded, "Not if the present government would turn around and say—all right—if they'd say 'uncle'..."

CONTRAdictions

In testimony before Congress in January 1985, then Assistant Secretary of State for International Affairs Langhorne Motley, claimed:

> The freedom fighters are peasants, farmers, shopkeepers, and vendors. Their leaders are without exception men who opposed Somoza.

In fact, former Somoza National Guard officers have dominated the military hierarchy of the FDN, the main contra force which has received the bulk of U.S. support. In a staff report, the Congressional Arms Control and Foreign Policy Caucus found that 46 of the 48 positions in the FDN's military command structure are held by former guardsmen: Strategic Commander, Regional Command Coordinator, all five members of the general staff, four out of five Central Commanders, five out of six regional commanders, and all thirty task force commanders. (The full report, "Who are the Contras?", appears in Appendix Two.)

To counter this Somocista reality, the CIA created a new six-member "political directorate," unveiled at a December 1982 press conference in Miami. Edgar Chamorro, chief public spokesman for the contra directorate until November 1984, recalls that the directorate was established "in a great hurry...in a week. We complained about this. They were just improvising, reacting to things. They said...they had to repackage the program in a way to be palatable to Congress."[10] The day before the press conference, the CIA held a briefing and rehearsal. Chamorro recalls:

> [CIA agent Tony] Feldman introduced two lawyers from Washington who briefed us on the Neutrality Act, the American law prohibiting private citizens from waging war on another country from U.S. territory. Feldman was worried we were going to tell the press that we were trying to overthrow the Sandinistas, which, of course, is exactly what we wanted to do. He emphasized that we should say instead that we were trying to "create conditions for democracy." After the briefing we asked each other the questions we were likely to face in the morning...
> "Have you had any contact with U.S. government officials?"
> The CIA men agreed there was no way to finesse this one. We simply had to lie and say, "No."[11]

Chamorro was ousted by the FDN because of his candor about the contra's standard practice of killing Sandinista prisoners and collaborators—later he would write "It was like stomping on a cockroach to them,"—his criticism of the CIA terror manual, and his outspoken assertion that "The Americans built up the contras officially to stop the flow of weapons from Nicaragua to El

Salvador. Privately, they promised us on many different occasions that they were helping us to overthrow the Nicaraguan government."[12] In 1983, in a further effort to display a non-Somocista appearance, the FDN had appointed Adolfo Calero as "President." Calero had been the Coca-Cola franchise holder in Nicaragua and is the former leader of the Conservative Party, the traditional rival of the so-called Liberal Party, which the Somozas came to dominate. Directorate member Alfonso Callejas, who served as Vice President under Somoza, admitted to the *Los Angeles Times* of March 4, 1985, that the civilians were treated as mere front men.

Edgar Chamorro wrote of his role as both a front man for the ex-guardsmen and the CIA in a *New York Times* op. ed. piece of June 24, 1985:

> My experience as a former rebel leader convinced me that the Nicaraguan Democratic Force cannot contribute to the democratization of Nicaragua. The rebels are in the hands of former National Guardsmen who control the contra army, stifle internal dissent and intimidate or murder those who oppose them. The rebels have been subject to manipulation by the Central Intelligence Agency, which has reduced it to a front operation.
>
> For example, in January 1984 after the C.I.A. mined Nicaragua's harbors, I was awakened at my "safe house" in Tegucigalpa [Honduras] at 2 A.M. by an anxious CIA agent. He handed me a press release written in perfect Spanish by CIA officials. I was surprised to read its claim that the Democratic Force had laid these mines. I was instructed to read this announcement on our clandestine radio state before the Sandinistas broke the news.
>
> Of course, we had no role in mining the harbors. Ironically, two months later, when a Soviet ship struck a mine, the same agent appeared. Out of fear of creating an international incident, he ordered us to deny that one of "our" mines had done the damage.

Nicaraguans commonly refer to the contra forces as the hated "Guardia." After four years of fighting, the contras have never captured and held any populated areas and remain tied to their bases in Honduras and Costa Rica. A contra government imposed by the United States would mean a new reign of terror for Nicaraguans. About a year-and-a-half before his conversion to open support of the contras in late 1984, Arturo Cruz expressed his fears of a contra takeover in an article in *Foreign Affairs*:

> Carrying perhaps an even greater responsiblity, those who sustain the forces inimical to the Sandinistas must not ignore the fact that idealist young boys and girls constitute the Revolution's rank and file. Therefore,

those who aid insurrection in my country—whose disen-
chantment with the Revolution's course and concern for
the security of their own country I do not dispute—
should be aware of the risk they take of bearing a
historical responsibility for contributing, albeit indirectly and unintentionally, to a possible mass execution
of the flower of our youth. A line of distinction should be
drawn, now more than ever, between "contras" and
armed dissidents [i.e. Eden Pastora, who Cruz sees as
seeking the redemption of the revolution rather than its
destruction].[13]

In a conversation over lunch in September 1983, Cruz told me
that Adolfo Calero had recently told him that if he expected to
wield any power in a victorious FDN, he was being overly
optimistic. At a later meeting, in June 1984, Cruz told me that he
had been talking with the "Key Biscayne mafia," the contra
leadership, and they had threatened that when they returned to
power they would hold a series of "Nuremberg" trials and Cruz
would be among the first to be tried. Cruz said he told them that he
would pay for his own air ticket to Managua to stand in the dock
and answer the charges. He recalled that when he told this to
Calero, Calero responded he would stand in the dock beside him.
Moreover, says Cruz, the "Key Biscayne mafia" threatened that
when they took power "the first persons they would hang from the
trees" would be the "Sandinistas arrepentidos," former Sandinistas who were now sorry for their temporary Sandinista association.

By January 1985, Cruz had become a public supporter of U.S.
aid to the contras. At a January 3 press conference, when asked
about charges of contra atrocities, Cruz blamed Sandinista "lack
of care." "If there is a truck with civilians and soldiers in it, it's
hard for the contras to know if it is a military or civilian group," he
asserted.[14] Cruz later lobbied Congress for renewed aid to the
contras, and on March 2, 1985 he embraced the "Key Biscayne
mafia" in the "Document on National Dialogue of the National
Resistance," issued in San Jose, Costa Rica. Cruz is now one of
three leaders of the United Nicaraguan Opposition (UNO) along
with Adolfo Calero and Alfonso Robelo, President of the Nicaraguan Democratic Movement (MDN), a faction of the contra
alliance ARDE. Eden Pastora, formerly Vice Minister of Defense
in the Sandinista-led government, and Miskito leader Brooklyn
Rivera of MISURASATA remain outside the UNO. The Nicaraguan government held a series of negotiations with Rivera in 1985,
but while some progress was made on amnesty for prisoners,
resettlement of Indian villagers, and other issues, the talks broke
down in May, in part over Rivera's demand that the Nicaraguan
government withdraw all troops from a large region of the
Atlantic Coast.

In April 1985, Arturo Cruz admitted that he had secretly
received money from organizations linked to the CIA.[15] Cruz has

been molded by the Reagan Administration as the democratic, "centrist" alternative to both Somocismo and alleged Sandinista totalitarianism. His on-again, off-again candidacy became the measure of legitimacy for the November 1984 Nicaraguan elections, much to the dismay of some Nicaraguan opposition leaders who did not live outside the country as did Cruz. After months of negotiations with Nicaraguan government officials, Cruz and the Democratic Coordinating Committee (CDN or Coordinadora)—an alliance of conservative political parties and the Superior Council of Private Enterprise (COSEP)—stayed out of the electoral process. The U.S. government labeled the elections a "Soviet-style sham." In the words of former *New York Times* senior editor John Oakes, "The most fraudulent thing about the Nicaraguan election was the part the Reagan Administration played in it. By their own admission, United States Embassy officials in Managua pressured opposition politicians to withdraw from the ballot in order to isolate the Sandinistas and to discredit the regime."

With over 75 percent of the registered electorate voting, the Sandinista National Liberation Front (FSLN) won 67 percent of the legally valid ballots (63 percent of total votes), electing Daniel Ortega as President and Sergio Ramirez Vice President, and giving the Sandinistas 61 of 96 seats in the new National Assembly. Most international observers—including the British Parliamentary Human Rights Group delegation, the Latin American Studies Association Delegation, and the observer mission sent by WOLA and the International Human Rights Law Group— deemed the elections to be free and fair, notwithstanding specific shortcomings cited by particular delegations. A system of proportional representation ensures the opposition parties a stronger voice in the National Assembly than a U.S.-style system would have. The Democratic Conservative Party (PCD), for example, has fourteen seats.

It's Not Too Late

Clearly, Nicaragua is not a totalitarian state and, just as clearly, the contras are not humanitarian "freedom fighters." It is not too late for the U.S. to stop supporting the contra terrorists and negotiate a peace agreement with Nicaragua. The foundation has already been laid in the bilateral talks in Manzanillo, Mexico which the U.S. broke off in Janaury 1985, and in the Contadora process.

In September 1984 Nicaragua signed a Contadora draft treaty which had been endorsed by the four sponsors—Mexico, Venezuela, Colombia, and Panama—after 20 months of negotiations with Central American nations. The treaty contained provisions for the withdrawal of foreign military advisers, prohibition of foreign military bases and interference in the internal affairs of other countries, controls on the level of arms and troops in the region, and support for the establishment of conditions for free elections. The Reagan administration encouraged Honduras, El Salvador, and Costa Rica to object to the treaty as unverifiable and favorable to Nicaragua. The real problem with the treaty was that it was unbiased, and not favorable to the United States. That is, it would prohibit U.S. military bases and advisers in the region—not just Cuban—and it would require suspension of aid to the contras. The Nicaraguans remain committed to the Contadora process and are very keen to resume the Manzanillo talks.

The Reagan administration prefers the "removal" of the Sandinista government to a Contadora Peace Treaty. A series of articles in the *New York Times* in June 1985 spelled out U.S. military preparations for an invasion of Nicaragua and reported that a growing number of U.S. government officials believe that a majority of Nicaraguans would welcome such an invasion. This dangerous assertion flies in the face of evidence from the elections and the battlefield. In over four years of fighting, the contras have never captured or held any populated area, and remain dependent upon their bases in neighboring countries.

The contras can terrorize the Nicaraguan people, and disrupt their new programs of social justice, but they cannot overthrow the Nicaraguan government. Only United States troops can put the contras in power, as they did the Somozas, at a cost of thousands of Nicaraguan and U.S. lives. The Sandinistas would lead guerrilla forces in a campaign to drive them out again. After reading the following report, let us hope that U.S. citizens will not permit the U.S. government to continue repeating the crimes of the past.

1. *Congressional Quarterly*, June 15, 1985, p.1139.

2. According to "A Statement on the Nature of Humanitarian Assistance" by U.S. Private and Voluntary Organizations, under the Geneva Conventions only civilians and noncombatants can claim humanitarian aid. Government donors must be recognized as neutral parties. Clearly, the contras do not qualify.

3. *New York Times*, April 30, 1985.

4. Remarks made to Jon Lee Anderson, associate of Jack Anderson, quoted in Jack Anderson, "CIA Joins with Extremists in Nicaraguan War," *Washington Post*, September 30, 1984, cited in an Americas Watch Report, *Human Rights in Nicaragua: Reagan, Rhetoric and Reality*, New York, July 1985.

5. *New York Times*, March 6, 1985.

6. An Americas Watch Report, *Violations of the Laws of War by Both Sides in Nicaragua 1981-1985, First Supplement*, New York, June 1985.

7. *U.S. Support for the Contras*, Hearing before the Subcommittee on Western Hemisphere Affairs of the Committee on Foreign Affairs, House of Representatives, April 16, 17, and 18, 1985, Washington, D.C.

8. Allan Nairn, "Endgame: A Special Report on U.S. Military Strategy in Central America," *NACLA: Report on the Americas*, May-June 1984.

9. See "Ex-CIA Analyst Disputes U.S. Aides on Nicaragua," *Washington Post*, June 13, 1984 and "In From the Cold and Hot for the Truth," *New York Times*, June 11, 1984.

10. *Los Angeles Times*, March 4, 1985.

11. Edgar Chamorro with Jefferson Morley, "Confessions of a 'Contra,'" *New Republic*, August 5, 1985.

12. Central American Historical Institute, *Update*, July 1984, 3:24.

13. Arturo J. Cruz, "Nicaragua's Imperiled Revolution," *Foreign Affairs*, Summer 1983.

14. *New York Times*, January 4, 1985.

15. See *Wall Street Journal*, April 23, 1985 and *Washington Post*, April 25, 1985.

Attacks by the Nicaraguan "Contras" on the Civilian Population of Nicaragua: Introduction to the Report

For the past three years, counterrevolutionary armed forces, commonly known as "contras," have carried on a guerrilla war in Nicaragua. Although unable to capture or hold any sizeable town or populated area, the contras have inflicted numerous casualties and caused substantial damage to the Nicaraguan economy. That much has been widely reported. Recently, however, accounts have surfaced with increasing regularity, and from a variety of sources, that the contras are directing their attacks against civilian targets—such as workers in the northern provinces attempting to harvest the coffee crop—and that these attacks have resulted in assassination, torture, rape, kidnapping and mutilation of civilians.

To probe the veracity of these reports, a fact-finding team, led by Reed Brody, a U.S. lawyer who volunteered his time, spent from September 1984 to January 1985 in Nicaragua. The team set out to locate victims and other eyewitnesses to contra attacks throughout northern and north-central Nicaragua—including Nicaraguan peasants and workers, as well as U.S. priests, nuns and lay pastoral workers—interview them, and obtain sworn affidavits recounting in their own words what they had seen or experienced. This report contains the results of this investigation.

The contra activities described in this report were carried out by the Fuerzas Democraticas Nicaraguenses (FDN) and its ally Misura. The FDN, by far the largest of the contra forces, operates in northwestern Nicaragua, along the border with Honduras and in central mountain areas. It began operations in 1980 and was officially founded in November 1981 under the military direction of Enrique Bermudez, a Colonel in the old National Guard and former President Anastasio Somoza's military attache in Washington. According to a 1985 report by the staff of the Congressional Arms Control and Foreign Policy Caucus, "46 of the 48 positions in the FDN command structure are held by former Guardsmen. (This report is reproduced in this book as Appendix Two.) Misura, a smaller force, operates in northeastern Nicaragua under the command of Steadman Fagoth, a Miskito Indian. Other small groups, operating in the south near the border with Costa Rica and whose activities are not examined in this report, are ARDE, led by Alfonso Robelo; the Frente Revolucionario Sandino, directed by Eden Pastora; and Misurasata, headed by Brooklyn Rivera.

The report is divided into 28 chapters, each one devoted to one incident, or to a series of incidents in the same vicinity or of the same nature. Each incident described in the report is substantiated by the eyewitness testimony of at least one, and usually several, affiants, and specific citations to the sources of each account are provided. The sworn affidavits themselves—145 in all—are available from the Washington Office on Latin America, 110 Maryland Ave. N.E., Washington DC 20002.

The investigation was structured to be as objective and professional as possible. A rigorous standard was applied: the report would include only those incidents and events that could be substantiated by reliable evidence of a kind that would be legally sufficient in a court of law. Thus, all of the facts presented here are based on direct eyewitness testimony. Each witness was reminded of the importance of relating only what he or she personally saw or experienced, and not what he or she had heard or read in the newspapers. (Parish priests and nuns, however, were allowed to testify generally about incidents they could verify in their parishes.) Each witness was challenged by the interviewer with questions designed to confirm the witness' *personal* knowledge of the events related ("Did you actually see that?" "What color were their uniforms?"). In most cases, the account of one witness was corroborated by the similar accounts of as many as fifteen others. Despite these precautions, it is possible that some of the testimony given to the team was false or exaggerated. Where the credibility of a witness was considered doubtful for any reason, however, the statement was excluded from the report.

Each witness' statement has been signed under oath. In some cases, the witness' testimony was initially tape-recorded and a transcription then typed and presented to the witness for signature at a second meeting. In most cases, the interviewer wrote down the testimony by hand and presented the handwritten transcript for signature. In each case, the affidavit was carefully read by (or to) the affiant, who made any corrections needed before swearing to its truth and signing it.

Each affidavit completely identifies the affiant by name (both patronymic and matronymic surnames), age, location, and, in most cases also by place of birth and complete mother's and father's names. This ensures that the authenticity of the statements can be subject to further verification. Some witnesses expressed their fear that by identifying themselves they would expose themselves to the danger of retaliation by the contras. Very few people declined the team's invitation to speak on the record, however. To the contrary, most appeared eager to tell their story.

The interviews were conducted during several trips to the areas of Nicaragua where the contra attacks have been the heaviest. In the northern provinces of Esteli, Madriz and Nueva Segovia the investigating team visited several individual towns and farms that had been attacked. In the provinces of Matagalpa and Jinotega the ongoing attacks made it impossible to travel outside the provincial capitals, so refugees and others from the outlying areas who could be found in the capitals were interviewed. In the northern Atlantic Coast region, for the same reason, the interviews were conducted with people in the provincial capital of Puerto Cabezas, with the exception of those conducted during a visit to the Miskito resettlement town of Sumubila. Still other witnesses were brought to Managua or to other locations by their parish priests and were interviewed there when it was impossible to visit the site of the incident.

After arriving in an area in which contra attacks were reported to have occurred, the investigators located survivors and witnesses through discussions with local religious people, local officials, health workers, and chance acquaintances. The Nicaraguan government was helpful in issuing a travel permit to the Atlantic Coast, providing transportation to remote or embattled areas when necessary and, on occasion, indicating where witnesses might be found. The Nicaraguan government did not, however, interfere in any way in the selection of witnesses or the interview process. All witnesses were selected solely by the investigative team (with the exception of one instance, noted in the text), and all interviews were conducted *outside* the presence of government or party officials.

This report is not intended to be exhaustive: because attacks on the civilian population of Nicaragua appear to occur frequently, this report by necessity can only cover a small sampling of them. (A more comprehensive chronology of contra attacks is provided in Appendix Three.) Even in the localities to which an entire chapter is devoted, the investigators could not attempt to inquire into every incident of which they were made aware, let alone interview every witness. Those incidents that have been investigated, however, reveal a distinct pattern, indicating that contra activities often include:

—attacks on purely civilian targets resulting in the killing of unarmed men, women, children and the elderly;

—premeditated acts of brutality including rape, beatings, mutilation and torture;

—individual and mass kidnapping of civilians, particularly in the northern Atlantic Coast region, for the purpose of forced recruitment into the contra forces and the creation of a hostage refugee population in Honduras;

—assaults on economic and social targets such as farms, cooperatives, food storage facilities and health centers, including a particular effort to disrupt the coffee harvests through attacks on coffee cooperatives and on vehicles carrying volunteer coffee harvesters;

—intimidation of civilians who participate or cooperate in

government or community programs such as distribution of sub-
sidized food products, rural cooperatives, education and the local
self-defense militias; and

—kidnapping, intimidation, and even murder of religious
leaders who support the government, including priests and clergy-
trained lay pastors.

Following are some excerpts from the affidavits themselves:

—Digna Barreda de Ubeda, a mother of two from Esteli, was
kidnapped by the contras in May 1983:

> [F]ive of them raped me at about five in the evening.-
> ..they had gang-raped me every day. When my vagina
> couldn't take it any more, they raped me through my
> rectum. I calculate that in five days they raped me 60
> times. (Chapter 28.)

She also watched contra forces beat her husband and gouge out
the eyes of another civilian before killing him.

—Doroteo Tinoco Valdivia, testifying about an attack in April
1984 on his farming cooperative near Yali, Jinotega:

> They had already destroyed all that was the coopera-
> tive: a coffee drying machine, the two dormitories for the
> coffee cutters, the electricity generators, seven cows, the
> plant, the food warehouse.
>
> There was one boy about 15 years old, who was
> retarded and suffered from epilepsy. We had left him in a
> bomb shelter.
>
> When we returned...we saw...that they had cut his
> throat, then they cut open his stomach and left his intes-
> tines hanging out on the ground like a string.
>
> They did the same to Juan Corrales who had already
> died from a bullet in the fighting. They opened him up
> and took out his intestines and cut off his testicles.
> (Chapter 14.)

—Roger Briones, 15, one of the survivors of a December 4, 1984
ambush on a truck carrying volunteer coffee-pickers which was set
afire by contra forces: "I could hear the cries and laments of those
who were burning alive." (Chapter 2.)

—Mirna Cunningham, a Black Miskito Indian doctor who is
now the government's Minister for the northern Atlantic Coast,
describing how she and a nurse were treated after being kidnapped by the contras in December 1981:

> During those hours we were raped for the first time.
> While they were raping us, they were chanting slogans
> like "Christ yesterday, Christ today, Christ tomorrow..."
> And although we would cry or shout, they would hit us,
> and put a knife or a gun to our head. This went on for
> almost two hours. (Chapter 28.)

—Maria Bustillo Viuda de Blandon told of how her husband, a lay pastor, and her five children were taken from her home near El Jicaro one night in October 1982; when she found them the next day:

> They were left all cut up. Their ears were pulled off, their throats were cut, their noses and other parts were cut off. (Chapter 12)

—Sister Lisa Fitzgerald, a North American nun, testifying about the aftermath of a mortar attack on a tobacco farm near Jalapa in April 1983 in which two women and three children were injured in their homes:

> All five were filled with shrapnel, particularly the backs of the women who had knelt over the children to protect them. The skull and chest of the one year old baby were dotted by shell fragments which I and another sister picked out by hand. (Chapter 8.)

—Mauricio Gonzales, a Miskito Indian, testifying about the April 1984 contra attack against the resettlement village of Sumubila:

> They shot my mother [age 64] in the leg. I opened the door and seeing that they had surrounded the house, I said to them that if we had arms like theirs, we would avenge the blood of my mother.
> Then they shot me in the head, on my patio, and I fell. After that I don't remember anything. (Chapter 6.)

—Inocente Peralta, a lay pastor, went out looking for seven people taken in an attack on a Jinotega cooperative in April 1984. He describes the condition in which the bodies were found; for example:

> We found [Juan Perez] assassinated in the mountains. They had tied his hands behind his back. They hung him on a wire fence. They opened up his throat and took out his tongue. Another bayonet had gone in through his stomach and come out his back. Finally they cut off his testicles. It was horrible to see. (Chapter 14.)

—Carmen Gutierrez described the death of her four year old daughter Suyapa in a June 1983 mortar attack on her border town of Teotecacinte:

> When we were all in the [bomb] shelter, my mother asked if any of the children were missing, so we called them by their names. Only Suyapa was missing. I went out... Then I remembered that I had seen her playing with a hen. I went there and saw her dead. Her face was blown away but I didn't realize it, I didn't even notice the mortaring. I picked her up and ran away like mad. Then

I realized that part of her face was missing. I went back to look and found the piece of her face. (Chapter 8.)

—Orlando Wayland, a Miskito teacher who was kidnapped by the contras in December 1983, testifying to tortures applied to him and eight others in Honduras:

In the evening, they tied me up in the water from 7 P.M. until 1 A.M. The next day, at 7 A.M., they began to make me collect garbage in the creek in my underwear, with the cold. The creek was really icy. I was in the creek for four hours...

Then they threw me on the ant hill. Tied up, they put me chest-down on the ant hill. The [red] ants bit my body. I squirmed to try to get them off my body, but there were too many.

I was on the ant hill ten minutes each day...

They would beat me from head to heels. They would give me an injection to calm me a little. Then they would beat me again. (Chapter 24.)

—Abelina Inestroza, a mother from Susucayan, testifying about events of the previous day in December 1984:

They grabbed us, me and my sister...and raped us in front of the whole family. They turned out the lights and two of them raped me and two others raped my sister. They told us not to scream because they would kill us. They threatened us with their bayonets. They pointed their guns at the others in the house. (Chapter 28.)

—Maria Julia Ortiz was hiding under the bed when the contras broke into her house near El Jicaro in October 1984 and killed her husband:

They grabbed my husband and they beat him and broke his neck with a rifle. They took him out of the room by one of the doors which was destroyed and they bashed in his head with a rifle and they took out his eye.

Then they threw him on the floor and they tied his hands and they cut his throat with a bayonet. He screamed and fought...and said that he didn't do anything wrong, but they wouldn't let him speak and put a green cloth in his mouth. (Chapter 12.)

—Martin Piner, a Miskito pastor, describing his treatment after being kidnapped by the contras and taken to Honduras in July 1984:

He grabbed me by the neck and put my head down in the water. When I couldn't take it any more, he picked me up and put me back in the water again. It was like that for half an hour.

> They took me from there and tied me to a pine tree in the camp for three days.
>
> After three days they untied me. I hadn't eaten for five days. (Chapter 25.)

—Noel Benavides Herradora, telling of the December 1982 abduction of Felipe and Mery Barreda, prominent church leaders from Esteli:

> Mr. Felipe Barreda...was bleeding heavily. He was being beaten and had blood all over him. [His wife] was also being beaten. They tied them. I was walking ahead, he was tied behind me, and she was tied further behind. He could hardly walk. I had to pull on the rope to help him along, because the pain prevented him from making it through some ravines, steep hillsides, over boulders and thick vegetation. He kept slipping and falling. And every time he fell they struck him and threatened to get rid of him right there so that he would stop being a burden. Then he would kneel and ask to be allowed to pray an Our Father... But they just beat him, kicked him, slapped him in the face and cursed him. (Chapter 3.)

The Barredas were later tortured and killed.

*   *   *

The members of the investigative team were:

Reed Brody. (Team leader and report author.) Mr. Brody, an attorney, is a member of the New York bar. He holds an honors degree in political science from Fairleigh Dickinson University, where he was student government president. A 1978 graduate of Columbia Law School, he was associated with the New York law firm of Weil, Gotshal and Manges, and then spent four years as Assistant Attorney General of the State of New York. He has taught at the Law School of the University of Paris (Pantheon-Sorbonne) and authored *Latin America: The Freedom to Write* (PEN American Center, 1980).

Sister Sandra Price. Sister Sandra is a nun of the Congregation of Notre Dame de Namur. She has been in Nicaragua since 1981 and in Siuna, in northern Zelaya province, since 1982. Sister Sandra collected affidavits in the Siuna region only.

James Bordelon. Mr. Bordelon was a student at the Antioch School of Law in Washington, DC. He received his law degree in June 1985.

The idea of an independent investigation grew out of discussions between Mr. Brody, Sister Lisa Fitzgerald, a nun and attorney who had lived in Nicaragua, and Paul Reichler of the Washington law firm of Reichler and Appelbaum, which represents the Nicaraguan government. The participation of Mr. Bordelon was arranged by the law firm. The participation of Sister

Sandra Price was arranged by Mr. Brody after he arrived in Nicaragua. The team members received no compensation for their work and no reimbursement for expenses. Each paid his or her own travel and living expenses except that, until they could find lodgings of their own in Managua, Mr. Brody and Mr. Bordelon lived in a house owned by the government. While they were in Managua, Mr. Brody and Mr. Bordelon were furnished office space at the government-funded Comision Nacional de Promocion y Proteccion de los Derechos Humanos.

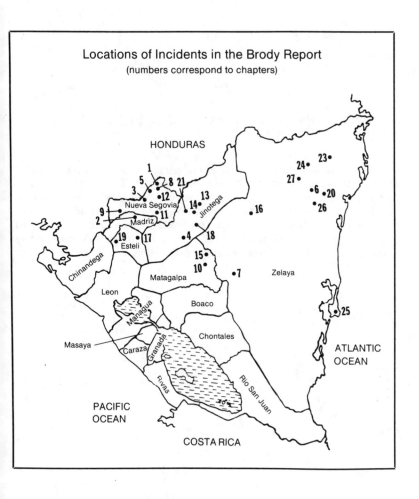

Locations of Incidents in the Brody Report
(numbers correspond to chapters)

HONDURAS

1
5
3 · 8 21
· 12
Nueva Segovia 14 13
9 · · 11 Jinotega
2 · Madriz · 16
19 · 17 · 4 18
Esteli
Chinandega · 15
· 10 · 7
Matagalpa Zelaya

Leon
Managua
Boaco
Masaya
Caraza Granada Chontales
Rivas Rio San Juan ATLANTIC
OCEAN
· 25

PACIFIC
OCEAN

COSTA RICA

Map of Nicaragua

Part I: Attacks On Coffee Pickers

Nicaragua is an agricultural country whose foreign exchange earnings depend in large part on its annual coffee harvest. During the harvest season—from November to February—civilian volunteers from all over Nicaragua (and many from abroad) travel to the coffee-growing areas and help with the labor-intensive task of picking the coffee beans. For the past three harvest seasons, the contras have staged direct attacks on these volunteers.

Chapter 1

Namasli
January 18, 1983

On January 18, 1983, several truckloads of civilian volunteers set out from the northern city of Jalapa to pick coffee in nearby Namasli close to the Honduran border. The last truck to leave Jalapa, at about 8:00 A.M., belonged to Abraham Reyes. Standing in the open-air back of the truck, which had side walls as tall as they, were some 25 to 30 volunteers. Two children, Guadalupe Ruiz and Pedro Cruz, both about 13, were riding on top of the driver's cabin. All were civilians, although at least two of them were carrying arms for their defense.[1] The volunteers went along "with high spirits, singing and shouting slogans."[2]

According to one volunteer:

When we were entering the farm where we were going to pick, in Namasli, about 12 kilometers from Jalapa, I saw two counterrevolutionaries in a coffee field on the left of the road. They began to shoot and we all threw ourselves on the floor of the truck.

I saw the blood flowing and I asked my friend Francisco, 'Don Chico, are you OK?' 'No,' he said, 'they got me in the foot.' I became nervous.

The child Pedro Cruz, who was traveling on top, fell on my legs...He didn't die right away, but later.

The girl Guadalupe Ruiz fell on my back, and lost the crown of her forehead. She died immediately.[3]

Elba Bucardo, 44, was riding in back:

We heard shots... The companeros told everyone to hit the floor...I did and listened to the firing.

...Emilio, about 16 or 17, was wounded in the arm and I gave him my scarf...

...I saw Guadalupe Ruiz almost dead...[and] Pedro Cruz, dying. I got up to get a little more comfortable and I saw Pedrito lying there, face-up, full of blood.

Then I felt a blow in the back of the head as if I were hit with a fistful of dirt. I felt back and saw blood on my hands and felt that the wood of the truck had fallen on me.[4]

Francisco Lopez, 46, a farmer, was on the floor of the truck when he received a shot in the foot, which broke it. "They fired 12-inch rockets which landed inside the truck, but did not go off."[5]

When the truck with the injured driver reached the farmhouse, the wounded and dead were immediately taken to a hospital in Jalapa. Pedro Cruz, one of the young boys, died in a hospital in Managua.[6] Francisco Lopez was taken to hospitals in Ocotal and then La Trinidad where he stayed seven months on crutches; he can no longer work in the fields.[7] Elba Bucardo was taken to Ocotal where they removed shrapnel from her finger but were unable to remove it from her head because it was too deep. She still has frequent headaches and goes to a hospital in Jalapa.[8]

Chapter 2

Telpaneca
December 4, 1984

On December 4, 1984, a contra task force ambushed a truck carrying volunteer coffee-pickers from the state communications company (TELCOR) near Telpaneca in the Department of Madriz. Twenty-one civilians, including a mother and her five year old child who had hitched a ride, were killed.

The group had assembled in Condega, in the Department of Esteli, and set off from there on December 4, headed for Telpaneca. Four of the pickers piled into a Toyota Land-Cruiser pick-up truck and the rest into a dump-truck.[1] Of the 32 people in the group, no more than 13 were given rifles for their protection in the event of a contra attack.[2] The group left at 7:45 A.M., stopping to pick up several hitch-hikers including a woman and her five year old boy.[3]

A few miles outside of Telpaneca, a contra task force was waiting. It let the pick-up truck pass and then opened fire on the dump-truck from about 20 yards, with a machine-gun, rockets, grenades and rifle fire.[4] The dump truck tried to keep going but, after about 100 yards, a rocket destroyed one of its tires.[5]

At that point, some of the pickers leaped from the truck as the fire continued. But "the majority of the people had already been shot," and were unable to get off the truck.[6]

Then the contras, some 150 to 300, advanced on the truck, firing.[7] As Roger Briones lay outside the truck with a bullet in his foot, pretending to be dead, the contras took off his boots and socks, stole his money and even turned him over. Certain that he was dead, they turned their attention to the others.[8] Another picker was lying near Roger with two broken legs. One of the contras killed him with his machine-gun.[9]

The majority of people were still in the truck—some alive, some dead, some merely wounded.[10] To orders of "to the truck," the contras climbed on and began to shoot the survivors and cut them up with their bayonets. A few nevertheless remained alive, at least for a while.[11] Then the contras took what they could from the truck, including backpacks, documents and money.[12] Next they set the truck on fire with gasoline.[13] From where Roger Briones lay, "I could hear the cries and laments of those who were burning alive."[14]

After burning the truck, the contras set off, taking with them Doris, a woman of about 19.[15] As they retreated in single file, carrying with them bodies of dead or wounded, they passed within five or six yards of where Jorge Luis Briones lay wounded, but they did not see him.[16]

When the Nicaraguan army arrived, about two hours after the ambush, they took away the dead and the few wounded. Brothers Roger and Jorge Luis Briones were taken to several hospitals and eventually wound up together in the hospital in La Trinidad where, for the first time, each realized that the other had survived. Both were there for six days and Roger now walks with crutches.[17] Lucio Rodriguez spent eight days in the hospital in Somoto; his arm is now in a sling.[18] All together, 21 people—all civilians—died, including five women and one child, and eight were injured.[19]

Chapter 3

Agronica Farm
Felipe and Maria Berreda
December 28, 1982

On December 24, 1982, a group of about 70 volunteer coffee-pickers left Esteli to join the harvest. The group, made up entirely of civilians, had a majority of women. All were adults, and the average age was quite high.[1] Among the volunteers were Felipe Barreda, 51, and his wife Maria ("Mery") Barreda, 49.

The Barredas were well known citizens of Esteli. Deeply religious, they were Delegates of the Word (lay pastors) and members of the Pastoral Council of the Diocese of Esteli. In the late 1960s and early 1970s they had organized Christian Family Movement retreats, taught courses on Christianity and helped form youth groups and cooperatives. During the insurrection against Somoza, they had worked with the Sandinista Front and helped build Christian base communities in Esteli. Following the revolution, Mery Barreda became a member of Esteli's City Council, and both she and her husband began to work in the poor "Omar Torrijos" neighborhood, promoting literacy and health, organizing a brick-making cooperative and continuing their courses on Christianity.

Leaving their neighborhood to join the coffee harvest on December 24 meant that the Barredas would miss the Christmas holiday. They believed, however, that Nicaragua's earnings from the harvest would mean more to their poor friends. Before leaving, Mery wrote to the people of the Omar Torrijos neighborhood:

> We have been awaiting this Christmas with real joy. Since we came to live among you, you have become a part of our lives. We love your children, your streets, your problems—in short, everything that is you. The best Christmas gift the Lord could give me would be to share this Christmas with you, and I was wondering what gift I could give you. But then I suddenly had the chance to give you a very fine present, although it means that I will not be with you at Midnight Mass. It is the chance to pick coffee for ten days. The little bit that I will pick will be transformed into health care, clothing, housing, roads, education and food for our people—that is why I am enthusiastic about going. In every coffee bean I pick, I will see each of your faces...[2]

The group the Barredas had joined reached one farm, Oro Verde, on the 24th and was then moved twice in three days. On December 27, 1982, they reached the Agronica farm near Honduras where, on December 28, they began to pick coffee.[3]

At about 11:00 A.M., one of the pickers came running, crying "Get down, get down right away, the contras are coming."[4] At that point, they began to hear intense firing of mortars, rockets, machine-guns, rifles and grenades.[5]

The pickers headed out on the only road from the farm, running parallel to a creek. As the road was elevated and the creek more protected, the group followed the creek until it turned off toward Honduras.[6] At that point, those who could climbed back up to the road.[7]

Upon reaching the road, Jose Ramon Gallo, 36, was received by machine-gun fire. As the attackers had the road surrounded from above,[8] he hid in a ditch from where he could hear voices, "Grab that son-of-a-bitch. Don't let anyone escape, especially not the women."[9]

The Barredas, older, lagged behind along with a few others. As that group helped each other up onto the road, they, too, came under fire.[10]

Gallo, who had been raised by the present Bishop of Esteli and had known the Barredas since participating in their Christianity course in the 1960s, saw Felipe make it to the road where the pickers' Toyota jeep was parked. Felipe started operating the jeep's radio to seek help when an explosion rocked the vehicle, destroying its hood and windows.[11]

While many of the pickers had made it past the contras before they closed their circle,[12] many others remained trapped. Gallo and two others hid for hours in a ditch as the contras fired.[13] Even after the firing stopped, the contras kept yelling for those in hiding to come out.[14]

Alicia Huete walked the road, where "Bullets were raining on us from all sides."[15] So she and those she was with got behind a hill and stayed there for hours. From there, she could see one of the contras with a machine-gun, looking down, who apparently did not see them.[16]

When the shooting stopped, at about five in the evening, the contras came down to about 100 yards from where Huete was. She could hear them saying "son-of-a-bitch, we're not going to leave even one of those son-of-a-bitch rabid dogs [contra slang for Sandinistas and their supporters]. We're going to kill them all."[17]

But the attackers did leave, and Huete and Gallo and most of the others made it back safely. Although thirty pickers were originally missing, little by little all but six showed up—four young men and the Barredas.[18]

Noel Benavides, one of the men who did not return, was hiding about a kilometer south of the farm when the contras spotted him. They tied him up, put on steel handcuffs and blindfolded him.[19]

Then, when they took him and three others to a point further on,

> Mr. Felipe Barreda and his wife were already there. He
> was bleeding heavily. He was being beaten and had
> blood all over him. She was also being beaten. They tied
> them. I was walking ahead, he was tied behind me, and
> she was tied further behind. He could hardly walk. I had
> to pull on the rope to help him along, because the pain
> prevented him from making it through some ravines,
> steep hillsides, over boulders and thick vegetation. He
> kept slipping and falling. And every time he fell they
> struck him and threatened to get rid of him right there so
> that he would stop being a burden. Then he would kneel
> and ask to be allowed to pray an Our Father before they
> killed him so that he would not die just like that, but that
> he wanted to pray to the Lord. But they just beat him,
> kicked him, slapped him in the face and cursed him.[20]

That evening they reached a post where Honduran guardsmen were mixed with contras. One of the soldiers said to leave
Mery there. They insulted her and told her she would be raped by
the whole troop, and she was left there.[21] The others continued
walking until, at three in the morning, they were presented to
another Honduran guard post. There,

> They started insulting us, threw us face-down on the
> ground and began beating us. One of the guards said
> that he would be the one to kill those dogs, to just leave it
> to him. He kicked us and said: 'Turn right-side up, take
> their blinds off.' They pulled our blindfolds off and
> placed their rifle-butts on our foreheads and fixed their
> bayonets. But one of the counterrevolutionaries said
> that he could not leave us there because the chief was not
> there and without the chief being there he could be
> sanctioned.[22]

Then they were made to carry the wounded as well as loads of
ammunition. Again,

> ...the guardsmen beat us and insulted us. And Don
> Felipe too, and they yelled at him, 'You are a Sandinista,
> you son-of-a-bitch,' and kept beating him. He moaned
> and told them not to beat him, but that was difficult. He
> asked them to loosen his handcuffs a little, for they were
> digging into his flesh, which was bleeding. Then one of
> the guards said, 'Tighten his handcuffs even more, let
> the old bastard's hands fall off!' One of the guardsmen
> proceeded to tighten all of our cuffs...
> Don Felipe could no longer walk because the blows
> had been too much for his age; he had lost too much
> blood and could not walk. As we went on in file we pulled
> him with the rope, which was the most we could do. He

walked on his knees or crawled, and thus we pulled him. At the top of a hill we could not pull him any longer. Then they said that we would eat his ears; that we were going to cut them off and we would eat one of his ears while he had to eat the other. And if he still would not walk, we would have to chop him to pieces until he was dead. And that if any of us got tired, the other had to do the same until we were finished off.

Thus we continued walking and walking, with blows upon rifle blows upon insults, and thus we arrived about two days later to a jail the counterrevolutionaries had on a hill. We had passed by camps where we heard strange voices, like from people who could not pronounce Spanish or voices I know not from what country. We were told these were military detachments. Where they took our blinds off for a while we saw along a hillside, in hollows, huge bundles covered with black, olive-green and camouflage canvas; in the woods we saw rainproof tents with many bundles.

In that jail, the prisoners were stripped.

They manacled us, tied us, blindfolded us once again and strapped us to trees. Three days after we arrived, Dona Mery [Barreda] arrived, quite beaten and hemorrhaging. She collapsed upon arriving due to the extenuation, the fatigue and the blows. They also stripped her of everything. They strapped her to a tree next to us. Thus we spent two days and two nights, strapped to the trees, standing, naked, barefoot, in the mud, and under the rain. They kept harassing us, and whenever a counter-revolutionary or a guardsman passed by he would threaten us with bayonets against our necks, against our chests, curse us and slap us in the face. They kept saying: 'Don't worry, for tonight you'll be dead. Don't worry, for tonight we are going to slit your throats. Right against those very trees, that's where you are going to die.'

The following night, still naked, they threw us into a gully, into a crevice. We moaned from the cold, the pain, the rain, the mud; the Barreda couple as well as the rest. Two days later they pulled us out of there. They interrogated them and us, they accused us, they beat us.

After five or six days of blows, torture, insults, interrogation, they said they would give us an opportunity to preserve our lives. They untied us, took our blinds off, and dressed us in U.S.-made suits: camouflage caps, camouflage brown and green packets, jungle boots and pants. They placed machine-guns, FAL rifles, all sorts of weapons on our chests, across our chests we had to wear

them. We were photographed and told to say that we had
come to Honduras to join them, to make an appeal to the
Nicaraguan people saying that we had left to join them
and the rest should do likewise...And everything they
told us to do we had to do, or else we would die.[24]

The Barredas, too beaten to travel, stayed in the jail[25] while
the other captives were taken to another camp.

They said they had a camp where we were going to be
taken, and whomever wanted could be trained in special
commandos, specialized in torture, in interrogations
and something like throat-cutting; they kept talking
about special training, that they could send us to a training camp or to the United States or a place like that for
classes...We were taken there at night forewarned of
what would happen to us should we try to escape, which
is what had happened to the three who had tried to
escape a day earlier: a boy about thirteen years old, one
of about seventeen and another of about twenty whose
throats were cut right in front of us by a special commando that took care, they said, of deserters.[26]

At the camp in Danli,

There were also many other people there—mothers,
fathers, brothers, children—relatives of kidnapped people who had been threatened that, if they escaped, those
held would be killed. Therefore the possibility of escaping was quite difficult.[27]

The four remaining pickers were given five lempiras (Honduran currency) each to get cigarettes.[28] Noel Benavides simply
announced that he was going to buy something in the store,
walked until he reached a telephone office, and called the Nicaraguan Embassy in the capital city of Tegucigalpa; and he was told
they could come and pick him up. He got his friends from the camp
and they hid in town until the embassy car came and took them
home.[29]

The Barredas were not as lucky. Nothing was known of their
fate until June, 1983, when the Nicaraguan government captured
a young contra officer named Pedro Javier Nunez Cabezas, alias
El Muerto ("The Dead Man"). Shown on national television, El
Muerto was identified by Noel Benavides and the others as the
man responsible for their maltreatment.[30]

In statements given to the Nicaraguan press, El Muerto described the execution of the Barredas:

At 1:30 P.M., more or less, they brought Felipe Barreda,
who had shrapnel wounds. Later, at about five in the
afternoon, they brought in Senora Maria Eugenia who
had been badly mistreated and had a bad vaginal

hemorrhage. I ordered that they be tied up [together with the four others] in a coffee plantation. The next day, the Barredas were brought blindfolded to a house to be interrogated. The interrogations were conducted separately. I applied psychological torture with the Senora but I gave Mr. Barreda a blow in the head with the butt of my pistol and kicked him all over when he refused to accept what his wife had said...

During some sessions, we would only hit them in their bodies, because we were waiting for the [counterrevolutionary television crew] and we didn't want them to appear with disfigured faces. Therefore the orders which I gave and executed were to kick them in the body, to hit them where it wouldn't leave any signs when the time came to show them on television...

That night they were both taken outside nude so they would spend the night under the rain. The next day [the television crew] interviewed them. After that, El Suicida [El Muerto's superior] told me to kill the Barredas and I carried out the order, shooting them in the head with the help of Juan and Tapir.[31]

Chapter 4

La Sorpresa
November 14, 1984

On November 14, 1984, a contra force of approximately 400 to 600 men attacked the state farm "La Sorpresa," 45 kilometers north of Jinotega, killing 17 of its members—all civilians—kidnapping others and destroying most of its facilities.

Like other farms in these fertile hills, La Sorpresa was preparing itself for the coffee harvest. A week later, it would have been the temporary home for hundreds of volunteer pickers who came to the Matagalpa-Jinotega region to help with the coffee picking, and that morning the members of the cooperative were at a meeting to coordinate the upcoming harvest.[1]

The head of the farm, Luis Amado Morales, left in a tractor to bring wood from nearby El Sarayal. As he approached his destination he was told that the contras were in the vicinity and he returned to the farm to warn the others.[2]

The farm was defended by only 20 resident civilian defenders who took up positions as the contras attacked with 79-millimeter grenades, hand-grenades, mortars, rocket-propelled grenades and rifle fire.[3] The attackers quickly surrounded the farm, killing 10 of the milicianos,[4] including Jamilet Sevilla, a pregnant 17 year old mother,[5] and forcing the others to flee.

Julia Picado Gonzalez was in her house with six of her eight children when the attack started. She grabbed the milk for her 18 month old baby and fled as the contras entered, yelling, "If we find the women of the rabid dogs in their houses, we'll cut their throats with the whole family."[6] As they left, the contras shot at them and they continued their retreat by crawling up a hill to a coffee plantation. From there she watched as the contras shot her husband in the shoulder, then hit him with a grenade which destroyed his head.[7]

When the contras overran the farm, they finished off the wounded and dying with bayonets, rifle shots and grenades.[8] Jamilet Sevilla was later found with a bayonet blow in her pregnant belly.[9]

The women and children fled the day care center where they had taken refuge. The contras shot at them, killing Telma Gonzalez and her 16 month old baby Jose Rodolfo Ruiz, as well as another four year old child, Carlos Jose Mejia.[10]

Santos Gonzalez was in her house when she heard the firing. She threw herself on the ground and watched from the cracks in the wall as the contras surrounded and then entered the farm. Her son, Jose Alejandro Pineda, was in front of the house. "They grabbed him alive, struck him on the forehead with a machete and his brains spilled. Then they burned him."[11]

As the contras retreated, they ordered two of their captives, Benito Talavera and Nicolas, to burn the houses. Benito went to the houses warning those still in them to "leave, because I'm going to set the house on fire."[12]

The attackers were able to destroy the coffee plant, 600 pounds of coffee, the coffee pulping machine, three dormitories, the offices, the kitchen, the houses and the food warehouse where beans, rice and fertilizer were stored, as well as the dormitories for the seasonal workers and the pickers. Only a few houses, two motors, the mill and the electric generator were not destroyed.[13]

The nearby Los Andes hacienda was also burned, including the main house and the kitchen.[14]

The contras took several captives as they left. Omar Gutierrez was forced to carry a chain saw and Nicolas Molina, the farm's accountant, two backpacks. Some Miskito Indians who had been resettled in the farm were also taken, and one was forced to carry two dead contras roped on to his back.[15]

Meanwhile, the 17 dead bodies of the victims of the attack were taken to nearby Abisinia. Luis Amado, the head of the farm, had his feet, his hands and his testicles cut up.[16] Mundo Cruz had bayonet wounds in his face and his testicles cut off.[17] Pedro Ortiz's head was smashed in and his testicles were also cut off.[18]

Also among the dead were three Miskitos, including a teacher, and two children: Elida and Renee Torres.

According to the *New York Times* account of this attack, after that Wednesday the contras:

> ...set an ambush along a nearby road for any relief column that might try to reach the devastated farm. The first vehicle that passed, however, carried Evenor Castro Ibarra, an official of the National Development Bank who was returning to the town of Jinotega after visiting several remote cooperatives. The rebel commandos killed him, left his body beside his jeep, and remained in wait for others.
>
> On Thursday morning, two top Sandinista officials from Jinotega, Ronald Paredes and Denis Espinoza, set out by jeep to assess the damage at La Sorpresa. Among the seven people accompanying them were a bank official concerned about Mr. Castro Ibarra's disappearance and a reporter from *Barricada*, 34 year old Juan Bautista Matus Lopez, a longtime Sandinista. All but one were killed when their car drove into the rebel ambush.[19]

Chapter 5

La Estancia
October 14, 1982

In the small community of La Estancia, outside of Jalapa, Julio Villareina Perez, 38, Juan Ramos Caceres, 22, and Margarito Rivera, 45—all civilians—were mutilated and killed by a contra band on October 14, 1982.

That morning, Rivera left his house at 4:30 A.M. to work in his cooperative. His wife, Maria Luisa Jimenez, had given birth only eight days before and was home in bed.[1] Later that morning, a group of 30 armed men in uniforms came through the village. When they passed the house of Feliciana, Rivera's daughter, they heard her say something about "dogs" and pointed their guns at her, but then went on to Rivera's house. When they passed by his house, which was flying a red and black Sandinista flag, they said, "It's ours. Let's mark it because it wil be our command post."[2]

They asked Rivera's son if he knew who the local health leaders were, who the party members were, and whether the contras had passed by. Before leaving, they marked the house, "with God, patriotism or death. FDN"[3]

Two of the band also passed the house where Juan Ramos Caceres lived with his mother, asking for Juan's brother Ricardo. When they saw that Ricardo wasn't there, they said they were going to take Juan away for an "investigation." Despite Juan's protests and his father's supplications, they then took him.[4]

A little later, shots were heard.[5] Then news came that Margarito Rivera, Juan Ramos Caceres and Julio Villareina had been killed.[6]

Mercedes Centeno Ramos found her husband Julio Villareina's dead body when it was already laid out in an aunt's house. "His face was swollen, his throat was slit, his arms were beaten and swollen. He had been hit so many times that he looked different." [7]

Antonia Caceres Centeno went looking for her son Juan, but could not find him. At about 9:00 A.M., she was told that they had found his body in the fields. By the time she got there the police had taken it to Jalapa. There, she saw her son's body.

It was shredded up, full of bullets. The legs were broken, there were bullets in its side and the back, and all cut-up with wire...it was disfigured and bloody.[8]

Margarito Rivera was not yet dead when his daughter found him lying in a hammock in the command post. He had two wounds in his throat. She accompanied him to the hospital in Ocotal where they gave him a liter of blood and where, unable to speak, he told her in writing what had happened:[9]

> He told me that they had taken him. The first group let him go. The group that came afterwards told him, 'you're coming with us.' They took him under a bridge and tied his hands behind his back... They asked him where Chico Caceres and Armando were and who was in charge of health and the CDS [Sandinista Defense Committee]. He said he didn't know. They told him if he didn't speak they would shut him up for good. They gave him a blue poison orally. He said that when they attacked him he didn't feel anything and when they gave him the first blow of the bayonet, he fell, got up and fell again and they left him for dead.[10]

They also stole 3,000 cordobas he had in his pocket. Margarito was taken to a hospital in Managua, where he died several weeks later.[11]

All of these families left La Estancia after this incident, but when a resettlement cooperative ("asentamiento") was built there, they and other refugees from La Estancia and other regions went to live in the cooperative.

Chapter 6

Sumubila
April 17, 1984

There are five communities on the road between Puerto Cabezas and Rosita, in Northern Zelaya province, to which Miskito Indians living along the Honduran border were resettled in 1982.

The largest of the communities is Sumubila, with some 3,200 Miskitos living in single-family wooden houses to which they have been given title.

On March 19, 1984, contra soldiers in the Misura Military Instruction Center (CIMM) in Honduras were told by "Chan," a former member of General Somoza's elite EEBI unit, that, on the orders of Miskito contra leader Steadman Fagoth, a force of 500 contras would leave the center to kidnap residents of Sumubila. Other troops were simultaneously ordered on other missions, including a group of 30 which was to attack the military base in Puerto Cabezas as a diversionary action. Another six men went to Esperanza, on the Rio Coco, to receive the kidnapped.[1]

On April 17, 1984, at about 4:30 A.M., the contra force began a surprise entry into Sumubila. They attacked the settlement from three sides with mortars, rockets, grenades and rifle-fire, easily overwhelming local resistance.[2]

Cristina Atoya, a nurse who was five months pregnant, was in the health center with her sick daughter when she heard the first shots, and hid with the child under the bed. Then she heard the contras draw closer, and shots entered the health center. One of the bullets ruptured the oxygen tank, setting the center on fire. There were four patients hooked to intravenous tubes. Ruth Gramm, the nurse on duty, unhooked them and they all fled the burning health center, crawling until they got to a pit on a nearby hill where they lay face-down for hours until the shooting was over.[3]

Along with the health center, the advancing contras set fire to the senior citizens' artisanry center, the cacao warehouse, the electricity plant, the settlement's only ambulance, the agrarian reform office and the fumigation center.[4]

A truck driver on his way from Puerto Cabezas to Matagalpa had parked his truck for the night in the settlement. The contras shot him and then stabbed him four times with their bayonets, killing him. His truck was destroyed as well.[5]

Mauricio Gonzales was in his house with his 64 year old mother:

> We had never heard firing like that day, so my mother got up to run from the house. I grabbed her and sat her on the bed.
>
> They shot my mother in the leg. I opened the door and, seeing that they had surrounded the house, I said to them that if we had arms like theirs, we would avenge the blood of my mother.
>
> Then they shot me in the head, on my patio, and I fell. After that, I don't remember anything.[6]

When Gonzales' niece, Cristina Atoya, returned after the attack, she found Gonzales and his mother lying on the floor. "My grandmother was bleeding, but she was already dead. Only [my five year old daughter, crying] covered with blood and hugging my grandmother, was alive there."[7] Gonzales had to be taken to the hospital in Rosita but did not recover consciousness until he reached the hospital in Puerto Cabezas, from which he was transferred to a Managua hospital. He remained there for two months.[8]

A bullet entered the house where Julio Obando, 55, lived with his wife and eight children, and hit him in the side, killing him on the spot.[9] Other bullets wounded Candida Lopez, 28, in the mouth and cheek, sending her to the hospital for four months.[10]

As some of the contras defeated the outnumbered local defense, others went from house to house pulling people out. Avelino Cox watched them:

> One of the contras came from another neighborhood, telling the others to get all the young people out. I could see through the corner of my window that they already had a lot of youths from my neighborhood...concentrated, under their pointed guns. The first people they took from my neighborhood were two of my brothers-in-law, Ricardo and Eduardo Coleman. To date, we haven't heard anything from them. Eduardo was pretty sick, very weak.[11]

After an informer pointed out that Cox worked for the agrarian reform ministry (MIDINRA) and had a pistol:

> Three contras came, aiming their heavy arms at my house, saying that if I didn't come out they would set my house on fire. Since I saw that the other houses that had been pointed out were burning, I was scared, but I didn't come out. A sister-in-law came out of her house and said 'my brother-in-law isn't here.' But [the informer] said no, I had come in at 9:00 P.M.
>
> Faced with that, I had to come out, my hands in the air as they had ordered. They shoved me and took me to a

Destruction caused by contra attack on Sumubila.

photo: Barricada

group they had kidnapped—approximately 10 or 15 others, all youths.[12]

The contras came four times looking for Evaristo Walden, who had hid in a tree trunk. They finally caught up with him there and, aiming their rifles at him, grabbed him and tied him up.[13]

In other cases, the whole family was first taken out of the house. Raul Davis, 21, was taken out with his father-in-law and all of his father-in-law's children. They were taken to where the contras were holding a group of 200 to 300 people, including children and older people. Davis was then ordered to join a smaller group of youths who were being held on the baseball field.[14]

The group of captives also included a 12 year old boy, Orlando Sosa;[15] the local doctor, Roberto Valle; the administrator of the health center, Jorge Ibarra;[16] and five women.[17] In all, more than 35 people were taken,[18] including Mercedes Thomas, a pregnant woman who was taken along with her husband.[19] When the group was all together, one of the contras got on his walkie-talkie and said: "We've captured the population of Sumubila and we're taking the people away."[20]

The contras commanded their captives, "March, civilian sons-of-bitches,"[21] and took the group off into the mountains. As they went along, the contras ordered their captives, "Run you sons-of-bitches. You're happy in your houses with your women and we're in the mountains fighting for you, to save you from communism."[22] When the wife of one of the bound captives, whose eight year old child was also being taken captive, asked to have her husband untied so that he could walk better, a contra replied, "Eat shit bitch, I'm not your brother."[23]

As the hostages were taken away by one contra group, another continued the attack. They took the volunteer police station, killing one man, Maximo Cano, and wounding another.[24] With the help of some communications company workers, the residents were able to retake the police station.[25] Then planes the residents had requested came from Puerto Cabezas and the contras set off back into the hills.[26]

Among the dead were a 12 year old boy[27] and a one year old child.[28] As the health center was destroyed, there was no medicine with which to treat the wounded, who were all taken to the mining town of Rosita.[29]

The flight of the planes also caused disarray in the contra group taking the hostages, allowing Raul Davis and Avelino Cox to escape. The contras fired at them as they fled and then chased after them, but they were able to make their getaway. After spending the night in the hills, they made their way back to Sumubila.[30] The contras continued on with the others, beating some of them[31] and warning them not to try to escape[32]. After about ten days Jorge Ibarra and Roberto Valle were able to escape, as was Evaristo Walden the following day.[33] Walden spent ten days walking through the mountains before finding his way back to Sumubila.[34]

Chapter 7

Bocana de Paiwas
August 1981—November 1984

The remote mountainous region of Bocana de Paiwas, in Central Zelaya—the geographical center of Nicaragua—is divided into 33 small, isolated townships. With the exception of Paiwas, these townships are accessible only by river or mountain path. There is no telephone system and no electricity. Lacking adequate protection by the regular army, the villagers have been subject to a series of contra attacks.

According to Father James Feltz, a U.S. citizen who is the area's parish priest, the contras:

> have tried to intimidate people who are working with the grassroots organizations. The greater the individual's contribution to the community, the more likely he or she will be singled out as a target by the FDN. These victims have included adult education workers, sugar distributors and coordinators of cooperatives.[1]

The first major attack in this area occurred in August 1981. Four campesinos, apparently singled out because they had joined a local militia unit, were assassinated in the township of Santa Rosa.[2]

On March 3, 1982, a contra band surrounded and then entered the small church in Copolar, where Father Robert Stark and Father Feltz were meeting with the local pastoral leaders. After rounding up the participants and questioning them individually about whether they had ever participated in the local militias, the leader warned everyone not to participate in the militia or education or health care, and not to report the incident to the authorities. Then he announced that his band had just shot someone on the road for encouraging people to participate in health, education and self-defense. The priests set out in search of the victim. Father Stark testified:

> Less than a kilometer from the chapel we found Emiliano [Perez's] body face down... [H]e was still struggling to breathe despite the blood also coming from his side and arm as well as the back of his head.[3]

According to Father Feltz, Perez, who died from the wounds:

47

...was one of the leading citizens of the community of Paiwas. Perez had worked closely with the parish for many years, serving as a Delegate of the Word for the previous 12 years. He was also a local judge and a father of ten children. The contra had long threatened to kill him...

The murder...made it more difficult to recruit students for adult education and volunteers for health brigades. The contra had expressly told the people of Copolar that Emiliano's death should be taken as a warning to anyone who participated in the grassroots organizations.[4]

Other participants in local organizations received similar messages. Felipe Oporta was coordinator of the Sandinista Defense Committee (the Sandinista neighborhood association) in El Jorgito and ran a store there selling sugar and soap—two important products in rural areas. When a townsman was stopped by the contras and identified himself as coming from El Jorgito, he was reportedly questioned at length about Oporta—because he was on their list. "What did he do?" "To whom did he sell his products?" The man was reportedly told that they had already had a lot of information on Oporta and would continue investigating his behavior.[5] Later, Oporta's son-in-law, who also sold basic products, was murdered and his body was found covered with bayonet wounds.[6]

In August 1982, and again in January 1983, the contras attacked the Flor de Pino cooperative in Malacaguas. In the first attack they broke in late at night to the home of Fausto Sanchez, the coordinator of adult education, killing him and wounding his brother. In the second attack, they decimated the cooperative, killing eight members and forcing the others to flee.[7]

In late August 1983, a band said to be composed of 350 contras and 150 kidnapped civilians entered the Paiwas mountains and launched attacks on four townships in the region: El Anito, El Guayabo, Las Minitas and Ocaguas.

In El Anito, the contras killed six unarmed civilians. After shelling the town, they forced the villagers to go to the chapel and lie face down while their houses were burned. Valentin Velasquez and Aristina Cerda, a married couple with ten children, testified about the attack:

[The contras arrived] at our house. We were all on the floor because they had mortars and gunfire. They stayed about an hour in the house, taking everything. When they finished that, they took us to the chapel along with the other persons of the community. They said they wanted to free the people from communism and that they didn't like the Russians. They were very proud of the arms that they received from Reagan, saying that the arms that the Sandinistas had weren't good. They asked for gasoline and burned down the houses, including the ENABAS warehouse [government center for the distribution of basic products] which we ran.

They left us naked in the street... They also killed six people from the community: Felipe Amador, an outstanding 15 year old who gave classes; Emilio Sotelo, an evangelist who was waiting for the boat; Tomas Mendez, the CDS leader who also had a sugar store—they beat him, broke his head and tortured him as an example to us; Roberto Mendez, Tomas's nephew; Geronimo Espinoza, who committed the error of saying that the 'compas' [Sandinistas] were good people and for this had his head cut off; and Natividad Ojera, also beheaded.

In addition to the deaths, they left us to beg for food and clothing... The destruction of the ENABAS store left many children suffering from malnutrition—about 2000 people used the warehouse...

And there is always the fear that they will return.[8]

Augustin Sequeira Rivas was the head of the local Sandinista Defense Committee in El Anito. When he heard the contras entering the town, firing and shelling mortars, he fled and spent eight days in the mountains before arriving in Bocana de Paiwas. When his wife and five children were able to join him, they told him what had happened.[9]

According to his wife, the contras surrounded, then entered, their house. After interrogating his wife, they stole 15,000 cordobas (about $500), food and medicine, and then locked her up in a room while they ate and slept. The next morning they let her out, told her that they had killed Augustin, took some mules to ride and carry their supplies, and burned the house down. Like Valentin Velasquez, and Aristina Cerda and Felipe Oporta, Sequeira and his family are among the many people who have taken refuge in Bocana de Paiwas.[10]

Father Feltz visited El Anito and the other sites shortly after the attack. In El Guayabo:

—nine people had been killed;
—a 14 year old girl had been raped repeatedly and then decapitated;
—three women were forced to lie in the mud while the contras took shots at them, killing one and wounding another;
—a woman was raped;
—ten year old Cristina Borge, who witnessed the killing of two uncles and another woman, was used as target practice and received four bullet wounds before being left for dead. Miraculously, she survived.
—four houses were burned.[11]

In Ocaguas, three campesinos had been killed. One was stabbed to death after his eyes had been gouged out. Another was found hung from a beam in his own house.[12]

In Las Minitas, the contras burned six houses and killed two local leaders. A Delegate of the Word who escaped told Father Feltz that one contra threatened to cut off his head so that they could drink his blood, while another suggested that they "hang him until his tongue sticks out to punish him for not telling us where his sons [militia members] are."[13]

After touring the area, Father Feltz calculated that 20 civilians had been killed, two women wounded, three women raped, 18 houses burned to the ground and 144 refugees forced to flee to the town of Paiwas.[14]

On Christmas eve, 1983, a band of 20 contras entered the comarca [district] of Calderon. At about 4:00 A.M., the attackers surrounded and entered the house where Julio Cesar Ortiz, 19, lived with his wife, two children and in-laws. They made Ortiz lie face-down on the floor and demanded that he tell them how many men were in the militia post and what kind of arms they had. When he refused, they made him and another man accompany them to the post.[15]

About 100 yards from the post, they made Ortiz and the other man lie face down again while they unsuccessfully attacked the post. Returning to where the two lay, they said, "Since we couldn't find your father [a civilian defender], you're going to pay," and shot Ortiz in the head, killing him. They also shot the other man in the back of the neck and left him for dead, but he did not die. After leaving the town, they killed Josefa Molinarez, the other man's wife. Like the others, Ortiz's family are now refugees in Bocana de Paiwas.[16] They have no work. Ortiz's father said, "We receive food and clothes. The small children and we are living hard times."[17]

The next major attack in the area took place in El Jorgito on May 13, 1984, when a contra band armed with mortars, hand grenades and machine guns surrounded and attacked a house where a group of unarmed civilian militia members were having a party with their wives and children. According to witnesses, the contras lobbed hand grenade after hand grenade, 30 in all, killing five women, nine children and 20 adult men. Some had their throats slit or faces peeled.[18]

On about October 15, 1984, the contras attacked two cooperatives in the township of La Paila. In one instance, they killed two elderly men and a a child, and seriously wounded one woman. They burned three houses and forced 48 people to flee. Their attack on the second coop was unsuccessful.[19]

In September and November, 1984, the contras stole about 1,500 head of cattle in the region, including some 800 from two state farms in El Toro.[20]

Chapter 8

Jalapa
July 1982—June 1983

The "beak of Jalapa" is an area of Nicaragua that juts into and is surrounded on three sides by Honduras. Only an old dirt road connects its rich plains with the rest of Nicaragua.

Because of its geographical situation, this rural area appears easy to isolate. One captured contra leader, Pedro Javier Nunez Cabezas, "El Muerto," of the FDN, said, "[Our] principal objective was the zone of Jalapa, to declare it a liberated zone and install a provisional government and ask for military aid from friendly governments such as the United States, Honduras and Argentina."[1]

Before July 1982, the region consisted of 120 villages scattered through the mountains and valleys. The town of Jalapa had a population of roughly 9,000, one-fourth of the overall population of the region.[2]

According to Sister Lisa Fitzgerald, an American nun who worked in Jalapa, in July, 1982:

> Incursions by 'contra' bands from Honduras began to make trips into the mountain areas very dangerous. We could no longer travel without an armed escort. After August of that year, travel was made impossible. Several months later, all of us, each nun and priest working in Jalapa, were named on the 'contra' radio station and threatened if we continued to participate in the national literacy program.[3]

Thereafter, attacks came with increasing frequency. Based on incidents she and the other nuns and priests in Jalapa had witnessed themselves or could verify by speaking with survivors they knew personally, Sister Lisa testified to some of the events in a two-month period in 1982:

September 22—A veterinarian and an accountant, both employees of the Ministry of Agrarian Reform, were ambushed near Santa Clara at five in the afternoon on the road between Jalapa and Ocotal. Contra forces cut their throats. A second vehicle was ambushed minutes later. Five farm workers were wounded. All seven were unarmed.

October 8—Two small store owners were killed in San Jose. The same group of contra forces cut off the arm of Angel Valenzu-

51

ela, a tractor driver in San Jose, when he refused to surrender his tractor to them. All three were unarmed.

October 15—Cruz Urrutia, a farmer in Siuce, was dragged from his home and his body found a day later, tortured, mutilated and his throat cut. He had been the community's Delegate of the Word, their health worker and promoter of adult education. His family identified the contra band who took him.

October 28—Leonilo Marin, a worker, was kidnapped by contra forces and found later the same day, his throat cut, near his home in German Pomares.

November 15—Celso Mejia, Mauro Mejia, Isidro Mejia, and Mateo Calderon, all farmers, were tortured, shot and their heads blown off by a grenade in front of their entire community of La Ceiba which was forceably assembled by a group of contras.

November 19—Pedro Carazo, Delegate of the Word for his community, was taken from his home in San Pablo by a group made up of contra forces. His body was found a day later on the path towards Jalapa on the outskirts of San Pablo; his throat was cut and the body half-eaten by dogs.[4]

During the last two months of 1982, "roughly 400 persons (men, women, and children) were forcibly taken to Honduras from the communities of La Ceiba, San Pablo, Las Filas, Zacateras, Terredios, Marcalali, Ojo de Agua, and Las Pampas."[5]

As a result of these attacks and raids, "nearly all of the mountain communities on the western side of [the]...region were abandoned by the campesinos, most of whom fled into the town of Jalapa."[6] By June 1983, the exodus swelled the population of Jalapa from 9,000 to approximately 20,000 as the number of communities in the area shrunk from 120 to fewer than 30.[7]

Sister Lisa and the other members of the pastoral team in Jalapa kept a journal of contra attacks they witnessed or could verify during the first six months of 1983. She summarized its contents:

> Three of the largest tobacco farms were totally destroyed. Others were partially destroyed by mortar rounds or arson. On two different occasions in April and May I was visiting families of tobacco workers at farms when shelling began. On a third occasion [April 8], I was visiting the hospital in Jalapa when two women and three children were rushed in by jeep; they were the family of a tobacco worker at El Porvenir... Their homes had been mortared two hours earlier. All five were filled with shrapnel, particularly the backs of the women who had knelt over the children to protect them. The skull and chest of the one year old baby were dotted by shell fragments which I and another sister picked out by hand.
>
> There were 337 abductions from mountain communities or as a result of road ambushes. Of these, 37 persons escaped. I interviewed five of them; all were forced to

carry equipment for the contras. They reported some of their friends were shot immediately after they were abducted and others were taken to Honduras.

Ambushes on the road to Ocotal increased in number and frequency. On several occasions, all the passengers from the ambushed buses were abducted. In May, a group of journalists were ambushed on this road. Since the hospital was over-crowded, we treated the lightly wounded in our home. Four were Americans. Several were European. One Nicaraguan journalist was severely wounded. The attack was by mortar from both sides of the road and took place without warning two miles from the center of town.[8]

The town of Teotecacinte, population 2,500 to 3,000, sits in the northern edge of the Jalapa valley, one-half mile from the mountains of Honduras. There, from May 22-25 and June 5-22, 1983, the contras, shelling the town from two sides, staged an intense attack.

The contras were able to take and temporarily hold the border post of Murupuchi and the small border town of El Porvenir and from there "they fired all day, every day" on Teotecacinte.[9] "They attacked with heavy artillery, mortars of 81, 106 and 120 [milimiters]. We calculate that there were about 1,000 [attackers]... They fired about 100 mortars each day."[10]

The town was defended by the resident civilian defense force of 70 plus the 25 army border guards until an irregular fighting batallion could be called up.[11]

During the battle, those who stayed in "Teote" and were not fighting spent their days and nights in the bomb shelters, while food was shuttled in from Jalapa.[12]

Carmen Gutierrez, mother of five including four year old Suyapa, who was killed on June 9, testified as to the events of that day:

[The day] began calmly. They had been mortaring for about eight days in a row, but it seemed like nothing was going to happen. At around 11 A.M., the girl was playing in the patio. We were confident and let her play because they had spent so many days in the bomb shelter.

All of a sudden, mortars started falling nearby, shaking our wooden, tile-roofed, house. One mortar fell near where she was playing... Another completely destroyed the latrine. When I heard them, I said to my mother, 'Gather up the little ones, they're mortaring.' She ran with them to the shelter which was a few meters from the house. When we were all in the shelter, my mother asked if any of the children were missing, so we called them by their names. Only Suyapa was missing. I went out... Then I remembered that I had seen her playing with a hen. I went there and saw her dead. Her face was blown away but I didn't realize it, I didn't even notice the mortaring. I picked her up and ran away like mad. Then I realized that part of her face was missing. I went back to look and found the piece of her face.[13]

Loencia Corea Canelo, who had moved with her husband and seven children to Teotecacinte in 1983, when the contras attacked their farm in Guanzapo, also lost a daughter to the mortars:

I was making tortillas with my eight year old daughter, Concepcion Ubeda...to send to [the other children] who were in the shelter. When I heard the mortaring, I took her by the rubber tree and huddled with her.

A mortar fell behind the ceibo trees...and knocked the rubber tree down on the child.[14]

The child never recovered.

After three days, she doubled up on the floor... I took her to the command post but she died...[that day] she was bleeding from the mouth, the nose, the ears. [15]

As the seige continued, the people of Teotecacinte fled to Jalapa. Numerous houses were destroyed and many still remain pock-marked with grapefruit-sized holes. By June 15, the entire population, with the exception of about 60 families, had fled to Jalapa.[16]

Chapter 9

Ocotal
June 1, 1984

Located near the Honduran border, Ocotal is the provincial capital of Nueva Segovia and, with a population of approximately 21,000, the largest city in northern Nicaragua.

On June 1, 1984, between 4:15 and 4:30 A.M., contra forces operating out of Honduras began an assault on the city. The Nicaraguan government has estimated that the force was made up of 500 to 600 contras divided into different commando units, some of them with special training. They were heavily armed with automatic rifles, mortars, rockets and incendiary materials.

The following description of the attack on Ocotal is based not only on the affidavits of several of the residents of Ocotal who were victims and witnesses, but also on the affidavits of American members of Witness for Peace, a U.S.-based Christian peace organization which maintains a permanent presence in the conflict zones of Nicaragua. Several members of Witness for Peace who were in Jalapa at the time of this attack went to Ocotal immediately after the attack, and, along with some American Catholic nuns living in Ocotal, interviewed victims and prepared their own report.[1]

One of the points of entry into Ocotal was Barrio Sandino, on the road to Jalapa. Maria de los Angeles Montalvan, who lived in Barrio Sandino, was awakened by the firing at 4:00 A.M. Then mortars began to fall. As she cradled her seven month old boy, Ezekial de Jesus, in her bed, a bullet ripped through the wall of their wooden shack, shot into her right ankle, exited further up her leg and then entered the baby's leg and lodged in his hip.[2] Because of the attack they could not be evacuated for one and a half hours and, when they were, the truck taking them to the hospital was fired upon, as was the hospital.[3] She was hospitalized in La Trinidad for 43 days, and was only able to walk on October 11 with crutches.[4] Her son had to be taken to a hospital in Managua where the doctors were finally able to extract the bullet. Ezekial was left with a five-inch scar.[5]

Juana Maria Carcamos also lives in Barrio Sandino. A mortar exploded in her backyard, destroying the outhouse, killing chickens and felling a tree. Three pieces of shrapnel from the blast lodged in her back. Thus far the doctors have been unable to extract the shrapnel.[6]

Once inside the town, the contra forces set about destroying its key civilian and economic installations.

The state-owned lumber mill and processing plant in Barrio Sandino, which produced an estimated 14,000 feet of processed wood daily, was attacked by machine guns, mortars and grenades. Incendiary bombs were then used to set fire to and destroy a plane, the saw and conveyor belt, the forklift, the lathe, and the mechanic shop including a small truck, a pick-up truck, two caterpillar tractor motors, one tractor, the electrical system, the welding apparatus and the stock of tools. The total economic damage was estimated at between 10 and 15 million cordobas and an estimated 250 persons were left jobless.[7]

Two days later the remains of the mill were still smoldering and hundreds of bullet jackets were found among the remains.[8]

At about the same time, administrative offices and a generator of INE, the state-run electric company, were attacked by a contra force using heavy artillery. The offices were destroyed but the generator was not.[9]

At 4:45 A.M. the contras entered the Pedro Altamirano coffee drying and processing plant across from the INE, using mortars and heavy gun-fire. According to a report given by the security guard at the plant, his work partner,

> Eusebio Quadra, 55 years old, was attacked by gun-fire as he ran towards the office building. He exited from the back of the office but died almost immediately. He left a pregnant wife and eight children as well as other dependents. The other security guard was injured but survived.[10]

The contras completely destroyed the office building, the machinery, nearly two tons of coffee and a part of the cement court used for drying coffee.[11]

At about 4:30 A.M. the contras attacked the offices housing Radio Segovia, the Sandinista Youth and the local Sandinista Defense Committee (CDS) in a residential area near Ocotal's central plaza.

Genaro Paguaga Reyes, a watchman on duty at the radio, was about 25 meters from the offices when he heard shooting. He ran towards the radio where he saw about 25 armed, blue-uniformed FDN men in front of the offices. Four of the men turned at him and started firing, yelling "Long live the FDN." Paguaga was able to dive into a nearby discotheque and make his getaway later in the ensuing crossfire.[12]

Ramon Gutierrez was already in the broadcast booth with his colleague Edmundo when they heard firing first in the streets and then in the adjacent offices. While the other radio employees were able to flee through the rear, they stayed in the booth, unseen by the contras, while the intruders set fire to the building. When the cabin itself caught fire, Gutierrez and Edmundo were forced to evacuate it, but were able to leave without being seen.[13]

When the contras had retreated, the radio installations had been destroyed, including microphones, tape recorders and typewriters.[14] Workers returning to the smoldering radio station also found the burned and mutilated bodies of 19 year old Juan Carlos Mendoza of the Sandinista Youth and Julio Tercero of the CDS, whose body had its entrails and liver cut out.[15]

Osmar Amaya, a dental technician whose home and office face the radio station, was four blocks away when he heard the shooting. Racing home, he saw that the station was in flames and the contras were moving in. As he climbed up to enter his house, the contras fired on him. A bullet entered through his back and went out his thorax, breaking four ribs and entering his lung. He lay by his door unconscious for almost two hours until neighbors could evacuate him to the hospital. He was then taken to the hospital in La Trinidad where he spent one month. He still has shrapnel in his forehead which the doctors were unable to remove.[16]

The contras also attacked six grain storage silos on the outskirts of town. These silos were the principal storage sites for the department of Nueva Segovia and contained nearly 1,500 tons of rice, beans, corn and sorghum.

The members of Witness for Peace who visited the affected sites in the days following the attack, made the following report on the granary, based on their interviews with eyewitnesses and an on-site inspection:

> A contra force entered the granary at about 4:30 A.M. They shot one of the watchmen on duty, and then launched a fierce attack on the silos and installations. After all six silos were destroyed they set fire to the grains. The value of the destroyed silos, auger and conveyors was approximately one and a half million cordobas. Grains that were lost: corn 6,950 quintales; beans 4,650 quintales; rice 2,475 quintales; sorghum 323 quintales. Also lost were 150 quintales of powdered milk, and small amounts of soap, cooking oil and salt. According to CEPAD [Evangelical Committee for Aid and Development], at least ten houses in the surrounding barrio were seriously affected by the attack.[17]

The religious team also reported these other incidents:

> Marvin Jose Lopez, the director of IRENA [Ministry of Natural Resources], was shot by contra forces while driving through the town in the early morning to pick up workers who were going to plant trees in the reforestation project. The contras fired at the truck, killing Lopez and shattering the glass and tires. The three women workers in the back of the truck survived the attack, sustaining minor abrasions. Jose Lopez left behind a wife and three young children.

At the offices of INRA [Ministry of Agrarian Reform] two trucks were completely destroyed by bullets and shrapnel.

According to a nurse who was on duty at the Ocotal hospital during the attack, the contras fired at the hospital and several bullets entered the nursery and women's ward. This report was verified by a patient in the women's ward. Pictures were taken of the bullet holes in the windows and door. No one was wounded.[18]

Before leaving Ocotal, the contras left behind "Freedom Fighters Manuals," subtitled "A Practical Guide to Free Nicaragua from Oppression and Misery by Paralyzing the Military Industrial Complex of the Traitorous and Sell-out Marxist State Without Using Special Tools and with a Minimum of Risk for the Combatant."[19] The comic book-style manual, which U.S. intelligence sources and the FDN have identified as produced by the CIA, gives suggestions on ways in which people can sabotage the Nicaraguan economy, such as by leaving lights and faucets on, making phony reservations, breaking windows, cutting wires and sabotaging roads and vehicles. Instructions are provided on how to puncture tires, cut electrical wires, plug toilets and destroy roads.[20]

Another pamphlet was left showing pictures of FDN leaders and urging the people to join them.[21]

The attack lasted several hours, trapping most residents in their homes. When the contras finally retreated, at about 10:00 A.M., seven civilians had been killed and many more wounded.[22]

Chapter 10

Rancho Grande
March 25, 1983

Dr. Pierre Grosjean, a French physician, came to Nicaragua in August 1982 as part of a cooperation agreement between a French medical school and the medical school in Leon, Nicaragua. His participation was financed by the French Foreign Ministry.[1]

After teaching a course in tropical medicine in Leon, studying malaria among workers and miners, and conducting an evaluation of the tuberculosis vaccination program in Chinandega, Dr. Grosjean went to the Matagalpa region to study lesmianosis, or mountain leprosy, a disease endemic to the coffee pickers of the zone.[2]

On March 24, 1983, Dr. Grosjean arrived in Rancho Grande, a small town on the road between Matagalpa and Waslala, to begin his research along with William Morales and Idalia Castro, microbiologists from the University of Leon; Maria Felisa de Solan, a French-Argentine doctor in charge of epidemiology for the Matagalpa-Jinotega region; and Zino Bisoffi, an Italian doctor.[3]

On the morning of March 25, the doctors:

> ...were already awake but on our mattresses when at 5:30 A.M. we began to hear shots and shouting like military orders. Later, the people told us that the contras had entered, yelling 'Get out, we're going to burn the town,' but I didn't hear that.[4]

The doctors dressed hurriedly in their wooden house in the local office of the national coffee company, and lay on the floor.[5] Dr. Solan remembers that when the attack was at the heaviest,

> Pierre [Dr. Grosjean] said to me, 'You assured me that we would be out of danger here.' It's true that I told him that—that in Rancho Grande we would be as safe as in Matagalpa, because that's what I believed.[6]

According to Dr. Bisoffi:

> At about twenty to six we heard a very, very loud noise, like a bomb which shook the whole house. When it was over—it only lasted an instant—I got up to see the others, to speak with them a little, to see what had happened. For two or three minutes we didn't realize that

Pierre had been hit by a bullet; he remained lying there, he was afraid. After three minutes, Idalia saw blood, and we jumped to see what was wrong. We took his pulse, and we could still feel it, but it was very weak and it soon stopped.[7]

Dr. Grosjean was not the only casualty of the attack. When the firing stopped at about 7:30 or 8:00 A.M., the doctors went out and saw that much of the town, totally built out of wood, had been destroyed and that four others had died, including the leader of the local chapter of the national women's organization. Seventeen people were injured including seven children and four women. One of the children had to have his leg amputated.[8]

The doctors set up a makeshift hospital in the local store, a building which offered some security, and gave first aid with the little medicine they had brought or found on hand.[9] An hour later, an army battalion arrived from Waslala—too late. The soldiers carried the wounded off to Waslala and Matagalpa. Then helicopters arrived to take Dr. Grosjean's body and the most seriously wounded to Managua.[10]

Dr. Bisoffi remembers:

Although [the townspeople] had their dead and wounded, they were extremely sad over Pierre's death, it was incredible. We were all well known, Pierre particularly ...they were all sorry, everyone in the village came to console us, while they had their own dead and their own wounded.[11]

Chapter 11

El Coco
December 18, 1983

One of the first resettlement cooperatives established in Nicaragua was the Augusto Cesar Sandino cooperative, known to most people as "El Coco," along the upper Rio Coco about 13 miles south of Quilali in the province of Nueva Segovia.

El Coco was founded in 1980 on land formerly owned by General Anastasio Somoza.[1] Its 680 acres, in a fertile valley, were well-suited for the growing of basic products—corn and beans—and provided good land for the formerly landless peasants of the area.[2] The houses of the cooperative were built with roofs donated by the Bishop of Esteli.[3]

After the cooperative received legal status in 1982, the majority of the people who came to live there were refugees from contra attacks further north, by the Honduran border.[4]

Throughout December 1983, the residents "knew that the contras were in the zone. They had a permanent presence and we didn't feel at ease."[5]

At 9:30 A.M. on December 18, the contras crossed a sorghum field and began attacking the cooperative.[6]

Carmela Gutierrez, the head of the local women's organization, was in her house preparing food when the attack came. She picked up her rifle and went to the trenches that had been prepared by the members of the cooperative to protect themselves against such attacks.[7] Her husband, Wenceslao, did the same.[8] The children of the cooperative, together with many of the women, ran to the bomb shelters where more than 100 of them huddled.[9]

The contras, mortaring from a nearby hill, surrounded the cooperative on three sides.[10] Carmela Gutierrez testified:

> The mortars flew as if they were stones. They began to infiltrate into the cooperative shouting for us to give up, saying that they were going to eat us alive.[11]

After local resistance by civilian defenders was overcome, and those in the shelter fled, the contras entered the cooperative and killed 14 people. One eyewitness, the evangelist Arturo Marin, told Carmela Gutierrez that Juana Maria Santos Ramirez, age 15, was raped as was Maria Cristina Espinoza, age 16 or 17.[12] This was confirmed by a captured contra leader.[13] The evangelist Marin also reported that an elderly woman, Julia Sanchez Hernandez,

61

and Marco Antonio Mendieta, a doctor from Leon, were literally cut to pieces.[14]

Two girls, Petronila Ramirez Zavala, 12, and Juana Francisca Ramirez, who were hiding under their bed, were shot when the contras entered their house.[15] Their grandmother was shot in the arm but survived. Altogether, six people from the Ramirez family died.[16] Aurelio Espinoza Sanchez, 60, his wife Julia, and their two sons were also killed.[17]

When the survivors returned, they found that the cooperative had been totally destroyed, including the food warehouses, the machinery and the tractors.[18] In addition, each of the 12 abandoned bomb shelters had been mortared and destroyed.[19]

After the attack, the families took refuge in Quilali, in the school and the Baptist church. Others moved to nearby San Bartolo, where they have been given some land.[20]

The attack on El Coco is also reported in the *Atlanta Constitution*.[21] This report, based on interviews with survivors, recounts in detail the killing, rape and mutilation of civilians and the destruction of the cooperative described above. It also reports that officials of the FDN "acknowledged that their men attacked and destroyed the cooperative."[22]

Chapter 12

El Jicaro
October 1982—October 1984

The northern region of El Jicaro-Murra, covering three towns and hundreds of small mountain communities, has been the scene of numerous contra attacks since 1982.

"The result of these attacks," says Father Evaristo Bertrand, a North American parish priest in the region, "has been hundreds of deaths and thousands of displaced people, including those who were taken off to Honduras as well as those who were forced to move to larger or safer places because of attacks or the danger of attacks."[1]

One of these incidents occurred on October 28, 1982, when five armed men dressed in blue FDN uniforms broke down the door of the house where Maria Bustillo, 57, was living with her husband, Ricardo, a Delegate of the Word, and five of their children.[2] The intruders ordered everyone to the floor, face down, and warned that whoever moved would be killed. After striking Ricardo and kicking the children, they tied them up two by two and led them away, telling Maria, "Careful you old bitch, you're going to find out tomorrow."[3]

When Maria went out the next morning to look for her family, she found her five children dead, about 50 yards from the house. "They were left all cut up. Their ears were pulled off, their noses and other parts were cut off."[4] Her husband Ricardo was found dead in a nearby town along with another man, Raul Moreno. "They were also left broken up. He had false teeth and they took them, his arms were broken and his hands were cut up."[5]

After the massacre, Maria took refuge in El Jicaro.[6]

The town of El Jicaro itself was attacked twice, on April 21, 1983 and August 24, 1983. During the first attack, the contras fired 87 mortars but were unable to penetrate the town, though one farmer had his throat slit, others were wounded and one man was kidnapped.[7] The attack occurred while mass was being held in the church, and many town residents spent the night there.[8]

The second attack on El Jicaro began at 5:15 A.M. with mortar fire. One resident, Marco Sevilla, a father of eight, upon hearing the firing, tried to leave his house to help in the town's defense, but his family would not let him go. Telling them that he would not let the contras kill him disgracefully in his house unarmed, he went out the back way toward the command post to get his gun.[9] Before he could get far from the house, however, the contras caught him and cut his throat with a bayonet.[10] One other man, Chilo Toruno, from Jalapa, was killed.[11]

Straddling the intersection where the main Segovias road from Ocotal and Santa Clara to Quilali forks off to El Jicaro is the town of Susucayan. In the early morning of October 11, 1984, the contras attacked the town with mortars, machine guns and rifle fire.[12]

Emelina del Carmen Merlo, a health worker, hid in her house. When the attack died down at about 6:40 A.M., she tried to get to the health center to attend any dead or wounded but the firing began again and she took refuge in a private home. When the firing stopped again at 7:30, she got what she needed from the health center and set up a first aid center in the middle of town.[13] Three men died: Pedro Gomez, Juan Tomas Ruiz, and Eusebio Rodriguez, Delegate of the Word and community leader, who was a refugee from the north.[14]

That same morning, the contras passed through the nearby community of Las Brisas, just outside the resettlement cooperative of La Jumuyca. At about 1:00 A.M., eight of them entered the house where Abraham Gutierrez, 66, was dying of a liver infection.[15] They demanded that Gutierrez' daughter, Dora, go with them, but she refused. Instead, they took an older man, Antonio Velasquez, who returned shortly thereafter since he was of no use to them.[16]

About an hour later, Gutierrez, the sick man, died[17] and his son Felipe went to La Jumuyca to report on the incident and find a coffin. While in a house nearby, some 200 contras ordered him and Antonio Olivas to go with them or be shot.[18] Olivas was ordered to carry one of their wounded.[19] The contras also captured Francisco Lopez about 200 yards on.[20]

Lopez quickly escaped, but after several hours of walking, the other two were put to work.[21] While the contras were resting, Olivas was able to escape as well, but Felipe, the dead man's son, is still missing.[22]

On October 24, 1984, shortly before 5:00 A.M., the contras came to the home of Luis Cardenas in El Pie de la Cuesta, between El Jicaro and Murra. Cardenas, 40, was a bricklayer and farmer. Accusing him of being an agent of state security (he was not), the contras demanded entry into Cardenas' house. When he refused, according to his widow Maria Julia:

> They broke down two doors and a window with rifles and three armed men, with olive-green uniforms, entered the house...
>
> They grabbed my husband and they beat him and broke his neck with a rifle. Then they took him out of the room by one of the doors which was destroyed and they bashed in his head with a rifle and they took out his eye.

> Then they threw him on the floor and they tied his
> hands and they cut his throat with a bayonet. He
> screamed and fought...and said that he didn't do any-
> thing wrong, but they wouldn't let him speak and put a
> green cloth in his mouth.[23]

Maria Julia was hiding under the bed with one of her three children and, during the incident, the contras did not see her. When the
child cried out "my daddy," however, they spotted her and tried to
take her away. When she refused, they beat her on the head,
leaving her lying on the bed, unconscious.[24] Then they left, after
stealing all the clothes and the utensils in the house.[25] That same
day, they also kidnapped Maria Julia's second cousin from the
same community.[26]

As a result of the attacks in the north, many refugees had
populated resettlement cooperatives ("asentamientos") around El
Jicaro, where they were given land and fields to plant. One of these
cooperatives, Las Dantas, was itself repeatedly attacked in the
first part of 1984, however.[27] Most of the families were therefore
forced to move again, to the Santa Julia cooperative, just outside
the community of San Gregorio.

On October 29, 1984, the refugees were attacked yet again. In
an early morning attack on the Santa Julia cooperative, the contras launched a mortar which landed in the cooperative's headquarters where three families were living. Maria Soza Valladares
was sick in bed, but all her children were in the middle of the room
"as if they were waiting for the mortar" which killed Marta Azucena, 11 years old, Carmelita Azucena, five, and Ronaldo Miguel,
three. Another child, Alexis, eight, was severely injured and died
on the way to the hospital.[28] Maria Soza, herself injured, tried to
rescue her dead and dying children, but it was too late. Her daughter Maria, six, covered with blood, walked all the way to the health
center in San Gregorio through the ensuing crossfire, despite the
wounds she had all over her body. Eventually, she and her mother
spent almost a month in the hospital, where she was operated on
twice.[29]

Aurelia Ortiz, eight months pregnant, was also in the room
with her children when the mortar exploded, killing Jose Rodolfo,
five, and Maura de Jesus, seven. A month later, she gave birth to a
stillborn child.[30] Not including the stillborn, six small children
died from the mortar.

Kidnappings continue to occur frequently. Father Bertrand
testified that it would be "impossible" to keep track of all of them.[31]
He added:

> The people in my area are now accustomed to the war.
> They are cautious as night comes on and as dawn
> breaks, but they have learned to live with it. They partic-
> ipate in their own defense because they know it's not
> play. As a rule, we don't go from town at night.[32]

Angela Diaz Montenegro

photo: Reed Brody

Chapter 13

Jacinto Hernandez Cooperative
December 16, 1984

On December 16, 1983, at 4:45 A.M., the contras launched an attack on the cooperative Jacinto Hernandez in El Cedro, between San Jose del Bocay and El Cua in Northern Jinotega. The cooperative was just getting underway, on land that had been abandoned. It had over 100 people, but was still mostly pastureland and cows.[1]

When the attack came, Angela Diaz Montenegro was at home with her eight children. Some months earlier she and her family had come to the cooperative, abandoning the 17 acres of land they had bought, because of constant threats against her husband, a local civilian leader, and fear for the safety of her young children.[2] Angela's 16 year old daughter and 13 year old son grabbed guns to try to repel the attackers while Angela and the younger children joined two other families in the bomb shelter near the house. When the contras entered the cooperative, however, the families took off, half-naked, for the hills nearby.[3]

From the hills, they could see and hear the contras, using machine-guns and mortars, take the cooperative against the defense of only 12 coop members.[4] In their hiding place, one of the attackers' bullets struck and killed Angela's 11 year old daughter Marta Rosalba.[5] Rather than attending to the dead child, Angela tried to calm the others so that they would not scream and attract the contras' attention. Even after the one hour battle was over, the contras continued firing in the direction of the family.[6]

When they could, the family headed toward a neighbor's house. There Angela learned that her two children who had been fighting—her 16 year old daughter and 13 year old son—were dead, along with five others from the cooperative.[7] The contras, she was told, had also burned down her house, as well as several other houses, the health center, the warehouse for basic foodstuffs, a tractor, two trucks and several animals.[8] Two women from the cooperative were kidnapped but thereafter returned.[9]

Angela and her surviving children took refuge in El Cua, but four days later that town was attacked as well. As the families took refuge in the church, the contras were fought off.[10]

Angela now lives in Jinotega but says she is tormented by those attacks. "Every noise I heard, I thought was gunfire. The Frente [Sandinista] sent me to see a doctor in Managua because I couldn't eat or sleep, thinking about what happened. I was going crazy...Now I'm better, only sometimes I get a case of nerves when I hear that someone died or that there was combat."[11]

Innocente Peralta

photo: Reed Brody

Chapter 14

Northern Jinotega
January 1982—November 1984

The mountainous area in the north of Jinotega province—the municipalities of El Cua, Bocay, Yali and Wiwili—has been a principal area of contra activity since the beginning of the war. This chapter describes just a few of the many attacks on civilians in this area.[1]

One cooperative alone, "German Pomares Ordonez," near Las Delicias, has been the target of eight attacks.[2] One such attack took place in mid-April 1984. A Nicaraguan helicopter flying over the cooperative was attacked by the advancing contras, tipping off the townspeople, but the contras were able to take away several members of the cooperative.[3] Inocente Peralta, 58, a Delegate of the Word (lay pastor), was one of those who went looking for the missing:

> We found [Juan Perez] assassinated in the mountains. They had tied his hands behind his back. They hung him on a wire fence. They opened up his throat and took out his tongue. Another bayonet had gone through his stomach and come out his back. Finally, they cut off his testicles. It was horrible to see.[4]

Peralta was told that six others had been found in similar condition, including one whose heart was cut out.[5]

Other attacks in this area over the last three years include the following:

—On January 12, 1982, in the area of Las Colinas, Jeronimo Lopez's private vehicle with 15 civilian passengers was ambushed by a group of about 100 counterrevolutionaries. Eight of the passengers, including an eight year old girl, were killed.[6]

—On January 22, 1982, a group of about 80 contras staged a 5:00 A.M. attack near La Pavona, surrounding several houses. One landowner, Manuel Alfaro Palacios, was taken out of his house and led to a nearby creek where the contras sat him down and shot a bullet into his head. Another man, Norberto Mairena, was killed by a grenade. The residents fought back, but when the battle was over, three campesinos were dead, and many others were forced to leave their homes.[7]

—One night in May 1982, the contras came to the house in Guapinol where Adrian Ferrufino was visiting Tomas Huetes and his family. Huetes had no political position, but was working to build a school and bring a teacher to his community.[8] The intruders knocked at the door and said that if Huetes did not open up, they would shoot.[9] As Huetes went to open the door, Ferrufino slipped out the back. From there he could see the contras tying up Huetes, and he ran further away.[10]

When Ferrufino returned in the morning, he found Huetes' dead body, its tongue cut up, its eyes cut up, and three stab wounds in the chest.[11] Huetes' wife, who was in a state of shock, told Ferrufino that the contras had done all of that in front of her and the children and that when she pleaded with them to leave him alone, they told her, "Shut up you bitch. We're going to kill you too because this son of a bitch is a rabid dog." Although she insisted that he was not a Sandinista but a simple campesino, they killed him and threatened her that if she told anyone what had happened they would kill her and her children.[12]

Later, when Ferrufino became active in the distribution of basic products and in school construction in his community in Penas Blancas, the contras began to look for him as well. Once they told a campesino that they were looking for him to kill him,[13] and they twice came to his house looking for him.[14] As a result, he was forced to move to Jinotega, and has left his farm in the care of a friend.[15]

—On April 25, 1983, in the zone of Villagual, north of Yali, a group of 500 counterrevolutionaries swooped down on Terencio de Jesus Flores and Fermin Valenzuela, two organizers of the National Union of Ranchers and Farmers (UNAG) who were working in the zone. They captured Valenzuela but Flores escaped.[16] The next day, Flores returned to the spot: "We found Fermin dead with his eyes gouged out as if with a bayonet and a stab wound in the throat and with a liquid in the face which left him burnt."[17]

—In September 1983, some 200 counterrevolutionaries attacked the town of Bana, killing five people including an 18 month old girl who was in her house when a bomb landed.[18]

—The town of Wamblan was attacked in the early morning of December 19, 1983, by a group of over 400 contras. Although the attack was repulsed by border troops in the town, two women and two children were killed when a grenade landed in the unfinished bomb shelter in which they had hidden.[19]

—In February 1984, the contras attacked the cooperative in Mollejones, less than two miles from the Honduran border, killing five people and wounding a 13 year old boy with a bullet in the eye.[20] Also in February 1984, the contras attacked the cooperative Georgino Andrades at 3:00 A.M., leaving three dead and five wounded.[21]

—On March 23, 1984, the contras burned the house of Irma Pineda, and killed her son, in the La Rica sector. The same day, they killed Manuel Gomez and burned his house, as well as the house of Jesus Mendoza and a truck carrying food estimated to be worth 1.5 million cordobas.[22]

—On April 8, 1984, the contras attacked the Las Colinas coffee growing cooperative, some eight or ten miles from the town of Yali. The farmers could not hold off the 400 contras, who came with mortars, grenades, rifles and machine guns.[23]

The attackers soon had the cooperative encircled and, after two hours, they sent in one company to take it by assault.[24] As the cooperative's defenders retreated, three of them were killed, but the others were able to make their way out, as were most of those in the bomb shelter.[25]

When the army arrived, at about 9:00 A.M. and the people returned to the cooperative:

> They [the contras] had already destroyed all that was the cooperative: a coffee drying machine, the two dormitories for the coffee cutters, the electricity generators, seven cows, the plant and the food warehouse.
>
> There was one boy, about 15 years old, who was retarded and suffered from epilepsy. We had left him in the bomb shelter.
>
> When we returned...we saw...that they had cut his throat, then they cut open his stomach and left his intestines hanging out on the ground like a string.
>
> They did the same to Juan Corrales who had already died from a bullet in the fighting. They opened him up and took out his intestines and cut off his testicles.[26]

—On September 15, 1984, Nicolas Chavarria, 15, and Marcelino Herrera were killed. According to their neighbors, they were taken from where they were working and brought to Villagual where they were killed.[27]

—On October 9, 1984, in La Pavona, near Yali, the contras killed Nortie Torres, Jose Navarrete Cruz, 30, Miguel Navarrete Cruz, 15, Jose Herrera and Inocencio Mejia, all campesinos. Their throats were slit and they had stab wounds in their bodies.[28] At the same time seven others were kidnapped. All of those who were kidnapped later escaped and reported that they were tied up and beaten on the head.[29]

—On November 7, 1984, 15 campesinos, including girls of 11 and 12 years old, were kidnapped seven miles from the town of Yali. Seven of them, including the girls, have escaped.[30]

As a result of these and many other attacks, numerous producers in Northern Jinotega have been forced to abandon their lands and move into the towns where they can live in greater safety.[31]

Chapter 15

Bernardino Diaz Ochoa Cooperative
November 18, 1984

The Bernardino Diaz Ochoa Cooperative was 16 kilometers from Waslala, in the province of Matagalpa. On July 19, 1984 a truck from the cooperative, carrying 40 unarmed members, was ambushed near Guabo. The shooting lasted an hour an a half, until an army unit came to chase the attackers away, and by the time it was over, Josefina Picardo, 29 and pregnant, Ricardo, 17, and Jose Perez, six, were killed, and fourteen people were injured.[1]

On November 18, the cooperative itself was attacked at 5:00 A.M. by a group of about 250 contras armed with machine-guns, rockets, mortars and rifles.[2] As the women and children fled to the road, the twelve civilian defenders in the cooperative tried to hold off the attackers.[3] The contras took the village about 500 yards from the cooperative, and went from house to house burning them down.[4] Then they began to take the trench where the defenders were, killing three of them, before the rest were able to retreat.[5]

The next day, when the people returned to their coop, they found three children burned to death in their house: Josefina, six, Rosalba, four, and Albertina, two. All the houses of the village were burned as was the whole cooperative including the main house, the machines and the animals.[6] One woman, Elda, 18, had been taken away by the contras.[7] As a result, the members of the cooperative have had to move to another coop.[8]

Chapter 16

Siuna
August 1982—November 1984

The rural zone of Siuna, in Northern Zelaya, has about 25,000 inhabitants, most of whom live and farm in the hills. In 1981, the area consisted of 58 communities. There are now only 47, however, the remainder having been attacked by the contras and destroyed.[1]

Father Enrique Blandon Vasconcelos, the area's parish priest, testified about some of the attacks in his parish:

—In August 1982, the contras attacked the Umbla cooperative of 40 families, killing one child and wounding three and causing the coop to shut down.[2]

—In March 1983, 130 contras invaded a cooperative of 90 families in Kaskita. They asked the leader, Miguel Martinez, to talk to them, but shot him in the back and head. They then gathered the families and threatened them if they continued to work in the coop. As a result, all those families, too, left for safer places.[3]

—In August 1983, the contras attacked the El Ocote cooperative, killing six people including three women, two men and a child. They then robbed the cooperative and destroyed the school and the community house.[4]

—At the end of January 1984, Candido Jarquin Jarquin of Kurrin was killed.[5]

—At the same time, the lay pastor Bernardino Sanchez of Los Baldes was kidnapped, managing to escape after 15 days.[6]

—On February 8, 1984 the catechist Fermin Cano was detained and his life threatened.[7]

—On February 15, 1984, seven people were kidnapped from Waspadito.[8]

—On February 16, 1984, Esteban Galeano was killed in Alo Betel.[9]

—On June 10, 1984, at a time when most of its defenders were away, the Waslalita cooperative was attacked by at least 600 contras. One 14 year old boy and one adult were killed, and three were injured. In May, the cooperative had also been attacked, but no deaths resulted.[10]

—In June 1984, 28 men were kidnapped from El Guayabo and are still missing. Only women and children remain in that community.[11]

—At the end of June 1984, 13 families were kidnapped, including the Evangelical pastor, from the community of San Pablo-Asa.[12]

—On June 14, 1984, Victorino Martinez Urbina was taken from his house in Cuicuinita and was cut into pieces with a machete.[13]

—On July 19, 1984, a truck from the cooperative El Naranjo-Iyas was ambushed and Javier Torres was killed.[14]

—Around the same time, the Delegate of the Word of Sarawas, Eusebio Perez Hernandez, was kidnapped. After a week, during which he was made to carry a heavy backpack, he was able to escape.[15]

—On August 15, 1984, more than 50 people were kidnapped from Waspuco Abajo.[16]

—On August 22 and 23, 1984, the contras passed through El Guayabo, stealing food, shoes and boots.[17]

—On August 26, 1984, Ancleto Palacios was killed with a machete by a contra group in La Union-Labu.[18]

—On September 12, 1984, the catechist Abelino Acuna, education coordinator, disappeared.[19]

The contra attacks have also disrupted the economic life of the region. The road connecting Siuna with Matagalpa has been the scene of many ambushes, which often are directed against trucks carrying food shipments.[20] Numerous health workers and school teachers have been kidnapped.[21]

The contras have harassed and threatened Father Blandon himself. In late January 1984, when he was leaving the community of Kurrin with two nuns, he was stopped by a group of 1,800 heavily-armed contras who had the road ambushed.[22] Some of them claimed to be Honduran and wore Honduran uniforms.[23] They made him get down from his mule and began interrogating him, calling him a communist and telling him that they "blow the heads" off priests who preach politics.[24]

Because some of the contras knew Father Blandon, and the nuns intervened, the contras let him go.[25] Later, the contras told local church leaders that if they ran into Father Blandon again, they would kill him.[26] Then, in September 1984, when he was in the community of Baka, Father Blandon received a note warning him that if he arrived in Luku Paraska his head would be blown off because he was preaching politics and communism.[27]

Because of the threats, Father Blandon renounced completion of his rounds[28], and in late September it was decided that Sister Sandra Price, an American nun, would go to visit some mountain communities accompanied by two Delegates of the Word.[29]

When they got to the community of Umbla, a commando unit of about 50 contras arrived and questioned Sister Sandra at length about Father Blandon, accusing her of lying when she said he was not with them. Finally, the commando left.[30]

Then a second commando unit came and took away a young couple accompanying the Sister to Siuna to be married. When Sister Sandra objected, the leader said that if the couple did not go voluntarily, he would have them tied up and taken away. They never returned.[31]

A few hours later, after the Sister had left town, four contras from the same group caught up with her and this time took away the catechist who was accompanying her. He never returned.[32]

In Cuicuina Grande, a river village, yet another commando unit forced the Sister and the two campesinos who had joined her to disembark in a house and held them there all night. The leader interviewed the Sister and boasted of all the aid that the United States had airlifted to them.[33] In the morning, the Sister was released but the leader insisted on holding the two campesinos. They, like the young couple and the catechist, are still missing.[34]

Florencio Godinez, a Delegate of the Word in Trignitara, had long received threats for having worked in literacy programs and for forming a credit and service cooperative. In June 1984, when the contras began to operate in his zone, he learned that a family was forced to give them the names of church and cooperative leaders, including his. Some friends then advised him to leave the area, and he did so on July 3.[35]

The next day, the contras came to Godinez's house. They held his daughters and daughter-in-law there for a day before leaving, promising to return. The whole family then decided to leave, giving up the cows, pigs, chickens and 17 acres of land they held.[36]

On July 24, the contras went to the house of Godinez's married daughter in Salto Verde and grabbed her husband. When the two tried to flee, Godinez' daughter was shot and killed.[37] (Godinez was not an eye-witness to these two incidents; his relatives described them to him.)

Cirillo Jarquin, a Delegate of the Word, was walking near his home in Coperna on June 23, 1984, when he crossed paths with four contras.[38] "You're coming with us," they said. The leader added, "Rabid dog, you're not going to escape. They call us beasts and it's true. We don't have pity for any rabid dog."[39] Although he was warned that "the slightest move" he made to escape, "[he would be] blown into the air,"[40] Jarquin was able to run away after spending a day with his captors.

The Siuna region was particularly hard-hit during October and November 1984.

On November 20, ten contras arrived at night, firing, at Gregorio Davila's house in Coperna Abajo. Davila's son Danilo, age four, and his six day old baby boy were sleeping. Another son, eight, was with his father. Upon hearing the shooting, Carmen, the mother, hid under the bed. Twelve year old Luz Marina, who clung to a wall, testified:

> The first shot hit my father and the same bullet entered my eight year old brother's leg. Another bullet

killed my four year old brother in bed. My mother was wounded in the head... Two contras entered the house and demanded that my father give up his gun but he hadn't one in the house. They shot Eulalia Cano Obando, 18, [my uncle Porfirio's girlfriend]... The contras grabbed my father and my uncle [Porfirio]. They shot my father four times and when he didn't die they cut his throat. My uncle died from one shot. Another contra came in and said of Eulalia, 'That fuck is the sister of the rabid dog Mariano Cano,' and shot her again.[41]

The contras then left. Luz Marina's wounded mother sent the surviving children to an uncle's house. When they returned the next morning, their mother was dead. They went back to their uncle's house but, when they returned to their house that afternoon, the bodies were no longer there.[42]

Three days later, the bodies of their father, their uncle Porfirio, Eulalia, their four year old brother and their mother were found in the river. Their mother's face was skinned and she and Eulalia were left naked.[43]

Other incidents in those months included:

—On October 13, a group of about 45 contras came at 7:00 A.M. to Valeriano Polanco's basic products post in the community of Fonseca and stole sugar, boots and other products.[44] They then took Polanco and some 30 other campesinos with them. They marched all day until they arrived near Siuna's landing-strip where, after night fell, the contras fired on the nearby homes with rifles and mortars.[45]

Douglas Spence, an American working with Witness for Peace, a U.S.-based Christian peace group, was in Siuna when the firing began. He testified:

We heard hundreds of rounds of automatic gun-fire, answered by slightly more distant fire. The shooting lasted about half an hour culminating in three loud mortar rounds...

The four of us huddled on the living room floor waiting to see what would happen next.[46]

Two days later, Spence visited one of the affected neighborhoods:

We saw the holes in the zinc roofs where people told us bullets had entered the night of the attack. We also saw three mortar craters, one within 50 feet of a little house, where the contra rounds had landed.

Fortunately, no one was injured or killed in the attack.[47]

—In the community of Uly, 50 contras surrounded a house on October 23, taking away six people on the three-day trek to Comenegro.[48] Pablo Perez Landeros, who escaped, saw 200 other hostages who, the contras said, were being taken to Honduras.[49]

—On October 28, ten contras arrived at the house of Pablo Perez Tercero in El Corozo. They tied up Perez Tercero and his brother and took them to where they were already holding their father and two other brothers.[50] After being handed over to another contra group, and held for 20 days along with ten other hostages, he began to run away. Realizing that he was fleeing, the contras fired upon him, but he made it safely out of danger. One of his brothers also managed to escape but they have not heard from their father or the other two brothers.[51]

—On October 28, in the community of El Dorado, the contras captured Leontes Velasquez, President of the local Electoral Board, and Eladio Rodriguez, Board Secretary, who had arrived in town by mule for a meeting held in preparation for the November 4 elections. The two were taken to where the contras were holding 40 others from El Dorado and then on to Monte de Oro, San Pablo de Asa and Lawas-Corozo. There, while the guard was not watching, Rodriguez escaped by throwing himself into the river.[52]

On the night of November 4, two contras, pretending to be Nicaraguan soldiers, came to Cristobal Grenado's house near Uly and told him and a friend that they had to go to guard the nearby cooperative. By the time they realized the trick, they were already being taken to a hill where they were made to spend the night. At 5:00 A.M. there was an attack on the cooperative and at 9:00 A.M. the contras brought the two down to the cooperative where other captives were being held. After walking seven hours they were held under surveillance for 22 days, with little to eat, before Grenado and a friend were able to escape into the mountains.[53]

—On November 26, the cooperative in Floripon was attacked by a contra force of about 120 with mortars, rockets, machine-guns and rifles. Because the 125 women and children of the cooperative took refuge in the shelters they had built in case of attack, only one cooperative member, a civilian defender, died in the fighting. After the contras left, however, an unexploded grenade was found and mishandled. It exploded, killing one woman and injuring thirteen.[54]

Chapter 17

San Jeronimo
May 16, 1984

In the valleys of a mountainous region 30 kilometers northeast of Condega, in the Department of Esteli, lie numerous small farming villages. Until May 16, 1984, many of the residents of these valleys were organized in the agricultural cooperative "Heroes and Martyrs" of Canta Gallo near the village of San Jeronimo.

On May 15, 1984, some campesinos from the valley noticed "something very strange—an airplane passed overhead flying very low...and dropped munitions to the contras."[1]

The next day, a contra task force invaded the valleys, attacking the communities of Santa Ana del Ojoche, Los Planes, Buena Vista, La Montanita, Robledalito and San Jeronimo.

In each community the story was similar: the outnumbered civilian defenders offered what resistance they could while the population was evacuated. When they were overcome, the contras entered the community and burned down the houses.

At about 6:00 A.M., the contras attacked Los Planes. The local residents fled on foot to the community of La Laguna.[2] According to the local offices of the Sandinista Front, when the contras entered the town they burned the houses of Juan Simon Herrera, Maximo Monzon, Prudencio Herrera, Alejandro Artela, Loaquin Artela and Amado Rodriguez.[3]

At around 9:00 A.M., the contras took positions on the hills around El Robledalito. The families were notified to leave because the village was not prepared to defend itself against such an attack. Filemon Zavala Cruz had the responsibility of moving the families out of the community and toward San Jeronimo. From San Jeronimo, the families fled to La Laguna.[4]

Once again, the contras set fire to the houses—this time 17 of the 20 houses were burned.[5] These included the houses of Victor Obregon, Carmelia Olivas, Cosme Cardenas, Visitacion Martinez, Luis Galeano, Nicomedes Galeano, Santos Cardenas, Filemon Zavala, Rene Martinez, Luis Martinez, Pedro J. Zavala, Isabel Galeano, Macario Rivera, Manuel Ortez, Marceliano Martinez and Luis Alfonso Cardenas, as well as the school.[6] Parish priest Father Enrique Alberto Oggier, who visited the village after the attack, testified, "In Robledalito, the only thing you can see now is burnt rubble, burnt cans."[7]

La Montanita was attacked shortly thereafter. Jose Ramon Castillo was working, getting the corn ready for planting, when he heard that the contras were coming. He got his rifle in case there was to be any attempt to defend the town. But the contras were advancing from two sides and he and his friends saw that they were vastly outnumbered and that any defense was hopeless. They concentrated instead on getting the people out of the village to El Bramadero.[8]

When the contras had left La Montanita, "the houses and everything having to do with corn were left burned."[9] The burned houses belonged to Juan Flores, Angelica Flores, Demetrio Galeano, Marcelino Cruz, Humberto Flores, Antolin Galeano, Reynaldo Perez, Estanislao Castillo, San Flores, Rosalio Flores, Modesta Cruz, and Francisco Corrales.[10]

Finally, the contras attacked the main cooperative Canto Gallo in San Jeronimo, which provided work for many of the people of the valleys. The cooperative—which, according to the managers, produced 120,000 pounds of coffee in the last year, as well as cattle—was left totally destroyed. According to Father Oggier, "only ashes remained. It was a very important cooperative for the people of the zone, especially the poor."[11]

In one day, hundreds of valley residents became refugees. That night, some 600 homeless people, mostly women and children, arrived in the town of Condega where they slept on the floor of the parish's communal house. They were then moved to the grammar school where they stayed another week.[12]

Today, many of the families live in overcrowded conditions with friends or relatives in Condega, having lost their land and possessions. In her crowded house in Condega, Angela Zamora says, "We never went back to see our house [in Los Planes]. They told us it was burned. We had animals, chickens, turkeys, pigs. We had corn. The riches of the poor."[13]

Ismael Cordoba Centeno, also living in Condega, had 60 acres of land, but now "the beans, coffee, rice and everything we had is gone."[14] Maria Espinoza Zavala, whose son was kidnapped in February 1984, had 17 acres of land in Santa Ana del Ojoche. Her family's houses there and in Los Planes were burned.[15]

Flora Cordoba Centeno's house was not burned, but she is afraid to go back even though she needs the corn that was left in Los Planes.[16] Maria Anita Hernandez had "a little land [in Robledalito] but it was enough to support ourselves." Now she and her husband and 12 children are staying with a family in Condega.[17]

In nearby Los Potreros, the contras broke into the home of Maria Guadalupe Rodriguez and Etemina Rodriguez on June 19, 1984, stealing a radio, clothes and 2,000 cordobas. Later that day, the contras kidnapped seven people, including their brother and sister. The sister was released immediately, but the brother did not return for a month. The same day, the contras killed Reynaldo Olivo and Laureano Flores, for whom the new cooperative is named.[18]

The refugees of the May attacks were dealt another blow in mid-August. The lumber mill in the valley community of El Bramadero, where wood was being cut and prepared to build new houses for the refugees, was destroyed by the contras. Says Father Oggier, "With this burning, we have another delay, and the people will have to wait much longer [for new housing]."[19]

The burning of the valley communities was the worst attack in the region, but there have been others. At the end of September, the huge grain silos in Palacaguina—which, according to the government records, stored 90,000 pounds of rice, 180,200 pounds of corn, 27,400 pounds of beans, 17,400 pounds of salt and 50 crates of soap[20]—were "totally destroyed by the counterrevolutionaries," according to Father Oggier. "I visited it the next day and saw how the people were trying to gather up the little that remained."[21] On other occasions the contras have raided towns and kidnapped civilians.[22]

Says Father Oggier, "The people of my parish are afraid. I am afraid, too. They tell me that I should not go out alone, only with a soldier. I don't go out at night to visit the communities, I always return earlier. At night I stay in my house."[23]

The state farm at El Castillo Norte after contra attack.
photo: Barricad

Chapter 18

El Castillo Norte
May 15, 1984

After the 1979 revolution, many farms under government control (formerly the property of General Somoza) were consolidated into state farms ("Unidades de Produccion Estatales," or UPE's) or cooperatives. These farms, which often serve as social service centers in their zone, have been frequent targets of contra attacks.

One such attack took place on May 15, 1984, against the UPE in El Castillo Norte, 65 kilometers north of Jinotega. It was a small farm with only 60 adults and their children. At approximately 11:00 A.M., a band of about 300 contras invaded the farm, overwhelming the 14 civilian defenders, and killing 20 people, kidnapping others, destroying the farm and its facilities and forcing the survivors to flee.

When the attack began, most of the unarmed members of the farm ran for the shelter they had built. As the battle raged, however, the shelter, too, was attacked by mortar fire. An 87 year old woman, Vicenta Castro, was killed by one of the mortars, and the others fled.[1]

Rosa Sobalvarro, a 15 year old civilian defender who was three months pregnant, was shot. She lay on the ground pleading for water and begging her fleeing mother not to leave her. Her mother was unable to help, however, and when she returned the following day, Rosa's "breasts were cut to pieces, her throat was cut. The poor girl was destroyed."[2]

Lucilia Chavarria Lanza, a mother of four who lost one son and one cousin, and whose father received a shrapnel wound, recounted what she saw after fleeing the shelter, helping her father and Ramon (Moncho) Castro, an injured civilian defender:

> When we got to the front of the store, they were chopping up a 'compa.' They had ripped out a bone and were tearing him apart. When we got closer, one of them grabbed a piece of his flesh and threw it in my face, saying, 'Maybe you're the mother bitch.'[3]

They passed by Francisco Castro, Moncho's brother, who "was filled with stab wounds...They hit him and blood flew and he was left standing as if lifeless. Then they killed him with a stick in his mouth."[4]

Another civilian defender, Rene Amador, "was carried off... They broke his arms and tortured him to death."[5] Another, Jesus Hernandez, "Chuno," who had been kidnapped previously but had escaped, was killed and then chopped up and burned.[6] Another was castrated.[7]

As Lucilia was helping Moncho, one of the contras hit him with the butt of his gun, then cut him with his bayonet and began to suck his blood, saying to Lucilia:

> 'Look bitch, this is thirst, this is the water we drink, the blood of these rabid dogs sons of bitches...' Then he took the blood and smeared it on me [saying] 'auntie, how tasty, bitch.' He shoved it in my mouth and made me drink it. Then he bathed the head of a little boy I was leading with the blood.[8]

Lucilia was then separated from Moncho, who was killed, and she fled with her father and daughter, but not before being bathed in gasoline,[9] as well as threatened and taunted.[10] When the battle was over, the entire farm was burned and destroyed, including the store, the office, the children's center, the center where the food was stored, the land and all the houses.[11] Other coop members were killed, and some were kidnapped.[12]

Lucilia Chavarria was relocated to the UPE La Colonia, but she is not well. "I can't sleep with the light off...because I see everything" that happened that day.[13] She also lost all her possessions: "We had our own house in the UPE. We had pigs, chickens, everything. The children ate. Now we have what people can give us."[14]

Like Lucilia, some of the survivors were relocated in La Colonia. Others were taken to nearby Abisinia and others to the farm La Fondadora. Maria Castro, who lost her mother Vicenta in the attack on the shelter, as well as her three sons, Francisco, Ismael and Ramon (Moncho), now lives in a shack on the outskirts of Jinotega with her daughter and her sole surviving son. Her house and adjacent land were burned, along with about 4,400 pounds of corn, beans and coffee.[15] "Before, food was never lacking—we gave it away. Now, without my sons, without the land, we hardly have anything."[16]

Chapter 19

San Juan de Limay
Sister Nancy Donovan
January 8, 1985

The town of San Juan de Limay in the province of Esteli has been the scene of numerous contra attacks in late 1984 and early 1985. Nancy Donovan, an American Maryknoll nun who is a missionary assigned to the town, testified that, between mid-December 1984 and mid-January 1985, almost 40 civilians were killed in the attacks. "The attacks have been made on civilian, not military, targets and they have been increasing."[1]

On January 8, 1985, Sister Nancy herself was detained and held captive by a group of contras.

That morning, at about 6:00 A.M., she left town to attend a clergy meeting of the Diocese of Esteli which had been called by the Bishop. To get there:

> I had to search for a ride in a private vehicle since the town's only bus had been burnt by counterrevolutionary forces on December 9 and now there is no public transportation. I found a ride with a refugee family which had been displaced by a counterrevolutionary attack on a village on the outskirts of Limay on December 27. This family was transporting their few belongings to Esteli. An 18 year old boy also had asked to be taken in the same pick-up truck. All were civilians and unarmed.[2]

After driving four miles, they saw a tractor in the middle of the road:

> Five armed men in blue counterrevolutionary uniforms with FDN marked on their uniforms came from behind the tractor and stopped our truck. They made us leave the vehicle and we joined about 25 civilians who were being held in a gully by the side of the road. After about ten minutes they told us we could continue on our way.[3]

After travelling another two and a half miles, Sister Nancy decided to return to Limay via back paths to warn departing vehicles of the danger. She got out of the car, which continued on towards Esteli. After walking a little over a mile:

I was stopped on the path by two armed men in FDN uniforms. They asked me where I was going and I told them to Limay. They spoke on walkie-talkies for some moments and then told me I could go no further and must stay in their custody. They directed me to a stone wall where there were more armed, uniformed men, about 20 in all... I was held there for approximately three hours. During that time three or four peasants and a woman and child also were stopped on the path and held with me. At about 8:00 A.M. I heard some gunfire from the old road where we had initially been stopped. There was a long wait of over an hour. Then I heard very loud automatic machine-gun fire and heavy artillery coming from Loma Atravesada which is further along the road to Esteli. I prayed for the lives of those who were involved.[4]

The contras then separated Sister Nancy from the three civilians, whom she never saw again. Despite her requests to leave, they marched her for another five miles, joined by 20 more contras, until they came to a group of still 20 more. There she was held for almost an hour while the contras "were boasting about the success they had had in the ambushes on the road."[5]

The 60 men who were now holding Sister Nancy:

were well armed and equipped. One of the men wore an arm patch which said 'Soldier of Fortune, Second Convention.' Another had 'U.S. Army' written on the front of his uniform. They showed me their new knapsacks and told me they had received new equipment recently. They told me that their supplies are dropped by planes which 'fly very quietly at night.' They hoped that they would be receiving new supplies that night to replenish the ammunition they had used that day.[6]

Sister Nancy again attempted to leave and was again prevented until four FDN leaders showed up:

These four men began to interrogate me about my work and identity. They searched my belongings and began to read my address book. After some time of discussion among themselves on the walkie-talkie they told me that I could go. I estimate that this was about 3:30 P.M.[7]

After returning to Limay on horseback, Sister Nancy:

quickly found out that 14 civilians had been killed by the FDN forces in different ambushes along the roads to Limay that same day. Nine were construction workers ambushed in Loma Atravesada, two workers from the Ministry of Natural Resources, two young coffee pickers,

Sister Nancy Donovan

photo: Barricada

and a tractor driver were killed along the road to Pueblo Nuevo. I saw four tractors which were destroyed. At least 10 persons were kidnapped, but there may be more. I also found out that the original vehicle in which I had been travelling had been stopped again by the FDN forces after I had left it to walk back to Limay. The 18 year old youth, Freddy Castellon, had been kidnapped.

We spent that night and the next day washing the bodies of the dead, comforting families and praying with them, and burying the dead from Limay.[8]

Chapter 20

CEPAD/TELCOR Ambush
September 1, 1984

On September 1, 1984, Jorge Barrow, an agronomist with the Evangelical Committee for Aid and Development (CEPAD), a private religious developmental agency, left Puerto Cabezas in Northern Zelaya in the organization's Toyota pick-up truck to drop off five workers in Sumubila. They picked up about ten hitchhikers, including a pregnant woman and some children.[1] Barrow, Federica Alvarez and her 45 day old child, and a nurse rode in the front and the others in back. Everyone in the pick-up was a civilian and no one was armed.[2]

As they passed a telecommunications company (TELCOR) pick-up, parked where men were working on the line, they heard a bomb and then rockets and machine-gun fire from the left of the road.[3]

Federica Alvarez had just finished breast feeding her baby and was burping her when the shots destroyed the window of the truck and covered them with shrapnel.[4] Barrow, the driver, kept going, driving with one hand as he tried to get glass out of his eyes with the other.[5]

Heavy fire landed in the back of the pick-up, lifting it off the ground. Barrow, looking in the rear-view mirror, saw everyone on the floor and thought they had all been killed.[6] In the cab, the baby was bleeding and the mother crying.[7]

They kept going until they reached the entrance to the Columbus settlement.[8] When Barrow was told that one of those in the rear, Alfredo Bushie, had been shot but was still alive, he drove on to the health center in Sumubila.[9] There, Bushie, age 20, died immediately.[10]

The baby and her mother were sent to the hospital in Rosita but the car taking them there lost control and Federica's sister-in-law, who rode with her to hold the blood serum, was injured as well.[11] The three were then transferred to Puerto Cabezas and ultimately sent to Managua. There, two delicate operations were performed on the baby, one on her intestines which had been pushed into her stomach by the impact of the shrapnel, and a week later another on her lung where the largest piece of shrapnel was lodged. After 26 days in the hospital, she was left with large scars and is in constant pain, unable to eat or sleep well.[12] The mother still has shrapnel wounds, and her right hand, which often falls asleep, cannot exert force.[13] The sister-in-law is still in the hospital.[14]

The contras also killed six or seven of the TELCOR workers.[15] Barrow saw the bodies when they were brought to the Sumubila health center. "Some had their heads bashed in, another had its forehead bashed in, one boy had his intestines out, others had their arms as if ground up."[16]

Chapter 21

Ambushes in El Cua
October 1984

In October 1984, Anibal Gonzalez, the alternate President of the Zonal Electoral Council for the Cua region for Nicaragua's November 1984 elections, suffered two ambushes while on electoral duty. The first time, he was travelling in a military truck from San Jose de Bocay, where there had been a contra attack the day before, to El Cua, when 80 contras ambushed the truck, killing one man and wounding three others.[1]

Eight days later, Gonzalez was travelling from El Cua to San Jose de Bocay to drop off ballot boxes, ballots and other electoral material. He was riding in an ambulance, along with six others, as part of a caravan including four trucks from the Ministry of Construction that were going to drop off provisions in Bocay.[2] Almost everyone in the caravan was armed. Gonzalez testified, "I want to emphasize that I am a civilian. If I go armed it's because in my zone, that's how one has to go."[3]

When they got to Frank Tijerino Valley, some 100 contras ambushed them with machine-guns, mortars and rifle fire from a distance of only 50 yards.[4] Everyone leaped from their vehicles. Gonzalez tried to get the ambulance driver, who had been shot in the head, rear and arm, out of the line of fire, but in doing so Gonzalez himself was shot in the ankle. He fell, but was able to crawl to the hills with the ambulance driver.[5]

Seven of the passengers were injured in the attack and one was killed before reinforcements came to drive the contras away.[6] Gonzalez had to spend 22 days in the hospital and was replaced in his electoral functions by Brigido Vargas Herrera.[7] At the end of October, however, Vargas was kidnapped in the Valley of Los Angeles while attending his daughter's funeral.[8]

93

Chapter 22

Six Examples

This chapter describes six individual cases of civilians kidnapped by the contras and taken to or toward Honduras in an attempt to forceably recruit them into the contra forces.

William Santiago Vasquez

William Santiago Vasquez is now 13 years old. He was 12 in December 1983, when he was kidnapped together with his father, Gregorio Vasquez, as they were leaving Ciudad Antigua, Nueva Segovia, where his father taught a course. A band of 170 contras came to the town that day. One part of the band attacked the town while the other kidnapped William and his father along with two other men. The four were taken to a hill where William was separated from the other three.[1] William later learned that all three, including his father, were killed that day.[2]

The next day, William was taken to the contra camp "La Union," still in Nicaragua, where he was kept for 15 days. There were about 400 men there, including five other kidnappees. William worked there as a cook's aide.[3]

Next he was taken ten kilometers by foot to the "La Lodoza" camp in Honduras:

> There were about 800 men there and about 50 people who had been kidnapped; men, women, old people, children, who were families which had been kidnapped from Chinandega, Matagalpa and other villages and towns. There were about 100 Honduran soldiers there; they were the ones who gave the orders.
>
> I was there about a month. I was trained by the Hondurans. There were also Nicaraguans there who were kidnapped and who were now part of the 'Guardia' [so-called because a number of contra leaders once belonged to Somoza's National Guard].
>
> I was trained in how to use a rifle and heavy artillery, then in ambush and counter ambush. The

training was dreadful; if you didn't participate, you didn't get any food that day.

Sometimes 'gringos' would come to take pictures; they would come as civilians. About five gringos came."[4]

After about a month, William was able to escape along a river and, after walking three days, made it back to Nicaragua. He now lives in Ocotal.[5]

Antonio Espinoza Morales

On October 23, 1984, two armed men entered the house near El Jicaro where Antonio Espinoza, a 32 year old farmer, was sleeping. They ordered him to leave: "You're going to march. We're the FDN."[6] When Espinoza told them he was sick—with a bad heart and nerves—they told him to get moving and added that they had medicine for him.[7]

The two men and their prisoner then joined a group of 30 or 35 other contras who had seven or eight other captives, and were taken on a march of five to six days to Honduras, through the hills, sleeping outside and eating little.[8]

The hostages were made to carry the contras' cargo. Espinoza carried a back-pack with ammunition.[9]

When they arrived at the Las Vegas base in Honduras, where there were about 1,000 men, the captives were split up. Espinoza stayed about two kilometers from the base, sometimes helping the cook with chores.[10]

After 43 days, Espinoza and some 34 others were sent back into Nicaragua, and he was given a blue FDN uniform and a rifle which he did not know how to use.[11] On the way back, he was able to make his escape between the guards while the group was sleeping.[12]

Espinoza testified that he will continue to work his fields but is moving closer to El Jicaro where he feels safer.[13]

Ernesto Pineda Gutierrez

Ernesto Pineda Gutierrez, a 43 year old coffee farmer, has been kidnapped twice. The first time, in September 1983, ten armed men came at 1:00 A.M. to the house in La Pavona, Jinotega, where he and his family were sleeping. They said they had orders to take Pineda and his niece Julia to their leader, because they supposedly worked with the army and had guns in their house. Pineda denies this.[14]

The two were taken about three kilometers to a house in the mountains where the contras were holding another 20 kidnapped campesinos. There, the leader told them that "they were going to kill us, that they weren't going to waste bullets but would hang us."[15] But they let Julia go and, after an eight hour march through the mountains, with Pineda protesting his "innocence," they let him go as well, telling him that "this time they would let us go but if we went around talking, they would behead us, hang us."[16] Some of the other campesinos never returned.[17]

The next time, on October 28, 1984, Pineda was running an errand with his brother when he ran into a group of 80 to 100 armed men leading 15 kidnappees. "They ordered us to go with them, without telling us why they were taking us. They only told us that they had orders to kidnap people, whoever they might be, because they had orders from their leaders."[18]

The group, with 23 kidnappees in all, including women, children and older people and Pineda's 14 year old nephew and two cousins, went to a farm where they met other contra groups, 300 men in all, holding other hostages. From there, the different groups set out separately on the same road, telling their captives, "We're not letting anybody go, and don't try to escape because if someone escapes and we find that person, we'll cut his throat."[19]

Pineda's group walked three days through the mountains, with the captives carrying the contras' backpacks, until they reached a mountain house were they stayed locked in for two days:

> They told us that they were taking us directly to Honduras for training.... They said that there in Honduras there were guards to train us and that we would return armed to Nicaragua to kill and kidnap more people. They told us not to say that we were forced to go because they would kill us in Honduras if we said that.[20]

After another day's walk, Pineda decided to try to escape. The next morning, while the contras were awaking, he and his nephew went out as if to urinate and were able to flee unnoticed.[21] His cousins still have not been heard from.[22]

Because the contras threatened to kill the deserters, Pineda has moved to Jinotega where he feels safer. There he has no work and is receiving support from cousins.[23]

Moise Fajardo Sambrana

Moise Fajardo was at his mother-in-law's house near Zungano, in Nueva Segovia, on September 2, 1984, when three armed contras came to the door and asked him to guide them because they did not know the area. When he said that he did not know it either, they told him that he had to come with them anyway.[24]

Joining up with a larger group of about 30 contras, they made Fajardo carry a heavy backpack on a 28-day trek through the hills towards Honduras, threatening that if he tried to escape, he would be killed.[25]

Fajardo was able to escape before the group got to Honduras, however, and after a three-day walk found his way back home.[26] He is afraid to live there now, however, and says he will move to a safer place.[27]

Jose de la Luz Padilla Rojas

At midnight on August 17, 1984, an armed contra, leading four kidnapped civilians, three with their hands tied, entered Jose de la Luz Padilla Rojas' house in Las Minitas in the Paiwas region and forced him out at gun-point. "When I left the house, he told me to get with the tied-up people and not to move. He told me that if I moved, or ran, he would shoot me."[28] They were joined by three other contras who had burned two other houses and were leading three other kidnappees, including Padilla's two adopted sons. Each of the contras unloaded a magazine (20 shots) in the air by the hostages' heads "until we were deaf,"[29] and then led them out of the town. When one of the men whose hands were tied stumbled, and Padilla tried to help him, one of the contras threatened him with his bayonet.[30]

That night the group stayed in the house of a campesino. The next morning, after one man was released, they continued on to a house where more captives were picked up and then to another where 15 kidnappees were already waiting. The contra leader took Padilla, a Delegate of the Word, out for questioning, taking out a notebook that already contained his name. He told Padilla, "'I'm going to let you go because you're old. What we need are people 30 and younger. You can go but watch out.' He told me that I should stop being involoved in organized things."[31] Padilla was released but he has had no news of his two adopted sons Jorge, 23, and Valentin, 24, or of the others who were taken by the contras.[32]

Amado Gutierrez

On October 15, 1984, Amado Gutierrez, 23, was in Waspuko in the Siuna region to pick up some cows. On the pretext of taking him to see the animals, a contra collaborator took him instead to where 50 contras were waiting. They accused Gutierrez of being a miliciano, which he denied, and burned his birth certificate and identity card. They held him there for 15 days as many other contras arrived, then took him on a day's walk to Copawas.[33]
Gutierrez tried to gain their confidence so he would be able to escape, and in Copawas they gave him a weapon, telling him, "We're going to collect people to liberate Nicaragua." Some of the group left and later returned with about 60 captives from San Pablo de Asa, Monte de Oro and Aserrin, including pregnant women and small children. The contras took the new group toward Waspuko, saying they would be taken to Honduras.[34]
Gutierrez stayed with the contras through battles in El Dorado, Monte de Oro and San Pablo before escaping on December 6 along with another hostage, as their captors slept.[35]

B. Mass Kidnappings on the Atlantic Coast

A recurring event on Nicaragua's sparsely-populated Atlantic Coast has been the mass kidnapping to Honduras of entire Miskito Indian villages by counterrevolutionary forces. While many Miskitos have chosen, for a variety of reasons, to resettle in Honduras, in a number of instances armed contra invaders have entered Miskito villages in Nicaragua and forced the entire populations to accompany them to Honduras. While some people in these villages undoubtedly wanted to accompany the contras, many others did not. All were obliged to leave, however.

In contra training camps in Honduras, new soldiers are given instructions in how to kidnap. One Miskito Indian, who had himself been kidnapped into the contra army and later escaped, testified:

> They told us that, arriving in a community to kidnap, we had to first surround the village and then shoot off our weapons to scare the people so they get out of bed, and not to let even one person escape, and to always do it at night."[1]

As the chapters that follow illustrate, this tactic has been used repeatedly by the contras.

[Note: The chapters on Slimalila, Set Net Point and Sukatpin are based on the affidavits of witnesses who were located, at the investigative team's request, by the Nicaraguan government. While this was a deviation from the team's policy of selecting each witness itself, the team spent over 12 hours with these witnesses—outside the presence of any government representatives—and is convinced of the veracity of their testimony.]

Chapter 23

Slimalila
April 23, 1983

One example of mass kidnapping occurred in the northern reforestation center of Slimalila where, on April 23, 1983, a contra task force took away an estimated 1,500 people, mostly Miskito Indians.

As it does each night, the village's electricity went out at 10:00 P.M.[1] About half an hour later, the residents began to hear shots and then mortar fire. As the town was defenseless,[2] the contras were easily able to enter.

Juan Bustillo Mendoza was at home with his wife and his sick mother when the firing and mortaring began. A mortar fell about four or five yards from his house. As the invaders shot indiscriminately, the family threw themselves on the floor and prayed.[3] Bustillo testified:

> After about an hour and a half, they began to yell for everybody to get out and I went to the window and saw that several houses were already burning. They mortared the iron water tank which made a great noise.
>
> Fifteen minutes later, we heard steps coming towards the house, they knocked at the door about three times. I didn't answer and they broke down the door and seven people entered with a flashlight into the room where I was with my wife, my brother and my nine year old sister. My sister started crying and they told her to shut up. My mother asked why she had to shut up, that she was very young. Then they threatened my mother with a bayonet and told her they were going to kill her. My mother asked why, if they call themselves Christians they did such things and they told her to shut up or they would shoot her. They said that if they killed, they did so in the name of God, and not because they wanted to.
>
> Then they told us to get out, because they were going to burn the house... They put a pistol to my mother's ribs and said that if I ran away, they would shoot her.[4]

Hereberto Siles Martinez, a non-Miskito who was in charge of the warehouse, was at home with his wife and four year old girl. On hearing the firing, they threw themselves on the floor and covered themselves with mattresses:

> About half an hour later, they began to bang hard on the door, shouting in Miskito. We were scared—we didn't know what to do because we didn't understand. I don't know how they realized it, but they began to shout in Spanish, telling us to get out or else they would set us on fire right there. We understood and opened the door.
>
> With a shove, they pushed me out, the same with my wife. I asked them if they would give me the time to get a blanket and some pants because we didn't have anything ready and they said they were taking us away. They refused.[5]

Nicolas Chan, 49, a half-Miskito, half-Chinese radio technician, was alone in his house as his family was in Puerto Cabezas. Crouched on the floor,

> I couldn't even raise my head because the bullets were flying near the roof. They passed by yelling in Miskito for everyone to get out of their houses...
>
> They said they were going to burn the houses.
>
> Some of the contras came and banged on my window, telling me to get out, that they were going to burn the houses. In the dark, I was able to grab a mosquito net, some pants, a shirt, and I went out.
>
> They told me to walk towards Yulnata and not to take one step backwards.
>
> I saw that they were burning the houses and the woods. First they burned by the workshop, the general offices.[6]

Two of the affiants give the number of people taken as 1,500. Of these, about 15 or 20 were people who apparently were expecting the attack (and may have helped prepare it), as they had all their belongings ready for the march.[8] Many of the others, who had nothing with them, were crying as they were taken away.[9]

That night the people were made to walk until dawn. In the dark, they had to cross a dirty river. Nicolas Chan and Hereberto Siles fell in, and were forced to continue on wet.[10] At seven the next morning, they came to the Rio Ulan and spent all day hiding in the hills because of the planes flying overhead.[11]

That evening the group set off again, walking until six the next morning through a pine forest. The group had no food, and the children and older people were having a difficult time. From 6:00 A.M. to 11:00 A.M. they walked through the hills until they reached the Rio Coco.[12]

That first day, Inocente Tinoco's wife gave birth. After she rested for just one hour, they had to continue marching and it was only the next day, in Honduras, that they were given a nurse to cut the umbilical cord.[13]

When they got to the river, the contras shot into the air as a sign. From the other side, the sign was returned and canoes began to take the group in crossings that lasted all day.[14]

Once in Honduras the group, which had gone three days without eating, was taken to a camp called Kiwastara where they were fed and allowed to rest for three days.[15]

They were then forced to march on, for one and a half days, toward Srumlaya. On the way, they passed through a provisional contra base where the contras took a census, separating out those men 15 to 20 years old, 20 to 25 years old and so on up to 40, telling them that they would be sent on to a central base for military training and return to Nicaragua to fight against the "communists."[16] There, a helicopter marked "U.S.A." dropped off munitions to the contras, as well as military boots which were then given to the ones who had been selected to fight.[17]

In Auka, the group was received by soldiers of the 5th Military Region of Honduras.[18] At 1:00 A.M. the group continued on to the abandoned hamlet of Tapamlaya, where they were told to choose houses from among those that which had previously been homes to other refugees.[19]

There, the contras separated out some 100 to 120 fighting-age men and took them away forceably. Only a few—"less than five percent" according to one witness—seemed to want to go.[20] Gregorio Winter, 29, a technician, was not sent to fight because of his educational level:

> One of the commanders told me that 20 of the boys in the line-up aren't worth what I'm worth and that its really difficult to bring educated people from Nicaragua and that I would be with them in their central office with the 'old man'—Steadman Fagoth. They even gave me a paper to present to the council of elders so I'd be sent to the central base.[21]

The remainder were then gathered together in a small Moravian church where they were told that foreign journalists and officials of the U.N. High Commissioner of Refugees (UNHCR) would be coming, and that the captives were not to tell them that they had been kidnapped:

> They said that the 'gringos' and the journalists were communists like the Sandinistas and that we had to say that we had come of our own free will, and that the Sandinista military had thrown us out of town, were persecuting us and that there was no freedom in Nicaragua. They said that if we didn't they would punish us, they would cut our tongues and make us swallow water by dunking our heads in the river.[22]

When the UNHCR arrived, they heard the story that the captives had been ordered to give.[23]

After 15 days, the people were moved, in Honduran army trucks, over four nights, to the town of Mocoron. They were told that the transfer was carried out nocturnally so that the role of the Honduran army would not be discovered by the UNHCR.[24] In Mocoron, where the refugees again lived in abandoned houses, they were again warned to tell the UNHCR and the many journalists who arrived that they were fleeing the Sandinistas.[25] Indeed, the people usually interviewed by the journalists were actually contras dressed in civilian clothes.[26]

In Mocoron, Juan Bustillo and Hereberto Siles and their families left the group and managed to find work with a company constructing a military base in Dursuna where contras would come and go. Once they saw U.S. advisors as well.[27] During their five months there, the contra leaders would often bring in tied-up contras who had tried to escape.[28]

There were many Nicaraguans working at the base, and one day a contra leader came to announce that they would all have to come, whether they liked it or not, to fight with them in their "final offensive."[29] Bustillo and Siles, who with their entire families had contracted malaria, then planned and executed a 17-day escape through the hills and rivers back to Nicaragua.[30]

After 15 days in Mocoron, on May 29, 1983, the remainder of the hostage group, some 500, marched for a day and a half to Wampu Sirpe where, after receiving eight days worth of rice and beans from the UNHCR, they were taken to a hill where most of them still live. There, as the rainty season began, they started to build their own houses of trees and leaves.[31]

In Wampu Sirpe, the refugees, almost without exception, began to fall sick with conjunctivitis, diarrhea, and malaria.[32] With only 28 malaria pills for the 500 who were there, virtually everybody contracted malaria, including Rosa Gutierrez, Gregorio Winter and their two children,[33] and Nicolas Chan, who also had conjunctivitis and boils.[34] In all, 13 people died in the first year the community lived in the hills.[35]

The 500 of Slimalila were not alone. On the neighboring hills, at least 13 other Nicaraguan Miskito communities, including Santa Clara and Tasba Pain, lived in similar conditions.[36]

The contras had left one "coordinator" to keep watch over the refugees,[37] making sure that they continued to tell journalists that they were living well.[38] Similarly, when officials of the Red Cross came to see if the captives wanted to write to their families, the coordinator warned them no to.[39]

The contras also raided the refugee camp four times looking for the remaining men to take them to fight.[40]

Escaping was difficult. Nicolas Chan tried to escape twice. The first time, travelling with local residents, he made it as far as Sir Sir, a one and a half day's walk, when he was intercepted by three dagger-wielding contras who asked him where he was going. When he said he was going to Puerto Lempiras, Honduras, to look for work, they told him that refugees did not have the right to work. They accompanied him half way back to Wampu Sirpe and told him that if they saw him again they would kill him.[41] The second time, after a day's walk with three other refugees, he was intercepted and sent back by the Honduran Army.[42]

Subsequently, after his two failed attempts, Chan smuggled a letter to the United States. Four months later, after 14 months in Honduras, his family arrived in Tegucigalpa and was able to arrange his return to Nicaragua.[43]

Rosalia Gutierrez and her family, and Inocente Tinoco and his family, all malaria-ridden, made their escape by spending almost a month on river boats, in hiding and on foot before arriving in the Honduran capital of Tegucigalpa. There, they were given food and lodging by the UNHCR but had to wait four more months before being repatriated to Nicaragua.[44]

The majority of those taken to Wampu Sirpe, however, still live there.

Orlando Wayland reading affidavit.
photo: Reed Brody

Chapter 24

Francia Sirpe
December 19, 1983

On December 19, 1983, a force of about 500 contras entered the town of Francia Sirpe, in Northern Zelaya[1], "shooting like crazy, with incendiary bullets."[2] When the people did not come out of their houses, the contras went "from house to house, taking all the people out with rifle-blows, and many old people, women, children and young people were crying out of fear, they didn't want to leave their town."[3]

Lucio Vargas, a 44 year old health worker, was in his house with his wife and children when it was surrounded by about 20 contras. "They said that if I didn't come out, they would machine-gun the house."[4] When they went out, they were grabbed. Vargas was separated from his family and taken away at gun-point.[5] He managed to get away, however, when the contras were not looking.[6] He spent the night in the mountains with three others who also were able to flee.[7]

Otto Borst, 50, who is half-German, half-Miskito, was hiding above his general store when the contras banged on the door demanding food. He gave it to them and then went back into hiding, but another group came and, breaking the window, dragged him off to one of their commanders.[8] Borst pleaded with the commander to let him go, saying that his wife was sick in the hospital. The commander, who called himself Luis Aguilera, responded, "Brother, it's war-time, march."[9] Nevertheless, Borst, too, was able to escape back to his house when the commander turned away.[10]

The contras concentrated the population in the middle of town.[11] There, Richard Thomas, who worked in popular education and with the volunteer police, tried to run away but was gunned down in the back.[12] The contras then sent out two groups, including civilians, one to ransack Jose Zuniga's store and the other to steal from Otto Borst's store.[13]

The group that had been sent out, including one of the commanders, began to ransack Borst's store, to which he had been able to return. They took away most of the merchandise he had on hand for the Christmas season (worth 185,000 cordobas), as well as 68,000 cordobas in cash and a radio.[14] Although they warned him that they would burn the house if he did not come out, Borst was able to make it out the back exit, and he hid in his out-house all night.[15]

Among the people gathered up by the contras was Monsignor Salvador Schlaffer, the Catholic Bishop of Zelaya province, who had arrived in Francia Sirpe that day. When the Bishop protested that he wanted to go back to Puerto Cabezas because he was infirm with arthritis, the contras responded that it would not be possible because the road back to Puerto Cabezas had been mined.[16]

When another woman complained that she was sick and did not want to leave with her five children, the contras shot in the air above her head and responded, "You want to stay as a communist spy, but you're coming with us."[17]

Those in the town who worked with the government, including Orlando Wayland who supervised the educational program and eight others who worked in health, education and welfare, had their hands tied behind their backs.[18]

The people were then moved out to the nearby village of Wisconsin. The men made the three hour march on foot while the contras used the Bishop's jeep to transport the women in several trips.[19]

The next morning, as those few residents of Francia Sirpe who had hid or were spared came out, they found a ghost town. Only 18 of Francia Sirpe's 1,250 people were left.[20] The doors of the houses were all broken in.[21] Jose Zuniga's store was as empty as Otto Borst's[22] and the road to La Tronquera had been mined.[23]

In Wisconsin, the road ended, and the contras and their captives began to march along a muddy trail. The contras, who had been getting drunk from the stolen liquor, began to fire their weapons to get the people, who were screaming and crying, to move faster.[24] In the group, in addition to the Bishop and other priests, was a journalist who identified himself as American. [25]

After camping for the night, the group marched onward when they heard fighting behind them. The leader of the contra group, Juan Solorzano, a former member of Somoza's National Guard now using the pseudonym Juan Blanco,[26] ordered the people to run, and they did until they reached the mountains.[27] The next day, at 3:00 A.M., they again marched all day until they got close to the Rio Coco. That day, two women gave birth. Their umbilical cords were cut and they were then forced to march on.[28]

The next day they reached Esperanza, on the Rio Coco, where Steadman Fagoth, the Miskito contra leader, was waiting for them. Upon seeing the dead and wounded contras from the rearguard fighting, he told the nine government workers "for these dead, you will pay."[29] They were then handcuffed and thrown down three or four yards to the river by contra commander "Evil Face." Orlando Wayman testified:

[H]e grabbed me by the hair and picked me up and began to drown me in the water. When I began to lose consciousness, he took me out, and I was left deaf, deaf. Then he began to beat both my ears and water came from my mouth and my nose.[30]

The other government workers received similar treatment.[3]

Everyone in the group, including the nine government workers, was then taken across the river in small boats and Fagoth told them that the boys were going to be recruited and the others would be sent to refugee camps in Wampu Sirpe (like the people of Slimalila). About 40 were taken to fight.[32] Once in Honduras, the others were taken toward Mocoron, on the way to Wampu Sirpe, while the government workers were taken to a military camp.[33]

In the military camp, the government workers were kept in a four foot high, poorly covered, muddy pigsty.[34] Orlando Wayland testified as to what their captors did next:

> The next day, the tortures began... They drowned me in the water in the morning. In the evening, they tied me up in the water from 7 P.M. until 1 A.M. The next day, at 7 A.M., they began to make me collect garbage in the creek in my underwear, with the cold. The creek was really icy. I was in the creek for four hours...
>
> Then they threw me on the ant hill. Tied up, they put me chest-down on the ant hill. The [red] ants bit my body, I squirmed to try to get them off my body, but there were too many.
>
> I was on the ant hill ten minutes each day, to get military information out of Nicaragua, they said. Sometimes it was only five minutes.
>
> Each day, they applied these tortures, to each of us, one by one.
>
> They would also beat me with a stick, which hurts. They would beat me from head to heels. They beat me hard and left me purple, purple in my back. Then they would give me an injection to calm me a little. Then they would beat me again.
>
> We stayed like that for, more or less, one and half months, with tortures every day, always sleeping, cold and wet, in the pigsty.[35]

After a month and a half, Steadman Fagoth approached them, saying "We are going to spare your lives." He urged them to join his forces and explained, "We tortured you because you deserved it, even God himself, when His son deviates from His word punished him, and we do the same."[36]

To avoid further torture, the workers agreed to join the contras and were given uniforms and sent to the Misura Military Instruction Center (CIMM) with Fagoth's brother Hilton Fagoth.[37]

There, the workers were trained by two instructors, "Chan"

and "Samba," who identified themselves as coming from the EEBI, formerly an elite unit of Somoza's National Guard, and by "Mercenary," who said he had received military training in Argentina.[38] The camp had three American supervisors who, Chan told the workers, were Vietnam veterans.[39] An olive-green helicopter with "USA" markings came to drop arms, including rifles, grenade launchers, mines and explosives, that the Americans received and gave to Hilton Fagoth for use in his camp. An olive-green twin-engine plane dropped canned food in white parachutes.[40]

Near this base was one called the "Chinese Base," which was run by six oriental instructors who, according to Fagoth and Chan, were South Korean.[41] There was also another base nearby called TEA—Special Area Troops—which was directly run by ten Americans and to which helicopters marked "U.S.A." arrived daily.[42]

On March 19, 1984, "Chan" called the troops together and announced that, on Fagoth's orders, they were being divided into groups to carry out several missions. He explained that one group was to go to Sumubila to bring back captives, another would attack the hydroelectric plant near Bonanza, another would mortar the military base in Puerto Cabezas as a diversionary action, while another would go to the Rio Coco to receive the captives.[43]

Orlando Wayland left with a group of 42 led by "Chan," another ex-EEBI soldier and a member of the Special Honduran Jungle and Nocturnal Troops (TESON).[44] After marching for eight days they arrived in Wisconsin, Nicaragua.[45] There, Wayland decided to try to escape. He tried to convince one of his fellow workers, Astin Ramos Brown, to flee, but Ramos was scared because his wife, children and parents were being held captive in Honduras and many people had said that the families of deserters were killed.[46]

On the pretext of going to pick oranges, Wayland ran away. He reached Francia Sirpe (by then deserted), and then reported to the authorities in La Tronquera. He now lives in Puerto Cabezas and, having heard threats against him on the contras' Miskito-language radio, he no longer leaves the town.[47]

Most of the Francia Sirpe residents who were taken to Wampu Sirpe have not since reappeared. Otto Borst lost some 50 relatives including a daughter, a grandchild, a sister, uncles, cousins and nephews. While he believes that some of the people of the town were willing to go with the contras, his family "Didn't want to go to Honduras."[48] He has not heard from them since, except via a letter from a niece in the United States, who told him the family wrote to her stating they are unable to leave Honduras.[49] In the ransacking of his store he lost everything he had, "everything I had fought to earn. I have ten children and my salary isn't enough to make ends meet."[50]

Lucio Vargas lost his wife, five children, five grandchildren, his sister and her six children, and other family members.[51] He has received a note from his wife through the Red Cross that they are in Mocoron along with his mother, who had been kidnapped from Andres with a brother and sister and their families, and with a brother who was taken from Santa Clara.[52] The note also said that one of their children had died, but it did not say how.[53] Like Otto Borst, he has written letters to try to get his family back, but thus far in vain.[54] Both Vargas and Borst now live in Puerto Cabezas.

Father Martin Piner

photo: Reed Brody

Chapter 25

Set Net Point
June 19, 1983

On the evening of June 19, 1983, a small contra band in a fishing boat landed in the Southern Zelaya fishing village of Set Net Point.[1] As the people were leaving a service in the Moravian church, the contras grabbed them and began to take them to the boat, which some residents identified as having been stolen from the village of Monkey Point.[2]

One of those taken was Martin Piner, the Miskito Moravian pastor. The contras searched him, took his identification papers as well as the card the government issues to priests for their protection, and pushed him on to the boat. "I didn't want to go...but I didn't have any choice. They said they were going to throw me in the ocean."[3]

In all, 107 people were taken on the boat, the entire town except for five families that managed to flee.[4] According to the pastor, "Some in the community wanted to go, but the others didn't want to go but were forced... The majority were not in agreement."[5] Caught by surprise, the people were unable to bring their belongings.[6]

After sailing 18 hours, the boat reached Puerto Limon, Costa Rica, where the people were met and given papers by Costa Rican immigration.[7] From there, a bus made several trips to take them to Pueblo Nuevo, Costa Rica, where the families were distributed to various houses.[8]

They stayed in Pueblo Nuevo. Each day, the Costa Rican authorities would take them to a kitchen to eat, while Costa Rican soldiers surrounded their settlement.[9] "We felt like prisoners there, because they said we couldn't leave."[10]

After 29 days, Father Piner was given permission to go buy cigarettes and, meeting with a contra, he asked to be taken to their base. There he met Brooklyn Rivera, a leader of the Misurasata contras. As a way to get back home, Piner asked Rivera if he could go back to Nicaragua with them. Rivera agreed and Piner was given a rifle and sent with eight others on an outboard motorboat towards Nicaragua.[11]

After two and a half days, the boat landed in Walpasixa in North Zelaya. There, while the others were sleeping, Father Piner managed to escape.[12]

Father Piner's encounters with the contras were not over, however. After reporting to the Nicaraguan authorities he went to live in the village of Sisin, where, as a result of his experience with the contras, he decided to work with the army, giving it information on contra movements. "As a pastor, I wanted to avoid more deaths."[13] One day, in June or July of 1984, on his way to his father's farm, he was stopped by two armed contras who, pointing their guns at him, led him to a hill where 36 others were stationed. There, the leader told him that they had been looking for him for some time.[14]

From there, he was marched for several days to the Rus Rus contra base in Honduras where he was presented to Steadman Fagoth, leader of the Misura contra group, who showed him a list of "Sandinista spies" on which his name appeared.[15]

Father's Piner's head was then shaved and he was left for three days with no food.[16] Next, he was taken to a river where "Jimmy," one of the contras:

> grabbed me by the neck and put my head down in the water. When I couldn't take it anymore, he picked me up and put me back in the water again. It was like that for half an hour.
>
> They took me from there and tied me to a pine tree in the camp for three days.
>
> After three days, they untied me. I hadn't eaten for five days.[17]

Father Piner then agreed to work with the contras, and they began to give him training. Each night, he was also given guard duty, but he often fell asleep and, five or six times, was punished with a similar water treatment.[18]

Father Piner was trained for 19 days. While most of those in the camp were Miskitos, there were also four oriental men in the camp who spoke no Spanish and who twice forced Father Piner to eat snakes.[19] Father Piner could not take the rigorous training and began to vomit blood. After spending six days in a clinic, he asked Fagoth to be allowed to preach. Fagoth agreed and sent him to Tapamlaya, Honduras, where he spent three months preaching to Nicaraguan Miskitos.[20]

At that point, Father Piner, along with eight others, secretly made their way to and across the Rio Coco into Nicaragua, and, on November 30, 1984, they reported to the Nicaraguan authorities.[21]

Father Piner is afraid to go back to his community, and now lives in Puerto Cabezas.[22]

Chapter 26

Sukatpin
October 1983

In October 1983, approximately 200 armed contras entered the Miskito town of Sukatpin in Northern Zelaya and occupied it for six days, preventing the inhabitants from leaving.[1]

After six days, the young people of the town, some 200, were taken away. Baudilio Rivera, 19, had tried to hide in his house but was given away by contra sympathizers. As a result, he was beaten in the back with a stick and dunked in the water as the contras led him and the rest of the group away.[2] Rivera testified that there were those in the town who supported the contras but that the majority did not.[3]

For two weeks the group marched, sleeping in the mountains, eating raw yuca and bananas, until they crossed into Honduras and reached Srumlaya.[4] After three days there, the group moved to Auka, then Rus Rus, then to the Misura Military Instruction Center (CIMM).[5] There, the group rested for several weeks because many of them had become sick on the journey.[6]

In the CIMM, those in the group were given blue military uniforms and began to receive training—exercises, how to ambush, how to blow up bridges, how to kidnap people. (The instructions Rivera received on kidnapping are described prior to the Slimalila chapter.) The captives received their instruction from non-Miskitos who spoke only Spanish. Honduran soldiers also came to the base, as did English-speakers who were identified by the commanders as Americans.[7]

After two months of training, a group was equipped and sent back towards Nicaragua intending to kidnap the people of Sandy Bay.[8]

They crossed the Rio Coco into Nicaragua at the village of Andres. After two days of marching, four of the captives escaped at night.[9] When they got close to Sandy Bay, Rivera escaped as well while on guard duty.[10] He now works in Puerto Cabezas as a tractor driver with the Construction Ministry.[11]

Chapter 27

Sangnilaya
December 11, 1984

On December 11, 1984, contra forces began an evening attack with gun-fire and mortars against the Miskito resettlement village of Sangnilaya, about 40 kilometers north of Puerto Cabezas near the Wawa River.[1]

After the firing stopped, "The contras went from house to house, collecting young people. They were well-armed, in olive-green and blue uniforms and rubber boots."[2]

Johnny Briman, an auxiliary nurse who was substituting for the vacationing regular nurse, hid in a back room in a neighbor's house when he saw the contras taking away the youths.[3] The contras yelled to the owner of the house in which Johnny was hiding. "Are you ready, let's go," calling him "son-of-a-bitch" and telling him he had to go. "Get a shirt and pants and let's go. Hurry up. Get your identification card, too."[4] When he could not find his identification card, the contras told him to light a match.

The man's wife was going to light a match but her husband stopped her, fearing it would give Briman away. The contras said "So, there's another boy?" but were apparently satisfied by the family's denial. Finally the owner of the house found his card and the contras started to take him, but his wife and step-mother put up such a fuss that, after hitting him with their rifle, they let him go.[5]

The contras took 30 people that night, however, 28 men and two women. Some were taken away tied up, others were beaten. To one boy, whose mother was crying, they said, "If we don't defend this country, who will, even if your mother is crying."[6]

The next morning, the mothers and relatives of the hostages got together, crying over their lost children. In the afternoon the Nicaraguan army came, but it was too late to help.[7]

Digna Barreda de Ubeda

photo: Reed Brody

Marta Arauz de Ubeda with her mother and daughter.

photo: Reed Brody

Chapter 28

Seven Examples

Digna Barreda de Ubeda

Digna Barreda de Ubeda of Esteli, a mother of two, is the neice of two well-known religious leaders, Felipe and Mery Barreda, who were tortured and killed by the contras [see chapter 3]. On May 3, 1983, Digna and her husband, Juan Augustin, were visiting the land they had received under the ararian reform program in the village of Zapote, near Susucayan, Nueva Segovia.[1] The couple was staying there with her uncle, who, it turned out, was collaborating with the contras and who had denounced the couple as Sandinista spies.

That evening after dinner, five contras came to the house, beat up Juan Augustin, stole a gold chain and watch Digna was wearing, and tied their hands and took the two of them away along with a one-eyed man from Managua.[2]

Three of the men went back to talk to the uncle. Upon returning:

> They beat my husband brutally.... And then, the three who talked with my uncle raped me so brutally that I still have scars on my knees. They put me face down. They raped me through my rectum too. And all this in front of my husband.[3]

The captives were then taken further on where they met a group of 55 contras. There they were interrogated and beaten and Digna was again raped in front of her husband.[4]

Two more campesinos were brought in, their hands tied, and the group continued on until they reached a safe house in the mountains.[5] After eating, they continued on until at 4:00 A.M. they reached a camp of tents marked "made in U.S.A."[6] There, while some of the contras slept, others interrogated Digna, "torturing me, pressing my eyes, separating my toes and raping me brutally again."[7]

Juan Augustin, who still was tied up, asked the contras to kill him, but he was told that they were going to take him to Honduras, beating him on the way, where "Benito Bravo," a contra leader, was waiting to kill him, and they "kicked him and beat him again and again."[8]

The contras said that they were with the FDN.[9]

On the fourth day, Digna promised her captors that she would collaborate with them if they would let her go. After discussing it with the leader and returning to talk to Digna's uncle, the contras agreed, but did not free her yet.[10]

That day, the contras called one of the hostages, Juan Valladares, and asked him if he loved Tomas Borge (Nicaragua's Minister of the Interior) and the revolution. When Valladares replied that he did, "they laid him down on the ground and they gouged out his eyes with a spoon, then they machine-gunned him and threw him over a cliff."[11] At the same time, the one-eyed man escaped.[12]

On the fifth day:

> five of them raped me at about five in the evening....
> They had gang-raped me every day. When my vagina
> couldn't take it anymore, they raped me through my
> rectum. I calculate that in five days they raped me 60
> times.[13]

That day, they let Digna go, believing that she would collaborate with them, but not before the contra who was assigned to lead her back to the road raped her.[14] On her request, the contras untied her husband's hands, which had been bound for five days. He was not freed, however.[15]

Back in Esteli, Digna reported to the authorities on these events and on the participation of her uncle, who had offered her a bribe not to do so.[16] She was taken to the hospital where she was treated and her vagina was cleaned. Her husband escaped during a battle 15 days later.[17]

Her difficulties were not over, however. Her house in Esteli was set on fire and she was forced to move.[18] Her father and two brothers were robbed and kidnapped. One of the brothers returned after having been taken to Honduras while the other is still missing. Another campesino was also kidnapped with her brothers, and reportedly his penis was cut off.[19]

Marta Arauz De Ubeda

Marta Arauz de Ubeda, 19, from Jinotega, was returning from Pantasma on September 24, 1984 with her sick mother and her two and a half year old daughter. They got a ride in a truck which was also taking five young teachers and several other people.[20]

When they got to Las Cruces, their truck was attacked by 500 armed and uniformed men. The attackers took the passengers out one-by-one, robbing them of their belongings. They were particularly severe with the teachers, calling them "the sons of bitches, teaching communism to the children."[21]

One of the contras recognized Marta because her husband had worked with the Sandinista Front in Pantasma:

> [He said] 'Get that woman down. She's a bitch, rabid dog.' I said I wasn't. Then about eight of them pointed their rifles at me. I yelled to my mother, 'Mama, Mama, they want to kill me.' My mother jumped out of the truck and said, 'Why are you going to kill my daughter?' They answered, 'You old bitch, you're not the one who decides, we are.'[22]

The contras brought Marta up close to where they were burning a beer truck, and the flames burned her. She tried to get away but they would not let her. Then they took off her shoes and forced her to march along with the teachers. "They made us walk about four hours through the mountains, I was barefoot and they made me carry sugar cane. The teachers were tied in a single file."[23]

During the march they pointed their guns at her, threatened to kill her, and asked her if she wanted to kill the teachers.[24] The group finally arrived at the house of a collaborator where they spent the night:[25]

> There, outside of the house they undressed me and wrestled me to the ground. They took me by force and raped me... I heard the screams of the other women and I'm sure they were raped too.
>
> I couldn't sleep. I spent the night outside with them. They asked me if I wanted to go to Honduras, if I wanted to be their woman. They told me they would take me to the United States and Honduras... I cried.
>
> We were there until morning, the teachers tied up. It was windy and the mosquitos were biting us.[26]

In the morning, when the group was leaving, Marta snuck into the house, telling the woman of the house that she had been told by the leader to wait there. Marta was able to hide in the house while the group left, and until the Nicaraguan army arrived and rescued her an hour later.[27] The teachers are still missing.

Mirna Cunningham

Mirna Cunningham, 37, is a half-Miskito and half-Black doctor who, in 1984, was named government Minister for Special Zone I, Zelaya Norte.

On December 28, 1981, she was returning to Waspam from a hospital inspection in her home town of Bilwascarma, with a driver, a nurse and the hospital administrator, Oscar Hudson:

> About 600 meters from the hospital gate, the car was attacked by a group of around 20 armed people who

started shooting at the car. When the shooting stopped, the hospital administrator was able to jump out and run into the bush. He got shot in the leg, one of his legs—two shots. The rest of us, we were taken out of the car and beaten with rifle butts all over our bodies. And after that they made us get into the car again. They forced the driver to go back into the village at knife point.[28]

They took the captives to a house on the Rio Coco where:

They tied us up, and said they were going to kill us, and they continued to hit us. They held us for several hours. Later they took two of the other doctors who were at the hospital; they were dragging them down to the river, also tied up and hitting them. When it got dark, they separated the doctors, and they took the nurse and myself to a hut, a little house near the river.

At this house, they had us there for seven hours. During those hours we were raped for the first time. While they were raping us, they were chanting slogans like, "Christ yesterday, Christ today, Christ tomorrow."

...And although we would cry or shout, they would hit us, and put a knife or a gun to our head. This went on for almost two hours.[29]

The hostages were then taken across the river to a training camp in Honduras. There they were told that they had been kidnapped because they worked for the government.[30]

Their captors, including Miskitos and former members of General Somoza's elite EEBI unit, told them that they had other bases and were receiving their equipment from Washington:[31]

They also said that they had Americans who came in and trained them for these camps that were deeper in Honduras. They said that they received help from the Honduran army. That they would come and help them transport their things. They were very proud of the help that they were receiving from the U.S. Government. They offered us Camel cigarettes, for example, as a proof that they were smoking good cigarettes. And they said they were getting canned food, good clothes and things like that, as a way to tell us why they were fighting."[32]

After two or three hours in the camp:

They told us that they were going to kill us, but they wanted to kill us in Nicaragua to leave our bodies as an example to the other people who work with the Nicaraguan government.

They made us walk to the river again and cross the river, on our way back we were raped again, by all the ones who were taking us to the village.[33]

In the village the captives were released, but they were told that they should leave the Atlantic Coast because the contras did not want doctors there.[34]

When they got back to the hospital:

> [W]e found Oscar Hudson in the bush with two shots in his leg. We were able to save him. We were all bruised for several days, bleeding. The nurse who went through this also was very disturbed emotionally.
>
> The hospital had to be closed also, because counter-revolutionaries went in the hospital. They stole instruments, medicine, things were broken and they terrorized the patients and the other health workers, who were afraid to continue working there. So we had to close the hospital.[35]

Mileydis Salina Azevedo and Ermelina Diaz Talavera

In October 1984, ten armed contras arrived at the Salina house in San Jeronimo de Chachagua, Nueva Segovia province, and told Mileydis Salina, 15, that she had to come with them. She and her mother pleaded with the intruders, but they insisted.[36]

The contras also went to the nearby house where Ermelina Diaz, 14, lived, and told her that she was coming with them. "I told them I didn't want to go, I was very afraid. They told me I had to go; they didn't say why."[37]

When the contras all joined together, there were about 100 of them, and they had taken three other hostages in addition to the girls.[38] After walking all day, they told the girls that they would both have to choose one of the contras to sleep with, or they would all rape them.[39] The girls did choose, "because that's what had to be done,"[40] and for the next 55 days, they slept with the men they had been forced to choose.

During that time, the band participated in nine combats, most of them with the Nicaraguan army, although on one occasion they ambushed a civilian pick-up truck, killing some of its passengers.[41] Although the girls had rifles, they did not fight, but carried backpacks with munitions.[42] They received little to eat.[43] Among the group were five soldiers who said that they were not Nicaraguan.[44]

The girls were finally able to escape while the group was resting, and they made it home the same day.[45] Both plan to move to Murra because they feel it is safer, and they had been warned that if they escaped and were caught, they would not get away again.[46]

[The team received a report, which we could not confirm, that two weeks after the girls returned to their homes, their throats were slit by the contras.]

Josefina Inestroza and Abelina Inestroza

On December 18, 1984, at 7:00 P.M., six armed, blue-uniformed, contras entered the Inestroza house in El Horcon, just outside of Susucayan. They said that they came to take away one of the boys, Purificacion, because he was a miliciano. When they could not find him, they turned on Josefina, 24, and Abelina, 20, both mothers. Testifying the next day, Abelina recounted:

> They grabbed us, me and my sister... and raped us in front of the whole family. They turned out the lights and two of them raped me and two others raped my sister. They told us not to scream because they would kill us. They threatened us with their bayonets. They pointed their guns at the others in the house.[47]

Before leaving, the contras told the family that they would return at eight the next morning "for coffee."[48] Early in the morning the whole family left the house for Susucayan where they gave this testimony. Even though they left everything in their house, they will not go back there but will move to Ocotal.[49]

Afterword

The contras—the forces which committed the acts described in the report—were organized, trained, supplied and financed by the United States Government. Between 1981 and 1984, the United States provided them with $80 million in "covert" aid and the administration is pressing for increased aid for 1985 and 1986.

The Nicaraguans interviewed for the report believed that once we, the people of the United States, know of the atrocities being committed in our name, we would put a stop to them. Now we know. Now we must act.

There are many things concerned citizens can do:

—*Write your congressperson,* telling him or her to oppose renewed aid to the contras;

—*Help rebuild what the war destroys.* Several organizations are working towards that end. Among them:

Let Nicaragua Live c/o Nicaragua Network
2025 I Street, N.W. Suite 1117
Washington, DC 20006
Tel: (202) 223-2328

Let Nicaragua Live is a campaign to send construction materials, school supplies, seeds, tools and medical equipment to Nicaragua.

NICMAC 1239
Broadway, room 802
New York, NY 10011
Tel: (212) 889-5188

NICMAC, the Nicaragua Medical/Material Aid Campaign, sends Nicaragua medicines, medical textbooks, hospital equipment and emergency medical kits that can be used in remote rural areas facing disaster and trauma situations. An important campaign is their Operation Wheels for Nicaragua, which sends bicycle tires and tools to help build wheelchairs for the 100,000 Nicaraguans disabled during the insurrection and by the continuing contra war.

OXFAM America
115 Broadway
Boston, MA 02116
Tel: (617) 482-1211

OXFAM America is sponsoring the Tools for Peace and Justice in Central America campaign: the 1985 goal is to send $500 thousand worth of agricultural tools to the people of Nicaragua.

*   *   *

—Visit Nicaragua and learn first-hand. Americans need no visa to enter Nicaragua, and several types of visits are possible:

Tours

Marazul Tours, Inc., 250 West 57th St., suite 1311, New York, NY 10107, (212) 582-9570 or (800) 223-5334.

Tropical Tours, Inc., 141 East 44th St., suite 409, New York, NY 10017, (212) 599-1441.

Center for Global Service & Education, Augsburg College, 731 21st Avenue South, Minneapolis, MN 55454, (612) 330-1159.

Schools

NICA (Nuevo Instituto de Centroamerica)
P.O. Box 1409
Cambridge, MA 02238
Tel: (617) 497-7142

Five week program of spanish study, family living and community work in the city of Esteli.

Casa Nicaraguense de Espanol (CNE)
141 East 44th St., suite 409
New York, NY 10017
Tel: (212) 946-4126

Two to eight week programs of spanish study and family living in the city of Managua.

Work

Nicaragua Exchange
239 Centre St.
New York, NY 10013
Tel: (212) 219-8620

Two to four week volunteer work brigades for agricultural harvests.

Peace Action

Witness for Peace
1414 Woodland Dr.
Durham, NC 27701
Tel: (919) 688-3880 or 688-5400

U.S. citizens maintaining a continuous presence at various locations on Nicaragua's borders with Honduras and Costa Rica to witness and report back the impact of U.S.-backed "contra" violence.

—*Work with others to change U.S. policy towards Nicaragua.* In addition to hundreds of local groups, there are several national solidarity and policy organizations. Among them:

National Network in Solidarity with
    the Nicaraguan People
2025 I St., NW, suite 1117
Washington, DC 20006
Tel: (202) 223-2328

The *National Network in Solidarity with the Nicaraguan People* promotes dialogue and ties of friendship between the people of the U.S. and Nicaragua. Its activities include: travel, direct assistance, community education, library and resource center, solidarity, political organizing/lobbying, and audio-visual media.

Witness for Peace
P.O. Box 29241
Washington, DC 20017
Tel: (202) 636-3642

A grassroots organization whose purpose is to develop a spiritually based non-violent resistance to U.S. military policy in Nicaragua by standing alongside the Nicaraguan people. *Witness for Peace* seeks to mobilize U.S. public opinion on this issue and welcomes those who vary in spiritual approach, but share a common purpose. Its activities include: travel, political organizing/lobbying, church liaison, speakers, and community education.

—*Learn more about Nicaragua.* News is hard to come by. The fact that the contras' three year war of terror has received only passing attention until recently is but one example. Several resources are suggested:

North American Congress on Latin America
151 West 19th St.
New York, NY 10011
Tel:(212) 989-8890

The *North American Congress on Latin America* (NACLA) is a non-profit research institute founded in 1966 to increase public awareness of issues affecting U.S.-Latin American relations. NACLA's bi-monthly *Report on the Americas* is a unique source of in-depth information on Latin America and U.S. foreign policy. NACLA organizes educational seminars, furnishes speakers, and provides consulting services to the media.

Washington Office on Latin America
110 Maryland Ave., NE
Washington, DC 20002
Tel: (202) 544-8045

The *Washington Office on Latin America* is a human rights advocacy organization which researches, monitors, documents, interprets, and disseminates data about Latin America and U.S. policies there.

Central American Historical Institute (CAHI)
Intercultural Center, Georgetown University
Washington, DC 20057
Tel: (202) 625-8246

CAHI is an independent research center affiliated with the Institute Historico Centroamericano in Managua, Nicaragua. *CAHI* publishes a monthly *Update* and provides information to journalists, church groups, human rights agencies, and politicians concerning events in Nicaragua and Central America.

Appendix 1

Verifications

This report was intended to open, not close, the debate over the contras' systematic violations of human rights. Each affidavit upon which the report is based identifies the affiant by complete name, age, location, and in most instances, place of birth and mother's and father's complete names. This was to ensure that the accounts in the report could be verified. Other groups were urged to independently examine the report and to conduct investigations of their own. Several did so. Following are excerpts from their reports.

Report of *Donald T. Fox, Esq.* and *Prof. Michael J. Glennon* to the *International Human Rights Law Group* and the *Washington Office on Latin America* concerning *Abuses Against Civilians by Counterrevolutionaries Operating in Nicaragua*

"In accordance with the request of our sponsors that we assess the reliability of Reed Brody's report, we interviewed 10 of the individuals previously interviewed by Mr. Brody. We sought geographic dispersion to the extent possible; 4 of those persons were therefore interviewed in Ocotal, 3 in Jalapa, and 3 in Estancia. To see whether similar incidents would be related by others who had not been interviewed by Mr. Brody, we interviewed 26 additional persons—16 in Ocotal, 6 in Jalapa, 3 in Estancia, and one in Condega...

"The affidavits on which Mr. Brody's report is based that we investigated are materially accurate. Based on our random sampling of these affidavits, and the other samplings performed by Americas Watch, [the *New York Times* and CBS], the probability is that other of the affidavits relied on by Mr. Brody are also probative. Given the number of incidents examined by Mr. Brody, the weight of evidence indicates that the contras engage with some frequency in acts of terroristic violence against unarmed civilians." (pp. 12 and 22)

An Americas Watch Report: Violations of the Laws of War by Both Sides in Nicaragua (March 1985)

"As part of our inquiry, we did make an effort to spot-check the findings of Reed Brody, a former Assistant Attorney General of the State of New York, who spent four months in Nicaragua starting in the latter part of 1984 and who collected some 150 affidavits from victims of and witnesses to *contra* violence against civilians. We also attempted to spot-check the findings of a U.S. church-based organization, Witness for Peace, that collected such information. In those few cases that we did spot-check, our findings confirmed their findings...

"The evidence that we have gathered shows a sharp decline in violations of the laws of war by the Nicaraguan government following 1982, though we have recorded abuses that took place as recently as a year ago.

"The most serious abuse currently attributable to the Nicaraguan government that we have found is its continuing failure to account publicly for what happened to victims of abuses in 1981 and 1982 and to provide redress to victims and their families...

"In combination, the *contra* forces have systematically violated the applicable laws of war throughout the conflict. They have attacked civilians indiscriminately; they have tortured and mutilated prisoners; they have murdered those placed *hors de combat* by their wounds; they have taken hostages; and they have committed outrages against personal dignity." (pp. 5, 6, 8-9)

New York Times

The *New York Times* chose four of the incidents in the report at random and conducted follow-up interviews "in Spanish, in the presence of other family members. No Nicaraguan police, army or other Government officials were present, and none of the interviews were arranged through official channels." The four incidents were confirmed, and various examples of the affidavits verified are given in the edition of March 7, 1985, p. A1.

CBS Evening News

Richard Schlessinger of CBS checked the report and on the night of March 7, 1985, the "CBS Evening News" showed two persons whose cases were included amongst the 145 affidavits.

Appendix 2

ARMS CONTROL AND FOREIGN POLICY CAUCUS

Rep. Matthew F. McHugh
Chairman

Sen. Charles McC. Mathias, Jr.
Vice-Chairman

Sen. Christopher J. Dodd
Vice-Chairman

Rep. Thomas E. Petri
Secretary-Treasurer

U.S. Congress
501 House Annex 2
Washington, D.C. 20515
(202) 226-3440

Edith B. Wilkie
Executive Director

WHO ARE THE CONTRAS?
_____

AN ANALYSIS OF THE MAKEUP OF THE

MILITARY LEADERSHIP OF THE REBEL FORCES,

AND OF THE NATURE OF THE PRIVATE

AMERICAN GROUPS PROVIDING THEM FINANCIAL

AND MATERIAL SUPPORT.

AN IN-DEPTH RESEARCH REPORT

PREPARED FOR THE MEMBERS OF

THE ARMS CONTROL AND FOREIGN POLICY CAUCUS

April 18, 1985

The Arms Control and Foreign Policy Caucus was formerly known as Members of Congress for Peace through Law.

Section 1: Who Are the Contras?

An Analysis of the Makeup of the Military Leadership of the Rebel Forces, and of the Nature of the Private American Groups Providing Them Financial and Material Support

The United States has been supporting armed opposition to the Nicaraguan Government since 1981. Over $80 million reportedly has been spent to build and maintain a force of from 10,000 to 15,000 "contras." In the next week [April 1985], Congress again faces the decision of whether to resume funding for the contras.

The purpose of this report is to analyze the leadership and membership of the contras, and the nature and goals of the private organizations which provide their financial and material support. The report is divided into two sections. The first describes and assesses the make-up of the contras; the second describes the private American organizations that assist them.

Information published by the Nicaraguan Government has not been used in this report. Instead, the report is based primarily on extensive interviews with former high-ranking officials of the primary contra force (the FDN), literature published by the FDN, and interviews with representatives of organizations that aid the contras. While we recognize there are limitations in this approach, the Executive Branch has thus far failed to respond to our requests for specific information on the structure and leaders of the FDN military command. We hope that publication of this report will focus closer attention on the significant questions it seeks to address.

Summary

In summary, the conclusions of the report are as follows:
* While the "foot-soldiers" of the FDN Army are largely peasants, the army is organized and commanded by former National Guardsmen. In the first publicly available organizational chart of the high command of the FDN military force, the report finds that

46 of the 48 positions in the FDN's command structure are held by former Guardsmen.

* While the FDN's civilian directorate has been cleansed to minimize the role of former Guardsmen and Somoza associates, the military leadership has not been. As a result, the key military strategist positions, including the Strategic Commander, are held by ex-National Guardsmen; as are *all* of the General Staff; four out of five of the Central Commanders; six out of seven of the Regional Commanders; and probably all 30 Task Force commanders.

* Up to 20 private groups in the United States have provided the contras with substantial financial and material aid (apparently some $5 million) in the past year. Most of these groups are not traditional relief organizations or other established groups recognized as providing humanitarian aid, but rather are ultra-conservative or paramilitary groups on the fringe of American political opinion.

* These groups are largely operated by a small group of about half a dozen men, mostly with military or paramilitary backgrounds, whose close association often means that the groups work in tandem.

* A major "relief" effort for the Miskito Indians living on the Honduran-Nicaraguan border has had the effect of maintaining the MISURA "contra" army. One of the groups contributing to this effort is funded in large part by Rev. Moon's Unification Church.

Who Are the Contras?
An Analysis of the Military Leadership of the FDN

Contrasting claims have been made about the background of the contras by the United States and Nicaraguan Governments. Nicaragua states that they are "basically former Somoza National Guardsmen who are engaged in terrorism against the Nicaraguan people," while the United States maintains that in the "democratic resistance...nearly all of the opposition leaders opposed Somoza." Our research indicates that the truth is somewhere in between.

This section attempts to resolve the differences between these two extreme positions by describing for Congress—to the best of our knowledge, for the first time in unclassified form—the military make-up of the Nicaraguan Democratic Force (FDN).

This section concludes that:

* FDN and U.S. Government claims that the FDN is largely a "peasant army" of Nicaraguans disaffected with their government are accurate.

* In contrast to FDN claims about the military leadership of the contras (which the State Department has given credence by publishing), 46 of the 48 positions in the FDN military leadership are held by ex-National Guardsmen. These include the Strategic Commander, the Regional Command Coordinator, all five members of the General Staff, four out of five Central Commanders, five out of six regional commanders, and all 30 task force commanders.

* While the core of the General and Central Command Staff is admittedly fluid, with personnel changing titles and duties over time, regional and task force commanders acquire personal control over their forces, and change infrequently. In any event, the over-all structure detailed here has existed for the past 16 months, and the personnel and duties listed were verified less than two weeks ago.

* Certain individuals in the leadership, including especially controversial ones such as Ricardo Lau (an ex-National Guard officer reputed to have engaged in numerous atrocities both in the Guard and in the FDN), have taken a less "visible" role in recent months in order to make the nature of the contra army more acceptable to Congress. Our interviews with former FDN officials, as well as the recent refusal of ARDE Commander Eden Pastora to ally his forces with the FDN because of the involvement of Lau and other ex-Guardsmen, indicate that these individuals nonetheless retain significant power in the FDN.

*Blanket FDN denials of the military structure and the Guard background of individuals as described in this section appear to lack credibility. The FDN representative in Washington, for example, claims that ex-Guard officers Armando "the Policeman" Lopez and Walter "Tono" Calderon Lopez, identified by three independent sources and numerous on-site news reports as two of the top three FDN commanders, serve in the minor ancillary roles of "warehouse keeper" and "supply assistant for a base camp." Further, the FDN representative denies that Col. Enrique Bermudez is the strategic commander who runs the military effort (this task is attributed to the civilian President of the FDN directorate), or even that a conventional military command structure exists in the FDN. These denials directly contradict literature published by the FDN in Honduras, which displays a military command structure, and places Bermudez at its head.

* While the Executive Branch will likely dispute some of the findings in this report at a later date, it has thus far failed to respond to a written request for specific information on the military leadership by Caucus Chairman McHugh, or to numerous telephone inquiries. At this point, the only information the Administration has made public about the FDN military command appears to concede that FDN claims may not be verifiable: rather than submit to Congress its own analysis of FDN leadership, the State Department attributes virtually all of its information to "FDN reports."

* * * * *

This section focuses on the FDN because it would receive the great majority (if not all) of U.S. funds approved for expenditure, and because the FDN is the only significant contra military force at present. Leadership struggles and lack of funds have combined to virtually bring to a halt major military activities by ARDE's roughly 1,000 fighters in the south, and the Miskito Indians' roughly 1,500 fighters in the north.

This section analyzes the military rather than the political leadership of the FDN for three reasons:

(a) because it is the military leaders who make the key decisions on military strategy and on the direction of the war. For instance, it is the military and not the political leaders who decide on military operations, on tactics, and on the disciplining of commanders and troops for human rights abuses;

(b) because it remains an open question whether the civilian leaders, who have little if any decision-making power now, would be able to wrest power from the military leaders, should the rebel forces gain victory; and

(c) because very little information has heretofore been made available on the military leadership of the FDN—in contrast to the wealth of material the Administration has provided on the "new" civilian leadership. Some critics call this leadership "repackaged": prior to a reorganization in 1982, nearly the entire FDN directorate was drawn from the 15th of September Legion, formed by ex-Guard officers and associates of President Somoza shortly after his ouster in 1979. For example, a recent State Department publication provides biographical information on 27 "top leaders" of the contras, only one of whom—Bermudez—is in the FDN military apparatus.

The conclusions in this section are based on extensive interviews with two former high-ranking FDN officials, and with one of the foremost American experts on the Nicaraguan National Guard. News reports, including those in the Central American press and those based on on-site interviews, formed the basis for the interviews. Information published by the Nicaraguan Government, which was found to be dated and of questionable accuracy, was not used.

The two ex-FDN officials, Edgar Chamorro Coronel and Salvador Icaza, served respectively as a member of the FDN civilian directorate and the FDN's communications liaison from 1983 to 1984. Both spent substantial time at the FDN's central base and other bases in Honduras, assisted in the investigation of regional commanders for alleged human rights abuses, and left the FDN largely because it failed to purge itself of high personnel with connections to President Somoza or the National Guard. In the course of the interviews, Chamorro checked with sources still in the FDN and brought this material up to date.

The academic expert interviewed was Professor Richard Millett of Southern Illinois University—a frequent Congressional witness who is widely respected as one of the most knowledgeable Americans on politics and power within Somoza's National Guard.

The following chart displays the current structure and leadership of the military command of the FDN. Most leaders are identified by their "Noms de guerre," as they are in the FDN. Of the 48 positions in the command structure, our two sources who were formerly in the FDN claim that 46 are filled by former National Guardsmen.

Military Command Structure: FDN

Strategic Commander: *Enrique Bermudez*
Supreme commander and chief of staff

Regional Command Coordinator: *W. "Tono" Calderon Lopez*
Coordinates from 8,000 to 12,000 combatants

General Staff
G-1, Personnel: *The Deer*
G-2, Intelligence: *The Bull*
G-3, Operations: *"Mike Lima"*
G-4, Logistics: *Armando "The Policeman" Lopez*
G-5, Psychological Warfare: *Invisible*

Central Commanders
Air Operations: *Juan Gomez*
Counter-Intelligence: *Ricardo Lau*
MISURA Liason: *Justiciano Perez*
Special Forces: *Little Bird*
Infantry Training School: *(name unknown)*

Regional Commanders
Direct from 500 to 2,000 combatants
Nicarao: *Comandante Mack*
Segovia: *Comandante Dr. Aureliano*
Jorge Salazar: *Comandante Quiche*
Rafaela Herrera: *Comandante Little Tiger*
Diriangen: *Comandante Dimas*
San Jacinto: *Comandante Renato*

Task Force Commanders
Two to eight Task Force Commanders serve under
a regional command. Each directs some 250 combatants.

General Description

In this command structure, the Strategic Commander is the director of military strategy and operations. He is assisted in planning and implementing strategy by his general staff and central commanders. All but one of the 12 top central staff were formerly in the Guard. Overall control of the primary combat units is given to the second-ranking officer, the coordinator of regional commands.

Each of the six regional commanders (five of whom were in the Guard) has a number of task force commanders operating under his control. The regional and task force commanders are referred to as "commandante," and command the personal loyalty of their troops. These are the key military field leaders. Our sources claim that most and probably all of the 30 task force commanders are former Guards. These commanders in turn break their 250-combatant commands into three "groups" of 70 (with the remaining personnel performing central command duties for the task force).

Roughly 80 percent of the group leaders have no prior service in the National Guard; this ratio is the reverse of what existed two years ago, before the expansion of the FDN. The groups are then broken down into three detachments of 20 combatants each (again, with the remainder performing central command duties for the group). Nearly all the detachment leaders have no prior Guard service.

FDN combatants are estimated at between 8,000 and 12,000, rather than the 15,000 claimed by the FDN. The lower figure was provided by Chamorro, who states that when he was responsible for public relations for the FDN, he was under instructions to routinely double the actual size of the FDN. Whatever the true figure, FDN combatants are largely peasants who are disaffected with Sandinista policies. In sum, the FDN is a peasant army with ex-Guard leadership.

Identification and Description of Military Leaders

Strategic Commander: Enrique Bermudez

Mr. Bermudez is a former Colonel of the National Guard. Along with *Aristedes Sanchez* (General Secretary of the FDN's civilian directorate, formerly a wealthy land-owner and close associate of the late General Somoza) and *Adolfo Calero* (head of the civilian directorate, and a leader of the business opposition to Somoza), Bermudez is part of the informal triumvirate that decides strategy for the civilian directorate. Bermudez controls military operations.

Bermudez, who led the Nicaraguan contingent in the OAS occupation of the Dominican Republic in 1965, was Nicaragua's military attache in Washington for the last three years of Somoza's rule. Following Somoza's ouster, he helped found the 15th of September Legion with some 60 former Guard officers, which was the nucleus of the FDN at its founding in 1981.

Bermudez increased his operational control over the FDN when he dismissed his Chief of Staff, former Guard officer *Emilio Echevarry*, and a number of his assistants in 1983 following a CIA-assisted investigation into Echevarry's handling of FDN funds. Bermudez did not replace Echevarry, and instead has assumed many of his functions.

Bermudez is assisted, in addition to the military staff described below, by a number of former Somoza supporters and National Guard officers who arrange for the procurement of weapons and supplies, and carry out a variety of special missions in surveillance, communications and special military tasks. These individuals are not part of the formal structure of the FDN, but an important operational component. They include: *Enrique "Cuco" [The Cuckoo] Sanchez*, a former land-owner and deputy for Somoza's party in the Nicaraguan parliament and brother of General Secretary Aristedes Sanchez; the *Teffel* brothers, *Jose* and *Jaime*, associates of Somoza; and two brothers, former Guard officers, the *"Shermans."*

Bermudez' presence in the FDN has been cited by some contra leaders, such as Eden Pastora and Brooklyn Rivera, as a primary reason why they refuse to join in a coalition with the FDN. Chamorro and Icaza left the FDN in large part because Bermudez would not remove his associates from the 15th of September Legion from the FDN command structure.

Coordinator, Regional Commands: Walter "Tono" Calderon Lopez

"Tono," a former Guard officer who was once a regional commander in the FDN, occupies this second-most powerful military position—the equivalent of what is known in western military parlance as a Theater Operations Commander. He directs the six regional commanders, and he can call on the general staff and central commanders to assist them. Tono is identified in a February, 1984 publication of the FDN in Honduras as commander of tactical operations, which appears to be the same functional role as regional coordinator.

General Staff, Personnel [G-1]: "El Venado" [The Deer]

"El Venado," a former Guard officer, was a Task Force commandante for the FDN. When he was badly wounded in an attack on the town of Ocotal, in the northern-most Nicaraguan province of Nueva Segovia, he moved to the general staff. G-1 is responsible for record-keeping and advises the Strategic Commander on personnel placement.

General Staff, Intelligence [G-2]: "El Toro" [The Bull]

"El Toro" was a colonel in the National Guard. G-2 is responsible for ascertaining the whereabouts and abilities of Nicaraguan military units. "El Toro" replaced *Edgard Hernandez*, a former Guard officer dismissed with Chief of Staff *Emilio Echevarry* in 1983.

General Staff, Operations [G-3]: "Mike Lima"

"Mike Lima," or "M.L.," was the most widely renowned of the FDN's regional commanders prior to moving to the General Staff. A former Guard officer, he led the Diriangen regional command, with up to 2,000 fighters. This was the most militarily active of the commands. While a regional commander, he was badly wounded in a mortar explosion, and lost an arm. G-3's responsibilities include planning overall requirements and strategy for operations, in consultation with the Coordinator of Regional Commands.

General Staff, Logistics [G-4]: Armando "El Policia" [The Policeman] Lopez

Armando Lopez, a former captain in the National Guard, was one of the founders of the 15th of September Legion; he is extremely close to Bermudez, and has been seen by some as his second in command at times. He has dismissed the possibility of negotiations with the Nicaraguan Government, although this is a stated goal of the FDN's civilian directorate: "He who speaks of dialogue with the Communists speaks of wasting his time." G-4's responsibilities focus on supplying the regional commands and task forces.

General Staff, Psychological Warfare [G-5]: "El Invisible"

"El Invisible," a former Guard officer, is responsible for planning activities that weaken the control of the Nicaraguan Government over its armed forces and the civilian population. Such activities can include distributing leaflets that offer rewards for desertion, or broadcasting information that discredits the Sandinistas. "El Invisible" replaced *Manuel Caceres*, a former Guard officer now living in the Dominican Republic. This staff position has rotated more frequently than others, and "El Invisible" may shortly be returning to Task Force command.

Central Command, Head of Air Operations: Juan Gomez

Gomez was a Guard officer who served as Somoza's personal pilot. He now performs the same function for Bermudez, as well as overseeing the operation of the small number of reconnaissance, cargo, and rotary aircraft that form the FDN's air force. Gomez was in the 15th of September Legion, as well as the original FDN directorate.

Central Command, Head of Counter-Intelligence: Ricardo Lau

Lau is a former Guard officer whose service in the FDN has been cited by contra leaders Eden Pastora and Brooklyn Rivera as a primary reason for their refusal to participate in a coalition with the FDN. Lau has recently been accused (by a former Salvadoran Army colonel) of procuring former Guards to assassinate Salvadoran Archbishop Romero in 1980—a new accusation which comes on top of long-standing charges that he has engaged in numerous atrocities, both as a Guardsman and in the FDN.

Lau was in the 15th of September Legion, as well as the original FDN directorate. In 1983, the FDN announced that Lau had been removed from the formal post of head of counter-intelligence, apparently to encourage the formation of a broad coalition of "contra" groups. Nonetheless, our sources contend that Lau continues to function as he had before, albeit with a lower public profile, and retains responsibility for preventing infiltration of the FDN by agents of the Nicaraguan Government and for enforcing discipline for Bermudez.

Lau's extremely close alliance with Bermudez leads our former FDN sources to believe that as long as Bermudez is Strategic Commander, Lau will play an important role in the FDN—

"forever." Lau is assisted in counter-intelligence by Armando Lopez' son, known as *"El Policito"* [The Little Policeman] and *"El Bestia"* [The Beast].

Central Command, MISURA Liaison: Justiciano Perez

Perez, a former Guard officer, has also been cited by other contra leaders as an unacceptable member of any military or political coalition. Perez commanded Somoza's infantry training school, and was personally close to Somoza. He too was formally removed from the FDN leadership in 1983, but continues in a key role as Bermudez' liaison with the MISURA military force, which operates in north-eastern Nicaragua under the command of Miskito Indian leader *Steadman Fagoth*.

Central Command, Special Forces: "El Pajarito" [Little Bird]

"El Pajarito" leads small groups (of up to 75 fighters) into Nicaragua to perform sabotage and other special missions requiring rapid movement. He is a young man, and although his father was a Guard officer, he was a medical student in Mexico during the revolution and never served in the Guard.

Central Command, Infantry Training School: Name Unknown

A former Guard officer commands the infantry training school at Las Vegas, which is currently diminishing in size. This officer replaced *Hugh Villagra*, a former Guard officer whom Bermudez allegedly ousted as a rival in 1984. Assisting the head of the training school in the recent past was a third *Sanchez, Victor*, whose two other brothers, *Aristedes* and *Enrique "Cuco,"* have been discussed above.

Regional Command, Nicarao: Commandante "Mack"

The Nicarao (a popular contraction of "Nicaragua") command is led by Commandante "Mack," a former Guardsman. His four Task Forces are all commanded by former Guardsmen, known as *"El Cascavel"* [The Rattlesnake], *"03,"* *"Ersi,"* and *"Ocran."* FDN publications in Honduras confirm Mack's identity as head of this command.

Regional Command, Rafaela Herrera: Commandante "Tigrillo" [Little Tiger]

The Rafaela Herrera command, named after a legendary Nicaraguan heroine, is commanded by Commandante "Tigrillo," the only Regional Commander (in fact, the only one of the top 48 military leaders in the FDN besides "El Pajarito," Head of the Special Forces) who is not a former National Guardsman. Tigrillo participated in the revolution, although commanders are all former Guards. Two of them are identified by their nicknames, *"Atila"* [Attila the Hun] and *"Tiro Al Blanco"* [Target-Shooter]. FDN publications in Honduras confirm the identities of Tigrillo, Atila and Tiro Al Blanco in these roles.

Regional Command, Diriangen: Commandante "Dimas"

The Diriangen command, named after a legendary Indian chief, is commanded by Commandante "Dimas." Dimas, a former Guardsman, had been a Task Force commander in Diriangen. He replaced *"Mike Lima"* when Lima was wounded and became G-3. All of Dimas' Task Forces are commanded by former Guards. FDN publications in Honduras confirm Dimas' prior role of Task Force commander.

Regional Command, Segovia: Commandante Dr. Aureliano

The Segovia command, named after the province of most FDN activity, the mountainous border province of Nueva Segovia, is commanded by a former Guardsman who also has studied medicine. All of Aureliano's Task Forces are commanded by former Guardsmen. FDN publications in Honduras confirm Aureliano's role in this regional command.

Regional Command, Jorge Salazar: Commandante "Quiche"

The Jorge Salazar command, named after a leader of the business coalition COSEP who was killed by Nicaraguan police in 1980 (and whose widow serves on the FDN's civilian directorate), is commanded by a former Guardsman. Commandante "Quiche" has adopted an Indian name, although he is not himself an Indian. He was a Task Force commander under Walter Calderon "Tono" Lopez, who left this regional command to become coordinator of the regional commands. All of Quiche's Task Forces are commanded by former Guards. One task force is led by *"Franklin."*

Regional Command, San Jacinto: Commandante "Renato"

The San Jacinto command, named after a famous battle in Nicaraguan history, is commanded by a former Guardsman. Commandante "Renato" presides over this smallest of the regional commands (probably some 500 fighters). His Task Forces are all commanded by former National Guards. Renato has been identified in this role in FDN publications in Honduras.

Section 2: Who Aids the Contras?

An Analysis of the Private American Groups Providing Financial and Material Assistance

Close to 20 privately incorporated U.S. groups have reportedly sent (or plan soon to send) aid, supplies or cash contributions to Nicaraguan refugees in Honduras and to the contras themselves. This section analyzes the activities of these groups and their backgrounds.

An analysis of these groups, with an emphasis on the six or seven which provide the lion's share of the $5 million in private funds which has reportedly reached the contras in the last year, shows the following:

* They are not the establishment conservative groups known to support administration policies in Central America, but rather are ultra-conservative, even approaching fringe, activist groups. For instance, one group helped provide mercenaries to protect the white government in Rhodesia and another has included in its international membership at least one neo-fascist party, whose chief had served in Mussolini's government.

* While some of these ultra-conservative groups have existed for decades, others have been formed in the last year or even in the last six months—with the primary if not sole purpose to aid the contras.

* The groups receive their funds from a wide variety of sources—including individual Americans, U.S. corporations (such as pharmaceutical companies who have contributed medical supplies), and Rev. Moon's Unification Church.

*Although many of the groups argue that they provide "humanitarian aid" only, they are not in any way associated with (nor do they coordinate efforts with) the broad community of recognized humanitarian organizations, such as Catholic Relief Service, the World Relief Organization, or the U.N. High Commission for Refugees (UNHCR). In fact, some of these recognized relief organizations have expressed concern that the private groups will politicize their relief efforts, and have contended that the so-called "humanitarian" aid to Miskito refugees on the Nicaraguan border actually sustains the MISURA contra army's military base camps.

* The individual driving forces behind the major groups are a small group of about a half dozen men, most of whom have military or paramilitary backgrounds or mercenary experience, and who often participate in more than one organization. For instance, three assistant editors of *Soldier of Fortune* magazine (which has sent direct aid to the contras) also run or are board members of three other separate groups seeking to aid the contras. And the chairman of the group which may have provided the most aid, retired Gen. John Singlaub, also is closely associated with four other U.S. groups aiding the contras. (Prior to being relieved by President Carter of his South Korean command, Gen. Singlaub headed the Unconventional Warfare Task Force in Vietnam.)

* While many of the groups work closely together, they have different stated purposes. Some openly admit their aid is for military purposes (and includes boots, uniforms and even personnel). Others insist their aid reaches only needy refugees, and is in no way related to the contra war. Most groups call their aid "humanitarian," but either privately or publicly acknowledge that some of it (e.g. medical supplies and food) ends up at contra camps. These groups also have conceded that their "humanitarian" aid to refugees (which includes families of the contras) may indirectly aid the contras by freeing up the contra accounts to purchase weapons and pay combatants.

The research for this section is based primarily on individual interviews with spokespeople or directors for virtually all of the groups, as well as publicly available information.

A description of each of these groups and their activities follows.

World Anti-Communist League

The World Anti-Communist League, formed in the 1960s by Nationalist Chinese to fight communism, claims to act as an "umbrella group" for many of the smaller and newer groups aiding the contras. Headed by retired Army General John Singlaub (who commanded U.S. troops in South Korea until he was relieved by President Carter, and who previously pioneered new techniques of unconventional warfare as head of the Joint Unconventional Task Force in Vietnam), the group coordinates fund-raising from U.S. groups, U.S. individuals, U.S. corporations, and foreign governments. According to Gen. Singlaub, funds raised by WACL have purchased food, medicine, boots, outboard motors, and office supplies, and have thus allowed the contras to use their cash for weapons and ammunition.

The WACL, in recent years, has been subjected to increasing charges of anti-semitism and neo-fascism. In 1973, charging anti-semitism, its British chapter resigned. Five years later at an annual convention, its Mexican delegation attacked NBC's

"Holocaust" program as "another gigantic campaign of Jewish propaganda to conceal their objectives of world domination." In the same year, WACL extended membership to Italy's principal neo-fascist party, which was headed by a member of Mussolini's government. One of its former chairmen has espoused the concept of genetic purity and calls for artificial insemination and sperm banks to maintain racial purity.

"Soldier of Fortune": El Salvador/Nicaragua Defense Fund

According to the magazine's editor, *Soldier of Fortune's* Defense Fund has provided boots and military uniforms to the Nicaraguan contras. In conjunction with several other groups (see Air Commandos, Refugee Relief International and Institute for Regional and International Studies), *Soldier of Fortune* is one of the larger and more aggressive recruiters on behalf of private aid to the contras.

Soldier of Fortune is a monthly journal widely considered to be a major source of information for mercenaries. Its classified ads offer information on how to obtain and use weapons and explosives, as well as references on individual mercenaries. It assisted the white minority government of Rhodesia in procuring mercenaries. Among its more recent projects have been the raising of funds for Afghan guerillas, and the offering of a $100,000 reward in gold to any pilot defecting with materials implicating the Russians for participating in biological warfare.

The Caribbean Commission

The Caribbean Commission, formed in 1979 with the help of pro-Somoza Nicaraguan exiles when Somoza's fall seemed imminent, has provided some 50,000 pounds of materials—particularly clothing and medical equipment—to Nicaraguan refugees on the Honduran border, including families of the contras. In addition, they have provided some specific medical equipment to the contras, including an x-ray machine.

The Commission is headed by Dr. Alton Oschner, Jr., whose father's similarly oriented organization (Information Council of the Americas) broadcast "truth tapes" throughout Latin America in the early 1960s warning about the spread of communism in Latin America. According to Dr. Oschner, he was also involved in establishing Friends of the Americas (see below).

The purpose of the group is to "maintain, promote and strengthen the free enterprise system in the western hemisphere in order to prevent totalitarian infiltration in this part of the world."

Friends of the Americas

Friends of the Americas was founded in April of 1984 as a charitable organization which aids, among others, Miskito Indian refugees in Honduras. According to its co-director Diane Jenkins, it has in the past year sent to Honduras ten medical teams, 5,000 pairs of children's shoes, and some food.

Ms. Jenkins vehemently denies providing any aid to MIS-URA, the major military arm of the Miskitos. However, Congressional staff members and Catholic Relief Service workers who have visited the area contend that aid from FOA and others has the effect of keeping the refugees directly on the border (rather than north of the border where the United Nations has bona fide refugee camps) and thus of sustaining MISURA base camps.

Further doubts about the ultimate destination of the aid are fueled by advertisements such as one which appeared in a FOA Newsletter last fall, which appealed for "cash contributions," for "a large airplane," for "boats and outboard motors," and for such militarily-oriented equipment as radios, walkie-talkies and a satellite dish.

Friends of the Americas is one of the better known groups in large part due to its leadership: Director Woody Jenkins, a Louisiana State Representative who resigned the Democratic National Committee in 1980 to campaign for Reagan, also now serves as secretary of the Conservative Caucus' research branch and as the director of the Council for National Policy. Mr. Jenkins (whose wife Diane is co-director) was the dinner-chairman of the Nicaraguan Refugee Fund (see below), which hosted President Reagan April 15 [1985].

International Relief Friendship Foundation

Funded largely by Reverend Moon's Unification church, the IRFF in the last year has shipped 1,000 pounds of clothing and seven tons of food and medicine to Miskito Indian refugees in Honduras. The group denies providing any aid to the military arm of the Miskitos, and asserts that much of the aid has gone to children.

According to the director of IRFF, the organization was started in 1976 with a $225,000 grant from the Unification Church. Ninety percent of their present annual budget of under $200,000 still comes from the Church.

Also according to the director, IRFF has worked with the political arm of the Church, Causa International, which he asserted had paid $3,000 to fly one of IRFF's shipments to Honduras last summer.

As with aid provided by FOA (see above), IRFF's aid is distributed to "recently arrived refugees" directly on the border, rather than to internationally-sponsored (e.g. UNHCR) refugee camps north of the border. As a result, this type of aid has been subject to criticisms from relief workers and Congressional staff that it has had the effect of maintaining the MISURA military base camps, which are also located directly on the border.

Civilian-Military Assistance

CMA, which received press notice when a helicopter carrying two of its men was shot down while participating in an attack in northern Nicaragua last fall, was formed in 1983 to take direct action against communism in Central America, and specifically to provide training and equipment to the contras.

According to CMA's director and Vietnam veteran Tom Posey, CMA has sent the contras over $200,000 (over 60 tons) in military equipment (not including humanitarian aid) including boots, canteens, and other supplies.

In addition, and perhaps more important, they have provided manpower: in the last year, CMA has sent Americans to work with the contras as mechanics and medical relief teams. CMA also claims that its personnel operate as forward observers alongside the contras inside Nicaragua, and, in some cases, have handled "small weapons." According to Mr. Posey, CMA provided "less than 100" Americans to the contras in the past year.

Most recently, in April [1985], 14 CMA-supported men were asked by the U.S. Embassy in Honduras to leave the area.

Air Commando Association

While the Air Commandos have not to date provided any aid to the contras, its director aims to start aid as soon as possible. The group is awaiting clearance from the Honduran government for delivery to the contras of a complete 25-bed hospital.

Air Commandos is run by retired Gen. H.C. Aderholt, who is also an assistant editor of *Soldier of Fortune* magazine. In addition, Mr. Aderholt served in Vietnam as deputy to Gen. Singlaub in the Joint Unconventional Warfare Task Force.

Christian Broadcasting Network (Operation Blessing)

Through Operation Blessing, its worldwide relief agency, news stories report that CBN has sent food, medical supplies and clothing to families of the contras. CBN refused to admit or deny these reports, asserting only that they "help starving, displaced people in Central America," and that while no "direct" aid is given to the contras, "aid is provided to needy people wherever they are."

Founded by M.G. (Pat) Robertson, CBN owns four TV stations and grosses over $50 million a year. Besides its regular show "The 700 Club," CBN provides news and prayer programming. In 1982, Robertson launched a political lobby named the National Planning Committee, which works to change First Amendment laws.

Refugee Relief International

Refugee Relief International, headed by one of *Soldier of Fortune's* editors, has provided an unspecified amount of aid to Miskito Indian refugees in Honduras—some in "direct funds" (cash), but the majority in medicine, food and clothing. According to news reports (*Boston Globe*, 12/30/84), a RRI pamphlet makes clear the ultimate military purpose of these funds, by saying "this type of (humanitarian) aid will defray costs that the U.S. government would ordinarily incur, thereby freeing a portion of its financial allocations for additional military and other assistance."

RRI is headed by Thomas Reisinger, the Assistant Director of *Soldier of Fortune* for Special Projects. On the Board of RRI is retired Gen. John Singlaub.

Veterans of Foreign Wars

Although the VFW voted in August of 1983 to establish a fund to provide food, medicine and other non-military aid to the Nicaraguan "freedom-fighters," the fund claims to have lasted only one year and raised only $2,000. The VFW turned the funds over to the American Security Council Foundation. The ASC Foundation claims to have transferred the funds to the International Red Cross. A spokesperson for the International Red Cross reported that after an extensive search, no record of this transaction could be found.

Institute for Regional and International Studies

The Institute for Regional and International Studies seeks to make available to Salvadorans and "perhaps" to the Nicaraguan contras (*Boston Globe*, 12/30/84) intelligence gathering and psychological operations.

The group is directed by Alexander M.S. McColl, military affairs editor of *Soldier of Fortune* magazine. It was founded in 1982 under the auspices of the World Anti-Communist League. *Soldier* editor-in-chief Dale Dye asserted he did not know if any contras have yet been trained at IRIS.

Nicaraguan Refugee Fund

The Nicaraguan Refugee Fund is presently seeking to raise $2-$5 million to aid Nicaraguans in Honduras—in part through a gala $250-a-head fund-raising dinner honoring President Reagan on Monday, April 15. A substantial amount is expected to go through FOA (see above), but to date, this group is not known to have provided any funds to the contras or to Nicaraguan refugees.

The sponsors and dinner committee of the NRF represent a virtual "who's who" of private U.S. citizens involved in aiding the contras—the dinner committee is chaired by Friends of the America's Woody Jenkins and includes J. Peter Grace (also affiliated with the Knights of Malta), Nelson Bunker Hunt, CBN's Pat Robertson, and Caribbean Commission's Dr. Ochsner. Its Honorary Committee includes conservative stalwarts such as Joseph Coors and W. Clement Stone; and its Special Committee includes Wayne Newton and Roger Staubach.

Although this group has not yet provided any aid to the contras or their families, it is noteworthy because the fund-raising dinner in its honor appears to be drawing key administration leaders, including the President—representing the first time U.S. Government officials have provided their names and stature to such a private pursuit.

Knights of Malta & Americares Foundation

The Knights of Malta, a 900-year old fraternal organization of Roman Catholics, has reportedly (*Washington Post*, 12/27/84) distributed $680,000 to Miskito Indian refugees in Honduras, in conjunction with the Americares Foundation. While the Knights deny raising any funds for the contras, a spokesperson at the Americares Foundation contends that Americares raised the money (targeted to six destinations in Honduras) and the Knights distributed the aid.

The head of the American division of the Knights of Malta is J. Peter Grace. The honorary chairman of the Americares Foundation is Zbigniew Brzezinski.

Other Groups Involved in the Private Aid Effort

Over half a dozen other groups, whose purpose was unclear or on which little information was available, have reportedly aided the contras in the last year. These include:

Causa International, the political arm of Rev. Moon's Unification church, which refuses to comment about aid to Nicaragua or Honduras, but which others (including IRFF) have asserted helps finance their efforts to aid the contras;

Human Development Foundation, reported by the *Washington Post* as aiding the contras and by *The Nation* as the unofficial operating arm of the FDN in the U.S.;

Nicaraguan Patriotic Association, which is reported to have collected half a million dollars in aid and to have provided daily food supplies for seven refugee camps in Honduras; and

Pro-America Education Foundation, which in the past year has sent $1 million in medical supplies contributed by major pharmaceutical companies to Nicaraguan refugees in Honduras.

* * * *

This report was prepared by the staff of the Arms Control and Foreign Policy Caucus. It does not seek to reflect the views of the members of the Caucus.

Appendix 3

Chronology of Contra Attacks on Civilians:
December 1, 1981—November 30, 1984

The accounts in the report were intended to be illustrative rather than exhaustive. Because of the frequency of contra attacks against civilians, the team was only able to investigate a small percentage of the incidents about which it heard.

The following chronology, too, is incomplete. No definitive catalogue of attacks exists. Nicaraguan civilians are killed, brutalized and kidnapped without any record being made. Nevertheless, by drawing on various primary and secondary sources, this chronology gives an idea of the magnitude of the war being waged against the Nicaraguan population.

Sources for the chronology include: *Bitter Witness: Nicaraguans and the "Covert" War*, by the Witness for Peace Documentation Project; the submissions of the Nicaraguan government to the International Court of Justice at the Hague; lists prepared by clergy in Nicaragua; America's Watch reports; Congressional testimony prepared by the Center for Constitutional Rights; the *Updates* of the Central American Historical Institute; and Reed Brody's notes. It includes only attacks resulting in the death, injury or kidnapping of civilians, or the destruction of farmland or private or communal property, and therefore excludes military skirmishes, rare contra attacks on military targets, overflights and economic sabotage (unless civilians were killed). In putting together the list, with the able assistance of Martin Putnam, we have not attempted to verify the incidents.

Incidents described in Reed Brody's report are marked with an asterisk.

Various acronyms for private and governmental organizations are employed in this chronology. The most common of these, with their denotations in English, are: CDS, Sandinista neighborhood committees; CEP, popular education committees; CEPAD, the Evangelical Committee for Aid and Development; ENABAS, the State grain trading company; ENCAFE, the State coffee trading company; INE, the State electric company; INRA, the Ministry of Agrarian Reform; IRENA, the Ministry of Natural Resources; MICONS, the Ministry of Construction; TELCOR, the State telecommunications company; TGF, the border patrol; UNAG, the National Association of Farmers and Ranchers; YODECO, the State lumber company.

153

December 2, 1981—A group of contras invaded the community of San Jeronimo, kidnapping and later torturing and killing a health-care worker.

December 4, 1981—Approximately 60 contras invaded the community of Asang, kidnapping and later killing Genaro William and Arles Escoban. They also robbed the local ENABAS warehouse of 600 quintales of rice and 35,000 cordobas in cash.

December 6, 1981—Aguedo Morales Reina, a Cuban elementary school teacher, was killed by contras in Chontales.

December 8, 1981—Armed contras coming from Honduras invaded the community of La Esperanza, ordering the inhabitants to cross over to Honduras and threatening with death those who refused. They also threatened those who worked for Government agencies.

December 10, 1981—Contras attacked and wounded Jesus Lorenzo Reyes in El Guabo, Waslala.

* December 28, 1981—Approximately 15 contras invaded the Miskito community of Bilwaskarma, kidnapping four people, including a woman doctor, Myrna Cunningham, and a nurse, Regina Lewis. The contras took the women to Honduras, where they were gang-raped.

December 31, 1981—Approximately 25 contras kidnapped a citizen from the community of Andres Tara. He was later found dead, his throat cut and the eyes removed from their sockets.

January 2, 1982—Approximately 60 contras attacked the town of Raiti, Zelaya Norte, from Honduras, killing three civilians. In a separate attack, 45 contras armed with shotguns, rifles and pistols invaded Limbaica, Zelaya Norte, stealing two vehicles, two boats, and various items of equipment. Later the same group burned a bridge at Alamikamba.

January 5, 1982—Contras invaded the community of Tuskrutara, Zelaya Norte, kidnapping a reservist and his wife.

January 22, 1982—Contras killed three campesinos near La Pavona, Jinotega.

February 4, 1982—Contras assassinated an activist in the CDS at Kuskawas, Matagalpa.

February 5, 1982—An FDN band attacked the towns of Las Pintades and San Roque, Nueva Segovia, robbing several houses and raping two women.

* March 3, 1982—An FDN band assassinated Emiliano Perez, a judge in Paiwas, Matagalpa.

March 9, 1982—In the community of Umbla, Zelaya, 20 contras assassinated two children, aged six and seven years, and wounded a campesino.

March 16, 1982—Union leader Timoteo Velazquez was shot outside of Nueva Guinea, Zelaya. On the same day, a campesino belonging to the union in Rama, Zelaya, was murdered and found with his tongue cut out.

March 18, 1982—At La Ermita, 60 contras attacked the building used by the local militia, killing two civilians, including a five year old girl. Three people were wounded.

March 21, 1982—Rio Blanco, Matagalpa. An FDN band of 40 attacked a farm at El Castillo, killing Alberto Soza Hernandez, 21, and his cousin Amalana Soza, five. Alberto's father and another relative were wounded, and his sister Leonor Soza was kidnapped. The same band burned down the local Ministry of Construction outpost, doing an estimated $30,000 in damage, in addition to stealing the life's savings of the woman caretaker.

April 4, 1982—In the district of La Ceiba, Somotillo, 20 contras armed with rifles kidnapped 22 campesinos, including 7 women and nine children.

April 5, 1982—In the district of Banco de Siquia, Zelaya Sur, 10 contras armed with rifles and grenades attacked the local cooperative, killing one civilian, beating the leader of the local civilian defense and burning his house.

April 6, 1982—In the district of La Danta, Zelaya Sur, 60 contras armed with rifles and shotguns attacked and burned the house of the leader of the local civilian defense, killing three civilian members and kidnapping four others.

April 7, 1982—Contras killed two campesinos in San Antonio, Matagalpa.

April 12, 1982—Contras attacked the village of Banu on the Rio Coco and kidnapped, tortured and murdered the head of the civilian defense; his family later found him in the woods with his tongue and ears cut off.

April 12, 1982—Contras kidnapped three civilian defenders at San Francisco, Nueva Segovia, killing one and wounding the others.

April 14, 1982—Thirty-five contras ambushed a caravan of INRA vehicles at Rio Wilika, killing one civilian.

April 24, 1982—Twenty-five contras invaded the district of Yale, Matagalpa, robbing and burning the command post of the civilian defense, injuring one.

April 26, 1982—Contras murdered four farmworkers, a woman and a nine month old child in El Recreo, Jinotega.

April 27, 1982—Six armed contras assassinated two voluntary policemen and two civilian defenders in the town of La Fonseca.

April 30, 1982—Eduviges Gomez, a Delegate of the Word, assassinated in Bana Centro, Nueva Segovia.

April 30, 1982—Marcelo Gonzalez, Delegate of the Word, killed in California, Nueva Segovia.

May 1982—Santos Mejia, Delegate of the Word, assassinated in San Pablo Arriba, Nueva Segovia.

May 16, 1982—Eight contras attacked the ENABAS post at Wanawas, killing three Nicaraguans and carrying off all of the merchandise and 6,000 cordobas in cash. One person was wounded.

June 2, 1982—On the Kukra River, near Bluefields, contras attacked a boat carrying civilian workers, killing one.

July 4, 1982—Forty contras kidnapped 16 Nicaraguans, including two women, at Ubu, Zelaya Sur, killing three of them and raping one of the women. The contras also robbed a store of 155,000 cordobas.

July 16, 1982—Approximately 60 contras seized the town of San Fernando, Nueva Segovia, killing one civilian, kidnapping four others, and burning government offices and a private house.

July 24, 1982—Fourteen Nicaraguans were killed, eight were kidnapped and four were wounded when contras supported by heavy artillery attacked the border posts of San Francisco del Norte and Guayabillo. Many of the victims were also tortured.

July 28, 1982—El Tuma, Central Zelaya. The contras took Alberto Rodriguez and 17 members of his family who were traveling on the road and held them in a safe house. Accusing them of supporting liberation theology and being Sandinistas, the contras beat and slashed them. Nine people were killed, some having their throats slit, others had their heads cut off. One contra collected the blood and drank it. One of Alberto's daughters and one niece were raped.

August 4, 1982—Twenty contras attacked the headquarters of the civilian defense at San Francisco de Kukra Rivers, Bluefields, killing one and kidnapping ten others.

August 8, 1982—Seventeen contras assassinated the CDS coordinator at Apatillo del Sabalar, Matagalpa.

August 11, 1982—At Musawas, contras assassinated three teachers, tortured several other Nicaraguans, and burned foodstuffs.

August 11, 1982—In the community of Malakawas, contras assassinated an adult education worker.

August 14, 1982—Twenty-five contras assassinated a woman member of the local CDS at Las Pampas, Nueva Segovia.

August 24, 1982—Twelve contras armed with rifles and pistols kidnapped two civilians in the El Trapiche district.

August 29, 1982—Approximately 70 contras wearing the uniform of Somoza's National Guard blew up the MICONS installation at Iyas, Matagalpa, killing one civilian and destroying 31 trucks, several pieces of construction equipment, a workshop and other facilities valued at a total of 12 million cordobas.

September 4, 1982—Contras attacked a government construction project in Comarca Betanit, Matagalpa, killing one worker and causing an estimated million dollars in damage.

September 11, 1982—Twenty contras kidnapped and assassinated an adult education worker at Los Chiles.

September 19, 1982—A band of 13 contras invaded the Tawa district, attacking three houses of local residents and raping a woman.

* September 22, 1982—At San Nicolas, on the Jalapa road in Nueva Segovia, a band of contras ambushed and killed two INRA technicians and wounded five other persons.

September 1982—Quebrada Negra, Nueva Segovia. William

Rodriguez, one of the first campesinos to receive land title under the agrarian reform, assassinated and mutilated while returning home.

September 1982—El Arenal, Nueva Segovia. Juan Alanis was kidnapped; his dead, mutilated body was later found.

October 3, 1982—Twenty-five contras kidnapped, tortured and killed a campesino at El Sanzapote, beating and tying up several members of his family.

* October 8, 1982—Contras killed three unarmed civilians in San Jose, Jalapa.

October 10, 1982—Contras ambushed a pick-up truck of INRA at Jalapa, killing one Nicaraguan and wounding three others.

* October 14, 1982—At La Estancia, Nueva Segovia, a band of 40 contras killed three civilians and kidnapped another.

* October 15, 1982—Contras maimed and killed Cruz Urrutia, Delegate of the Word, in Siuce, Jalapa. In a separate attack, 12 contras invaded the La Providencia farm in the Saiz district, kidnapping three Nicaraguans.

October 26, 1982—Approximately 25 to 30 contras kidnapped five farm workers in the El Quemazon district.

* October 28, 1982—Contras mutilated and assassinated 6 peasants in the community of La Fregua, near El Jicaro, including Ricardo Blandon, a Delegate of the Word, and his four children. The same day, contras slit the throat of Leonilo Marin near German Pomares, Jalapa.

October 28, 1982—Approximately 14 contras kidnapped three INRA employees at Haulover; they also robbed the local commissary of 5,000 cordobas, foodstuffs and a boat and motor.

November 6, 1982—Ten contras tortured and killed a civilian defender at Pantasma, Jinotega.

November 9, 1982—At 2:00 in the morning, 30 armed contras kidnapped 42 workers from three farms in San Jose de Las Manos, Nueva Segovia.

November 15, 1982—Contras torture and shoot four farmers in La Ceiba, Jalapa.

November 16, 1982—In Ciudad Antigua, Nueva Segovia, a band of some 50 contras kidnapped three campesinos from the Ramon Raudales cooperative. Their bodies were found the next day.

November 16, 1982—A contra unit kidnapped 60 campesinos from a farm at Rio Arriba, Jalapa. Also kidnapped were two children of a man who worked for State Security.

November 19, 1982—Contras maim and kill Pedro Carazo, Delegate of the Word, near San Pablo, Jalapa.

November 21, 1982—In the community of Buena Vista, Jalapa, Nueva Segovia, 30 contras intercepted and assassinated 3 campesinos.

November 22, 1982—A band of approximately 80 to 100 contras armed with FAL, BZ and M-16 rifles invaded the district of El

Pantasma, kidnapping a member of the FSLN and his 16 year old daughter.

November 22, 1982—A group of 21 contras armed with rifles and revolvers kidnapped five people at El Caimito.

November 24, 1982—A band of 25 contras assassinated a UNAG delegate and an army officer at Buena Esperanza, on the Okawas River.

November 30, 1982—Jalapa, Nueva Segovia. Twelve campesinos were kidnapped to Honduras.

December 4, 1982—At the San Ramon farm in the El Bambucito district, two members of the local CDS, a man aged 45 and a woman aged 54, were assassinated by contras.

December 6, 1982—In La Tronca, Matagalpa, some 15 contras kidnapped eight members of one family, including four members of the militia.

December 18, 1982—A band of contras appeared at the El Jicaro farm in the Saiz district, kidnapping a father and one of his sons. The other members of the family were beaten.

* December 28, 1982—An FDN unit entered the Agronica coffee plantation near the Honduran border, where they kidnapped several civilians, all of whom were volunteer coffee pickers, and took them by force to their military base in Honduras. Felipe and Maria Eugenia Barreda, a highly esteemed Catholic couple from Esteli, were among those kidnapped, and were later tortured and murdered.

December 30, 1982—La Pampas, Nueva Segovia. Twelve peasants were kidnapped to Honduras.

January 1, 1983—Contras kidnapped seven people, including 5 children, in the Chaquital sector near the Honduran border. In a separate attack, a band of 30 to 40 contras armed with rifles invaded the town of San Rafael, kidnapping 67 people (10 families).

January 3, 1983—Seven contras armed with shotguns, rifles and pistols invaded the community of Labu, Siuna, killing a 65 year old woman who headed the local CDS and a man who belonged to the army. The bodies showed signs of torture, and their throats had been cut. The contras also kidnapped two members of the military reserve.

January 5, 1983—Thirteen contras seized the civilian defense post in the district of Wana Wana, killing two brothers and burning the house of their father, a CDS member. The contras also burned a schoolhouse which served as a command post. Two people were wounded.

January 7, 1983—A band of approximately 40 contras assassinated two volunteer coffee pickers at the El Amparo farm in the sector of Cerro Helado, Jinotega. One person was wounded.

January 8, 1983—At 4:30 in the morning, a group of 15 contras armed with rifles, grenades and mortars invaded the San Francisco sector south of Jalapa, kidnapping two sons and a daughter from one family. The kidnapped woman was the coordinator of the local center for popular education. The contras also kidnapped an employee of the same family.

January 10, 1983—Contras invaded the Santa Julia farm in the community of San Gregorio, kidnapping three volunteer coffee pickers.

January 12, 1983—Contras ambushed an INRA pick-up truck in the Punta Mico sector, killing two INRA technicians and wounding another.

* January 16, 1983—Contras armed with rifles and mortars ambushed a private truck near Namasli, killing two children aged 11 and 12, residents of Jalapa. Eight people were wounded.

* January 21, 1983—In Las Colinas, near Yali, Jinotega, contras armed with rifles and grenade launchers ambushed a pick-up truck, killing four civilians (one of them an eight year old girl) and two soldiers. Six people were wounded.

January 24, 1983—Five contras armed with rifles appeared at a house in Las Quebradas, stating that it was their intention to kidnap a certain member of the Auxiliary Forces. Not finding him at home, they kidnapped his wife and held her for four days while they interrogated and raped her. They then released her, threatening her with death if she denounced them.

January 24, 1983—Yali, Jinotega. Contras ambushed a passenger bus, killing six civilians and wounding two militia members.

January 25, 1983—Six coffee pickers were kidnapped from the farm of Noel Ortez in Las Puertas, Jalapa.

January 26, 1983—Twenty-six coffee pickers were kidnapped in Rio Arriba del Limon.

January 29, 1983—Rio Blanco, Matagalpa. Contras killed eight campesinos on a cooperative.

January 29, 1983—A band of contras attacked the civilian defense headquarters at Walakawas, killing seven people and wounding one. One woman was missing.

February 3, 1983—Some 60 contras invaded the community of Bella Vista, Nueva Segovia, kidnapping 21 residents of the community.

February 7, 1983—A group of 60 contras armed with rifles and heavy machine guns kidnapped 11 coffee cutters in the sector of El Ural.

February 10, 1983—A group of 20 contras armed with pistols and rifles kidnapped two campesinos at Santo Domingo, near Jalapa, taking them toward Honduras.

February 26, 1983—A group of approximately 100 contras armed with rifles, grenade launchers and mortars invaded the district of Canada La Castilla, Jinotega, kidnapping 20 campesinos from one cooperative and killing the leader of the local militia.

February 27, 1983—Approximately 200 contras armed with rifles, machine guns, mortars and grenade launchers attacked the civilian defense post at San Jose de las Mulas, killing 20 and wounding ten. Before retreating the contras also burned the schoolhouse and a health center.

March 1, 1983—Contras invaded the Escambray sector, kidnapping two campesinos. They also kidnapped two residents of San Jose de Las Manchones.

March 2, 1983—Sabana Larga, Nueva Segovia. Contras ambushed a civilian truck, killing four and wounding six.

March 3, 1983—Three farmers were kidnapped from El Escambray, the site of a cooperative worked by refugees from nearby mountain communities. Two of the three escaped a few days later.

March 4, 1983—Two hundred contras invaded the zone of Cerro Colorado, burning the Santa Rosa State farm and kidnapping three civilian defenders.

March 5, 1983—Eighty contras seized the San Carlos farm near Muy-Muy, Matagalpa, burning the farmhouse and kidnapping the farm manager. Later they kidnapped two campesinos at the Santa Rosa farm.

March 6, 1983—Some 150 contras armed with machine guns, rifles and rocket launchers seized the community of Kaskita, Zelaya Norte, for three hours, kidnapping four people. In the ensuing combat, a civilian member of the local militia was killed.

March 10, 1983—A group of contras ambushed a jeep at Puente Rio Viejo, Matagalpa, killing eight people, five of them campesinos from the El Castillo Cooperative.

March 11, 1983—A group of contras kidnapped 31 members of the community of Esperanza, Zelaya Norte.

March 12, 1983—A group of 150 contras assassinated five members of a popular education committee who were meeting in a school in the El Jicaro district.

March 14, 1983—Contras kidnapped four CDS members at San Francisco, department of Boaco.

March 15, 1983—Five contras assassinated two campesinos in the sector of Valle Datanli, near Jinotega. In a separate attack, in the community of El Cuje, a group of 25 to 30 contras armed with rifles and grenade launchers burned an INRA pick-up truck and kidnapped the local CDS coordinator and four civilian members of the militia.

March 18, 1983—Contras intercepted and burned an INRA pick-up truck near San Jose de Los Remates, Boaco; its three passengers are missing. In a separate attack, approximately 300 contras invaded the locale of El Achiote, Yaoska, kidnapping two people who worked with the FSLN. Near Rio Blanco, contras kidnapped education administrator Maria Martinez Alvarez. Her body was later found with her throat slit and her breasts cut off.

March 21, 1983—Near Valle El Naranjo, 60 well-armed contras kidnapped seven people, including two employees of the National Development Bank.

March 23, 1983—Ambush of the bus which runs between Jalapa and Ocotal in San Nicholas. The passengers, all civilians, were taken from the bus by contra forces. A confrontation ensued between Nicaraguan soldiers and militiamen, on the one hand, and the contra forces, on the other, after a passenger escaped and alerted Nicaraguan soldiers at the army post in Santa Clara. Four Nicaraguan soldiers/militiamen were killed; one was wounded. During the fighting, the bus passengers escaped.

* **March 26, 1983**—Two hundred contras attacked the district of Rancho Grande with mortar fire, killing two members of the civilian defense, two other Nicaraguan civilians and Pierre Grosjean, a French doctor. Seventeen people were wounded, including seven children. On their retreat the contras burned a house in Canada La Castilla.

March 27, 1983—Thirty contras ambushed an ambulance of the Modesto Agurcia Hospital near San Fernando, Nueva Segovia, killing the driver. In separate attacks, contras kidnapped 7 campesinos from Buena Vista de Ventanilla, near Wiwili. The following day another group of contras kidnapped six campesinos from the nearby La Pita district. Also, 40 contras appeared at the community of El Carbon, Ciudad Antigua. Falsely identifying themselves as members of the army, they kidnapped three members of one family.

March 28, 1983—Contras kidnapped three campesinos in the Las Canas sector.

March 29, 1983—La Esperanza, a tobacco farm in Teotecacinte was attacked under cover of mortar fire from Honduras. One worker was wounded. Two barns were destroyed.

March 30, 1983—Contras attacked the Quinta Del Carmen State farm near San Juan del Rio Coco, killing three civilian defenders and wounding another.

April 6, 1983—La Carranza, Nueva Segovia. Contras assassinated two members of a National Farmworkers Union cooperative, Mauricio Rocha and Gerenias Rocha.

April 7, 1983—Twelve campesinos were kidnapped by contras in the sector of Mozonte, Nueva Segovia.

April 8, 1983—Contras attacked the State farm at Los Laureles, Jinotega, killing the manager and burning two trucks and a jeep. In the ensuing battle, 11 Nicaraguans (including 4 civilians) were killed and 19 were wounded. In separate attacks, 60 to 80 contras armed with rifles robbed the health center at La Movil of all of the medicines it contained. Also, a detachment of contras attacked the town of Ciudad Antigua, Nueva Segovia, with rifle fire and rocket launchers. Three people were wounded and the local health center was partly destroyed. In another attack, 12 contras broke into a campesino's house at Cano Wilson, near El Rama, raping his sister and beating him and both of his parents. On the same day, fifteen year old Concepcion Lopez Torres, from the town of Barriel in Nueva Segovia, was kidnapped and tortured by ten contras. He was hit with a rifle butt and pinned to the ground and tortured with an electric shock instrument. Although he managed to escape, his face is permanently disfigured by the electric shocks. Also the same day, El Porvenir, a tobacco farm near Teotecacinte, was attacked. Over a hundred mortars were shot from the Honduran side of the border onto the farm, destroying 3 houses in the workers' quarters and wounding three girls between the ages of one and five, their mother and grandmother. Under cover of mortar fire, members of the contras crossed over the border into the farm and set fire to six tobacco barns, four of which burned to the ground.

April 10, 1983—A group of ten contras attacked a boat used for the "Inter-Terrestre" canal project near Bluefields, Zelaya Sur, assassinating two people and kidnapping three others.

April 11, 1983—A group of 90 to 100 contras armed with rifles, mortars, grenade launchers, and machine guns attacked the La Colonia State Farm near La Presa Mancotal. After burning the farmhouse to the ground, they kidnapped a woman teacher (a Salvadoran national) from nearby Santa Isabel.

April 12, 1983—Contras destroyed the Rural Infants' Service center at the La Colonia state farm; a campesino family that lived in the center is missing. The same day in San Jose de Bocay, Jinotega, contras entered the school in Agua Sacra Abajo, tying up teacher Hector Rivas and beating him in front of the children. After breaking his ribs, they put two bullets in his head. Nine educators died or disappeared in this area between then and August, 1984.

April 13, 1983—Contras intercepted a vehicle in which the chief of the police sub-station at Palacaguina was riding, killing him and wounding a campesina.

April 14, 1983—In El Cocal, Zelaya Sur, contras seized an INRA motorboat, kidnapping five people. In a separate attack, contras ambushed a civilian truck in the Achuapa sector, near Jalapa, killing two people and wounding two others. They also burned three State vehicles. Also, in La Pedrera, Zelaya Norte, approximately 35 contras ambushed a pick-up truck, killing 4 civilians.

April 16, 1983—Contras assassinated the manager for UNAG at Pantasma, one day after he was kidnapped.

April 18, 1983—Sixty contras invaded the sector of Chusli, near Jalapa, kidnapping a soldier and two campesinos.

April 19, 1983—Fourteen contras armed with rifles and rocket launchers invaded the Vado Ancho sector, cutting the throat of a civilian defender and kidnapping 12 other civilians, among them four health-care workers and five children. In a separate attack, contras kidnapped 30 campesinos in the Monte Frio sector, near Jalapa.

April 20, 1983—Thirty-six men, women and children were kidnapped from La Florida. The same day, 19 people were kidnapped from Monte Frio, Jalapa.

* April 21, 1983—Contras attack El Jicaro with heavy artillery, killing one and wounding others. In a separate attack in the vicinity of Cerro El Toro, near Wina, contras kidnapped 3 people who worked as technicians at the Siuna mines; they also burned the vehicle in which they had been traveling.

* **April 23, 1983**—Approximately 80 to 100 contras armed with rifles, rocket launchers, mortars and other weapons attacked the town of Slilmalila, Zelaya Norte, forcing the entire population of 1,250 to accompany them to Honduras, and damaging the facilities of INRA, IRENA, the medical dispensary, and the Office of Transport of that community.

April 24, 1983—A group of 200 contras burned a MICONS truck and assassinated the driver in the Las Canas sector, near Wiwili.

April 25, 1983—Contras maim and kill Fermin Valenzuela in Villegual, Jinotega. In a separate attack, contras ambushed a pick-up truck at La Belleza, near San Juan de Rio Coco, killing the local head of the Farm Workers Association.

April 28, 1983—Contras kidnapped three tractor drivers and three farmers between Las Uvas and Las Mercedes, four of whom managed to escape.

April 29, 1983—In the district of Cruz Verde, five armed contras robbed and kidnapped Alberto Rodriguez, the local UNAG coordinator and ENABAS manager.

April 30, 1983—Zompapera, Jinotega. One hundred FDN contras ambushed and assassinated 14 people on the road near Wiwili. Two nurses, Adelina Ortega and Dolores Lopez Hernandez, as well as Isabel Molina, an employee of the National Development Bank, were raped and killed in front of the men in the group. Filadelfo and Ramiro Cruz were tortured and then murdered. Also murdered were Reinaldo Mairena, Ronald Blandon, Jose Albergaran, Alvaro Martin Trana, Francisco Reyes, Carlos Cisneros, Francisco Ballesteros, and Albrecht Pflaum, a German doctor who had volunteered three years of service to Wiwili.

Late April 1983—An ARDE commando passed through three small and isolated villages near La Azucena, Rio San Juan, torturing and later murdering 11 peasants who had worked in education, rural cooperatives, and the militia. Another ten peasants were kidnapped. More than 20 families were told that they would be killed if they did not join ARDE's military activities.

May 2, 1983—The bus traveling from Ocotal to Jalapa in the morning was ambushed. Thirty-two people were kidnapped, representing all the men on the bus; six of them were teachers in the high school in Jalapa. Four escaped later in the week. Two vehicles belonging to IRENA were also ambushed.

* **May 3, 1983**—Contras kidnapped three people, including Digna Barreda whom they raped 60 times and a campesino who they tortured and killed. In a separate incident, the bus traveling between Jalapa and Teotecacinte was ambushed. The contra forces opened fire on the bus, wounding a ten year old girl and her mother. The four occupants of a pick-up truck which had been ambushed ahead of the bus were kidnapped. The dead bodies of

three—David Osorio, Alfredo Moran and Gerardo Casco—all small farmowners, were later found with their throats slit and signs of severe torture. The fourth was also later found dead.

May 5, 1983—In the Zacateras sector, contras kidnapped 9 civilians. In a separate attack, a group of 15 contras killed 2 campesinos in the Kuskawas sector.

May 5, 1983—San Juan del Norte, Rio San Juan. Contras attacked a boat carrying food and supplies to a community near here, and kidnapped Alfredo Ballesteros, Cesar Ballesteros, and Cesar's son, German Monterrey.

May 6, 1983—Approximately 200 contras invaded the El Galope State Farm near Rancho Grande, assassinating the TELCOR service manager and kidnapping eight campesinos. They also burned a TELCOR vehicle, a tractor and a warehouse with a large quantity of tools. In a separate attack, in La Dalia, Jinotega, 60 contras ambushed a TELCOR jeep, killing the assistant manager of the TELCOR project in that zone. The same day, an unknown number of perople were kidnapped from Monte Frio near Jalapa.

May 8, 1983—A group of approximately 60 contras armed with rifles, mortars and machine guns, attacked the civilian defense post at Las Papayas, killing two and wounding another. They also took away 78 people, some equipment, and 80 head of cattle.

May 9, 1983—In the district of La Laguna, Nueva Segovia, a band of approximately 30 contras kidnapped 17 campesinos and took them to Honduran territory.

May 12, 1983—A group of 15 contras kidnapped six campesinos from the district of El Ocote.

May 17, 1983—Fifty contras kidnapped 20 campesinos in the Las Canas sector. Also, in separate attacks, 20 contras invaded the Cerro las Torres sector, Nueva Segovia, burning a tractor belonging to the State, and two campesinos were kidnapped from the San Pablo de Kubali farm in the jurisdiction of Waslala.

May 19, 1983—Upa, Jinotega. An attack on the Miskito resettlement area killed three and caused the disappearance of 10 to 15 families.

May 22-24, 1983—Thirty contras kidnapped four campesinos at Bilwas, among them a member of the local CDS.

May 25, 1983—In the Las Tiricias sector, on the Rio San Juan, a boat carrying three West German journalists was attacked by contras. All three journalists were kidnapped (one of them wounded) and two members of their military escort were killed. Four soldiers were wounded.

June 1, 1983—Approximately 120 contras invaded the communities of Las Barandas, Guayabo, Kaskita, Platano, and Puerto Cabezas, kidnapping seven campesinos and a soldier.

June 2, 1983—Twenty-three contras armed with rifles, machine guns and grenade launchers kidnapped a family of nine at Las Carranzas, near Somoto.

June 3, 1983—Ambushes between El Corozo and Siuce killed two civilians.

June 4, 1983—A band of 45 contras armed with rifles and machine guns invaded the community of Sarawas, kidnapping 3 persons.

June 5, 1983—A detachment of contras invaded the State Farm of Lisawe, Rio Blanco, Matagalpa, kidnapping three civilian defenders from that sector. On their retreat the contras burned and looted the State farm there; the losses are valued at over one million cordobas. The contras kidnapped 60 campesinos from the Pita del Carmen zone.

* June 5, 1983—The contras continued their seige of the town of Teotecacinte, shelling it with mortars, killing three people, injuring three others, and destroying eight houses. Also, a force of 500 to 600 contras seized the El Porvenir sector after a 15 hour battle, taking 50 Nicaraguans with them to Honduras. Nineteen people were listed as missing.

June 6, 1983—A group of approximately 60 contras armed with rifles, grenades, and machine guns, invaded the community of Kuikuinata, kidnapping three people.

June 10, 1983—A group of 50 contras intercepted a pick-up truck belonging to the State lumber company and an IRENA jeep at a bridge on the Dipilto highway. They blew up the pick-up truck on the bridge with C-4 explosives, damaging the bridge and completely destroying the truck. They also kidnapped seven people, including a woman nurse and two IRENA employees.

June 11, 1983—Approximately 150 to 200 contras supported by mortars and rifle fire attacked the town of Ciudad Antigua, Nueva Segovia, kidnapping four persons and burning a store, the health center, and the headquarters of the militia. They also cut the electric and telephone lines.

June 12, 1983—In the La Pita sector, a group of 13 contras ambushed a pick-up truck in which seven civilians and a soldier were traveling. One civilian was killed and the other occupants were wounded.

June 13, 1983—Reymundo Escoto, of Mosante, Nueva Segovia, was kidnapped. He was used as a pack animal and told he would be trained to fight with the contras before escaping.

* June 19, 1983—Contras forced 107 people from Set Net Point, South Zelaya, to go with them to Costa Rica.

June 25, 1983—Contras kidnapped the manager of the La Patriota farm near Matiguas, Matagalpa.

July 2, 1983—Contras ambushed a jeep from INE, killing one person and wounding two others.

July 2, 1983—San Juan del Norte, Rio San Juan. Contras entering Nicaragua from Costa Rica attacked this town with mortars and machine gun fire. The attack was repelled by the town's civilian defense, but two people were killed.

July 3, 1983—A group of 100 to 120 contras divided into two groups and armed with rifles, heavy machine guns, mortars, and grenade launchers attacked the community of Sinsin and the bridge there, killing an old man and wounding three children under five years of age.

July 4, 1983—A group of 70 contras kidnapped 18 campesinos from Oyote, Madriz, and took them to Honduras.

July 5, 1983—A group of approximately 40 to 60 contras assassinated two civilian defenders at Macuelizo, near Ocotal.

July 10, 1983—Contras ambushed a boat at Boca Tapada, Zelaya Sur, killing four people including the boat's captain. One woman was injured.

July 20, 1983—A group of 30 contras raked an INE vehicle with automatic-weapons fire, killing the driver, an electric-company employee. In a separate attack, at El Carmen, near San Juan de Rio Coco, contras kidnapped the mother of the head of the local militia and burned a farmhouse. In another attack, contras kidnapped 152 people in Mozonte, Nueva Segovia, including 77 children aged a few days to 12 years, and a pregnant woman who gave birth on the road to Honduras. Almost all were later returned to Nicaragua after spending 7 to 10 months in refugee camps in Honduras.

July 21, 1983—A group of about 20 contras burned the State farm at Daraili.

July 23, 1983—A group of contras invaded Pena del Jicote, Chinandega, kidnapping nine persons and taking them toward Honduran territory.

July 24, 1983—A group of contras intercepted a truck and a jeep near Las Manos, Nueva Segovia, kidnapping three civilians and taking them toward Honduras.

July 28, 1983—Contras kidnapped four campesinos in the sector of El Aguacate, near Ococona.

July 30, 1983—Contras kidnapped eight campesino families from the district of La Escalera.

July 31, 1983—A group of contras burned the school and hermitage of Aguas Calientes, near San Jose de Bocay.

August 2, 1983—Thirty contras ambushed an INRA jeep between Telpaneca and Los Ranchos, Nueva Segovia, killing an INRA technician and wounding four people, including a woman and a child.

August 7, 1983—A group of contras kidnapped a campesino in the sector of Las Canas; later, they kidnapped two other Nicaraguans in the El Limon sector.

August 8, 1983—San Carlos, Rio San Juan. ARDE contras murdered Never Antonio Oporta Gomez, member of the departmental directorate of the National Farmworkers Association.

August 9, 1983—Contras ambushed a MICONS tractor near Morrillo, assassinating a worker and kidnapping 25 people.

August 10, 1983—Contras ambushed a pick-up truck used for public transportation at Valle Los Cedros. Of the 18 people riding on the truck, 15 were assassinated.

August 15, 1983—San Rafael del Norte, Jinotega. One hundred contras attacked this town, the first major attack on a semi-urban center in Nicaragua, and killed more than a dozen people.

August 16, 1983—A group of contras kidnapped two campesinos at El Lecher.

August 18, 1983—A group of 18 contras kidnapped 11 campesinos from Los Caracoles.

* August 24, 1983—El Jicaro (Ciudad Sandino), Nueva Segovia. Two hundred contras assaulted and attempted to occupy this town, but were repelled by civilian and military defense units. Two people died in the attack.

August 26, 1983—Rio Blanco, Matagalpa. Contras murdered five members of an agricultural cooperative.

August 30, 1983—Contras attacked the town of San Pedro de Potrero Grande with mortars, rifles and heavy machine guns. Two people were killed and three were wounded. In a separate attack, a group of 60 to 80 contras burned 11 houses at the Santa Fe farm near San Carlos and kidnapped 11 campesinos who worked there.

August 31, 1983—Three contras came to the house of a citizen of Negrowas, kidnapping two of his children, aged seven and 15 years. In a separate attack, a group of 80-120 contras attacked the State Farm at Abisinia, killing two people. Also, contras kidnapped ten campesinos at Ohriwas and later killed four of them.

* August 31-Septemeber 3, 1983—Contras attacked four villages in the Paiwas region. In El Anito, six campesinos were assassinated. In El Guyabo, nine were killed and a woman and a girl raped. In Las Minitas, two local leaders were killed. In Ocaguas, three campesinos were mutilated and killed. Houses were burned in all the villages.

September 3, 1983—Contras kidnapped and then cut the throats of 18 campesinos in El Guayo. Among the victims was a teacher for the Evangelical Committee for Aid and Development. They also burned 22 houses.

September 11, 1983—A group of 20 contras attacked the cooperative at Chalmeca, Zelaya Sur, killing a civilian defender and kidnapping three other persons. One person was wounded.

September 15. 1983—Twenty contras burned a coffee farm and a private house in El Zapote.

September 17, 1983—Contras assassinated two campesinos at Aguas Rojas.

September 21, 1983—In the district of El Tabaco, contras assassinated four campesinos who were members of the local civilian defense. On the same day, two campesinos were kidnapped in the Paiwata sector. In a separate attack, 150 contras killed six people and wounded six others at the Quipo cooperative in Siuna.

September 23, 1983—Contras attacked the Yakalwas cooperative in Quilali, killing four people and wounding seven others.

September 25, 1983—In Las Hatillas, a bus carrying a group of merchants from Managua was ambushed. Some of the passengers were beaten, and two immigration workers were reported missing.

September 27, 1983—Approximately 100 contras invaded the town of Ciudad Antigua, Nueva Segovia, cutting the telephone line, burning government offices, and painting FDN slogans. The town was defended by 16 civilians, one of whom was killed and one wounded in the attack.

October 2, 1983—Approximately 200 to 250 contras ambushed a caravan of five trucks carrying MICONS workers at Cerro Los Chiles, kidnapping 29 people, including a Delegate for the FSLN in that zone.

October 3, 1983—Contras ambushed an INRA pick-up truck at Cerro Blanco, near San Juan de Rio Coco, killing INRA technical workers. In a separate attack, contras kidnapped a group of campesinos at Terreno Grande, near Palacaguina.

October 9, 1983—Eight contras ambushed a pick-up truck carrying 12 persons in the Yolai sector. One person was killed and two were wounded.

October 10, 1983—A speedboat armed with M-50 machine guns and a 20 millimeter cannon fired on the fuel tanks at the Port of Corinto, setting one on fire. The fire spread to the diesel tanks at the port. A Korean tanker anchored at the Port was also fired on in the attack. A Korean seaman and a woman in the port area were injured. In a separate attack, contras kidnapped a woman civilian at El Tablazon.

October 12, 1983—Los Chiles, Rio San Juan. Contras ambushed a Ministry of Construction truck bound for La Azucena, killing a 12 year old boy.

October 14, 1983—Contras kidnapped two people in the community of Balsamo.

October 18, 1983—A 300 member FDN force devastated Pantasma, Jinotega, destroying the school, two peasant cooperatives, the bank, the Agrarian Reform office, a sawmill, the coffee warehouse, three foodstuffs dispensaries, and eight tractors. The contras murdered 40 citizens; seven of the town's 20 civilian defenders were killed trying to fend off the attack. Material losses came to 34 million cordobas. A few days later, FDN leader Adolfo Calero was quoted in the *Miami Herald*: "There will be more Pantasmas." In a separate incident, a group of up to 40 contras kidnapped four workers from the La Flor farm near Penas Blancas.

* October 1983—Contras forced some 200 young people from the Miskito village of Sukatpin to accompany them to training camps in Honduras.

October 20, 1983—Fifty contras attacked the "Heroes and Martyrs" Cooperative of San Jose de Bocay killing two, including a civilian defender, and wounding four. In separate attacks, a speedboat armed with cannon fired on the docks at Puerto Cabezas, hitting a ship at anchor, killing one and wounding 11 civilians, among them three children. Also, contras burned the Galilea farm at Guapinol and, near the town of Somotillo, contras using C-4 explosives destroyed a tractor belonging to INRA.

October 29, 1983—Three hundred contras invaded the community of Siawas, Zelaya Sur, kidnapping two popular-education coordinators.

October 30, 1983—Approximately 100 to 150 contras burned the State farm at Las Delicias, wounding a civilian defender.

November 2, 1983—Contras kidnapped nine campesinos from the locale of Macuelizo. In another incident, three heavily armed contras detained U.S.-born Father Francisco Solano while on a pastoral visit to El Coco, south Zelaya. Solano, who had received frequent death threats, was interrogated and asked to join the contras. Before releasing him, the contras told him—three times—to "be very careful."

November 14, 1983—In the district of El Ojoche, 150 contras attacked a civilian defense post, kidnapping several civilians.

November 18, 1983—About 300 ARDE contras attacked Cardenas, three miles from the Costa Rican border, with cannons, mortars and rockets. Three civilians were wounded and two soldiers killed. Several houses and the new health center were destroyed.

November 30, 1985—Contras ambushed a vehicle carrying Father Augustin Sambola from Rosita to Tasba Pri, but the priest escaped unhurt. He had often been threatened on the contras' radio broadcasts.

November 1983—Wali, Nueva Segovia. Catelino Vanegas, a religious student, was beaten to death and shot. His brothers also were beaten, but escaped.

December 11, 1983—Contras ambushed a boat near Barra Punta Gorda, Zelaya Sur, killing three people and wounding five.

* December 16, 1983—Contras attacked the Jacinto Hernandez collective at El Valle Los Cedros, killing eight, burning eight trucks, and kidnapping a woman nurse and four campesinos.

December 17, 1983—A group of contras invaded the encampment of INRA near the Punta Gorda frontier post, kidnapping all of the personnel there.

* December 18, 1983—Approximately 300 contras attacked the settlement of El Coco, killing 16 civilians and totally destroying the settlement.

* December 19, 1983—Four hundred contras attacked the town of Wamblan, Jinotega, killing five people, including two women and two children.

* December 19, 1983—Contras entered the Miskito village of Francia Sirpe and forced the entire population to accompany them to Honduras. In a separate attack, contras burned the Santa Ana farm near the Colon frontier post and kidnapped the entire family.

December 20, 1983—Some 500 contras attacked the district of El Cua, killing nine people and wounding 16.

December 22, 1983— Contras and Honduran soldiers attacked the cooperative at Los Cedros, Nueva Segovia, killed 15 campesinos, and burned the ENABAS and MICONS warehouses.

December 23, 1983—Approximately 30 contras ambushed a

civilian pick-up truck in Las Playitas, kidnapping two workers for ENCAFE.

* December 24, 1983—Contras killed two people and wounded one in an attack on Calderon, Paiwas.

December 25, 1983—Eighty contras kidnapped 20 campesinos in the El Rosario sector and took them to Honduras.

January 1, 1984—Two launches attacked a fishing vessel near Puerto Sandino, killing Noel Briceria.

January 3, 1984—Contras ambushed 12 people who were going by boat on the Torsuany River south-west of Bluefields. Two Nicaraguans were killed, two wounded and three missing. In separate attacks, contras attacked the town of Ciudad Antigua, Nueva Segovia, killing one civilian defender and wounding two unarmed civilians before being driven away; and contras burned the houses of Fila Las Marias, Nueva Segovia.

January 5, 1984—At 12:40 A.M. "piranha" boats fired on Puerto Potosi, killing a civilian defender and wounding two others. Two customs workers were also wounded.

January 8, 1984—MISURA contras killed Miskitos Nolasco and Francela Valisco, who had returned from Honduras to Lapan, Zelaya Norte, and had been granted amnesty by the Sandinista government in December.

January 9, 1984—A mine on the highway between Mozonte and San Fernando destroyed a truck, killing the driver.

January 12, 1984—Approximately 30 contras kidnapped 12 campesinos from the locale of Tito Izaguirre.

January 16, 1984—Contras kidnapped 30 campesinos from El Tablazo, near Dipilto in Nueva Segovia, and took them to the "Las Difficultades" camp in Honduras.

January 21, 1984—Loma Quemada, Rio San Juan. ARDE contras entered Nicaragua 14 km northeast of San Carlos, kidnapping six topographers and three campesinos, and taking them to Costa Rica.

January 24, 1984—ARDE contras kidnapped 30 campesinos between the ages of 13 and 20 from El Zapote, Rio San Juan. In Wiwili, Nueva Segovia, FDN contras attacked the "El Zapote" coffee farm owned by Felix Pedro Medina, and kidnapped six young men.

January 25, 1984—In the Wilike sector, approximately 20 contras ambushed a pick-up truck from the Ministry of Construction, killing two civilians and wounding eight.

January 30, 1984—Approximately 60 contras invaded the town of Pueblo Nuevo, Atlanta sector, Zelaya Sur, kidnapping five civilians who were members of the militia.

February 7, 1984—Approximately 50 contras ambushed a civilian truck near La Azucena, injuring nine civilians, including two pregnant women.

* February 5, 1984—Contras invaded the community of Waspado, Siuna, kidnapping seven persons.

February 16, 1984—A fishing boat (El Pescasa No. 22) exploded two mines set opposite the Pescasa dock. Three of the five crew members were wounded and two were missing. In separate attacks, approximately 35 contras kidnapped ten workers northeast of Atlanta, and contras killed Esteban Galeano in Alo Betel.

February 20, 1984—Approximately 30 contras kidnapped five campesinos at Playa Hermosa and El Cedro.

February 21, 1984—Contras kidnapped 30 campesinos at Cano La Cruz.

March 2, 1984—Contras assassinated two workers in Ruben Dario, cutting out their hearts and feeding them to dogs.

March 4, 1984—Approximately 50 contras kidnapped five campesinos in San Pedro, near San Jose de Bocay.

March 5, 1984—Contras assassinated a member of the FSLN south of Nueva Guinea.

March 6, 1984—Contras and Honduran troops attacked Santo Tomas del Norte, Chinandega, killing one year old Carina Cardenas Rivas.

March 7, 1984—Contras launched a rocket attack from the sea on San Juan del Sur.

March 8, 1984—The Panamanian ship "Los Caribes" hit a mine in the Port of Corinto, injuring three persons and seriously damaging the ship.

March 9, 1984—In Cano Mollefones, contras assassinated five campesinos. In separate incidents, contras kidnapped 25 civilians who were traveling in a MICONS boat in the Siwas canal near La Cruz de Rio Grande. Also, contras kidnapped three civilian members of the militia in La Pedrera.

March 11, 1984—Approximately 100 contras burned houses in Copapar and killed three civilians in Perro Mocho.

March 11, 1984—Approximately 60 contras assassinated 5 campesinos in Fila Los Mojones.

March 12, 1984—Fifty contras invaded La Cuesta El Guayabo, killing two people, kidnapping four others, and burning a truck.

March 13, 1984—Contras kidnapped nine campesinos plus a newspaper boy and an agricultural student from the San Jose farming cooperative in Pueblo Nuevo, Rio San Juan.

March 14, 1984—Contras attacked San Jose, Rio San Juan, killing an eight year old boy and wounding four other children. In a separate attack, contras killed three campesinos and burned the entire village of El Copalon, Rio San Juan.

March 16, 1984—San Ramon, Jalaguina, Matagalpa. Contras kidnapped, mutilated, and beheaded eight farm workers, including Francisco Gonzalez, Guevarra, a teacher; Arturo Calero, local school director; and Jose Zavala Casco, head of the local Sandinista association.

March 18, 1984—Contras kidnapped several campesinos from San Jose, near San Juan de Limay, and retreated to Santa Martha, where they kidnapped 11 more campesinos.

March 19, 1984—Five campesinos were killed in an ambush in San Jose de Cusmapa, Madriz.

March 20, 1984—The Soviet tanker "Lugansk" was damaged by an explosion caused by a mine set near the buoys at Puerto Sandino. Five people were injured. Also, about 200 contras kidnapped two civilians at La Patriota, Matagalpa.

* March 23, 1984—Contras killed two people and burned two houses and a truck in La Rica, Jinotega. The same day, contras killed 13 and wounded 15 in San Rafael del Norte, Jinotega; they also stole medicine from the health center and destroyed the gas station, children's library, and many homes.

March 24, 1984—Fifty contras invaded Quebrada El Agua, kidnapping an adult-education worker.

March 25, 1984—Contras ambushed a MICONS truck in Cuesta Las Brisas, kidnapping all of its occupants. In a separate attack, approximately 100 contras killed five people and kidnapped 13 others at the Las Brisas cooperative.

March 26, 1984—One hundred contras attacked the State farm at El Arco, near San Sebastian de Yali, killing 23 civilian defenders.

March 29, 1984—Approximately 300 contras attacked the border post at Sandy Bay, kidnapping 80 residents of the town, killing four people and wounding eight.

April 1, 1984—Approximately 35 contras attacked the Serrano district, killing the local police chief and kidnapping the head of the local CDS. In a separate attack, 60 contras attacked the Colonia Fonseca, near Nueva Guinea, killing two Nicaraguans and wounding 11.

April 2, 1984—Contras burned two houses and killed a child at Santa Cruz, near Quilali.

April 3, 1984—About 1,000 contras attacked the village of Waslala, central Zelaya, and surrounding areas, killing 37 and kidnapping at least 210. Among the incidents: A family with a newborn baby was taking cover in a ditch. The father was dragged off, tortured by having his fingertips and then his right hand cut off, and then killed with bayonets. Finally, the contras beheaded him and carved a cross in his back. The contras also shot the wife and threw a grenade into the ditch, lodging shrapnel in the woman and her children. On the same day, three children were kidnapped, and the bodies of five campesinos, too disfigured by torture to identify, were found in the nearby hills. Three teenage boys, returning home after hiding in the hills all morning, were attacked with bayonets. Two of the boys, one 14, the other 16, died from their wounds. The third, who had been stabbed five times in his stomach and all over his body, survived. In nearby El Achote a band of contras dragged an agrarian reform worker from his home, and in front of his wife, 11 month old son, and three year old son, cut him into pieces with their bayonets. The man's wife was then shot, but she lived to watch them behead her 11 month old baby. She was later found hidden in the hills, near dead.

April 4, 1984—Some 150 contras attacked and burned the State farm at La Colonia, near San Rafael del Yali, killing six Nicaraguans.

April 5, 1984—Contras ambushed three State trucks near Kusuli, kidnapping the civilian occupants of the vehicles and burning the trucks. They also burned the school at Kusuli. In a separate attack, contras assassinated a civilian member of the militia and kidnapped 30 campesinos from Laguna Verde. They retreated toward El Morado hill, where they assassinated an adult education teacher.

April 6, 1984—Approximately 30 contras burned houses and health centers in Valle El Guadalupe sector.

April 8, 1984—Contras invaded the community of Maniwatla, killing five and kidnapping 15 people.

April 9, 1984—Contras kidnapped 12 campesinos at La Pita.

April 10, 1984—Contras kidnapped 15 campesinos near Valle El Cua. In a separate attack, contras attacked the ENABAS post in the Kurinwas sector, near Nueva Guinea, assassinating four members of a cooperative, kidnapping one person and taking 500,000 cordobas.

April 15, 1984—Las Chichiguas, La Concordia, Jinotega. Contras kidnapped 12 year old Pedro Martin Herrara Duarte along with four neighbors; Herrera escaped 22 days later.

April 16, 1984—Approximately 150 contras kidnapped 25 civilians at Teocintal hill. In separate attacks, 40 contras burned a State farm located at San Gabriel Hermitage, near San Sebastian de Yali. Also, 30 contras ambushed a MICONS truck four kilometers south of Mulukuku, killing two civilians and wounding one. In addition, 70 contras attacked the settlement of Los Chiles, killing three civilian defenders and wounding two other people.

* April 17, 1984— Three hundred contras attacked the settlement of Sumubila with mortar and rifle fire, killing several civilians, wounding 14, and kidnapping 37. The contras also destroyed the headquarters of the Sandinista Police, the Health Center, the machinery of the cacao project and the INRA warehouses, the senior citizens center and the ambulance. The Moravian Church was also damaged. In a separate attack, approximately 400 contras kidnapped seven campesinos at San Jose de Kilambe.

April 18, 1984—Contras kidnapped 21 families at Wamblancito and took them toward Honduran territory.

April 19, 1984—Fifty contras destroyed the State farm at La Paz, near San Sebastian de Yali.

April 23-24, 1984—Three contra task forces kidnapped three campesinos and destroyed the local medical station, the militia headquarters and two houses in the La Rica district.

April 24, 1984—Twenty contras burned State farms at San Luis and Buena Vista.

April 25, 1984—Approximately 20 contras ambushed an ENABAS truck south of Nueva Guinea, killing the driver and an assistant.

April 29, 1984—Seventy contras burned the cooperative and a house located in Valle Santo Domingo.

May 1, 1984—Contras burned State farms at Las Brisas and La Esperanza.

May 2, 1984—Four contras dressed in uniforms of the militia invaded the community of Cano Azul, kidnapping 9 campesinos, including two minors.

May 3, 1984—In Limbaica, Zelaya Norte, a service truck of the Corporacion Forestal del Pueblo, carrying several Miskito Indians, was ambushed by approximately 70 contras. Nuno Cornelio, Napoleon Dixon and Tomas Campbell were tortured and killed, while Luisa Solorzano and German Aragon were seriously injured. The vehicle was burned by the contras.

May 4, 1984—Approximately 50 contras kidnapped nine campesinos at Colonia La Providencia, near Nueva Guinea.

May 5, 1984—Eight contras kidnapped 14 persons in the sector of Jocomico and took them toward Honduran territory.

May 7, 1984—One hundred contras armed with rifles, machine guns, and mortars, attacked the border post and settlement of Palo de Arco, kidnapping 40 civilians. In addition, six civilians were killed and three were wounded when the contras threw a grenade into a shelter.

May 9, 1984—Six contras kidnapped two civilian defenders in the Quebrada Las Pilas sector, later assassinating one of them.

May 11, 1984—Health worker Ricardo Benandes was ambushed by contras on the road from Telpaneca. The contras machine-gunned him and then set fire to his truck.

May 12, 1984—In San Jose, near Quilali, contras burned a State farm.

* May 13, 1984—Sixty contras attacked the Jorgito district, killing five women, nine children, and many men. In a separate attack, 400 contras burned the La Ventana Cooperative in El Jilguero. One person was killed and ten were missing.

* May 15, 1984—Five hundred contras attacked the state farm at Castillo Norte, Jinotega, killing more than 20 and destroying the farm.

* May 16, 1984—Contras attacked and destroyed the communities of Los Planes, Las Montanitas, El Robledal, Buena Vista, and San Jeronimo, Esteli, causing damages of ten million cordobas and causing hundreds to flee.

May 19, 1984—Contras attacked San Juan del Rio Coco, Jinotega, destroying farm equipment, installations, fuel and food. They also stole cattle, horses, fowl and cash, and burned several houses. They killed Lydia Perez, coordinator of the AMNLAE, and Carmelo Martinez was reported missing.

May 23, 1984—Contras attacked the El Garrobo cooperative near Waslala, burning ten houses. In a separate attack, 60 contras kidnapped 11 families in the Tumarin sector, Zelaya Central.

May 26, 1984—Contras kidnapped four campesinos in the Colonia Providencia.

May 28, 1984—Approximately 250 contras burned the Moises Herrera cooperative near San Jose de Bocay, later killing one civilian and kidnapping seven others in the Bocaycito district. In a separate attack, 100 contras invaded Alamikamba, kidnapping six members of the militia and 40 other civilians and assassinating one member of the militia. They also attacked the local ENABAS post, from which they took 15,000 cordobas, and fired on two IRENA pick-up trucks. Also, three hundred contras invaded Valle La Union, kidnapping three campesinos.

* June 1, 1984—Contras attacked the town of Ocotal, killing 16 Nicaraguans and wounding 27. In addition, they burned the State lumber yard, the electric company building, the silos of ENABAS, the coffee plant, the radio station, and other buildings. In a separate attack, at Limbaica, contras burned State facilities and kidnapped several civilians.

June 2, 1984—A group of contras attacked the district of El Pajaro, kidnapping three people. In a separate attack, contras ambushed two trucks in the Las Brisas sector, killing two civilians, wounding one, and kidnapping three others. In addition, the contras burned 150 quintales of grain.

June 5, 1984—Contras kidnapped 63 people in the localities of Alamikamba, Sumugila, La Agricola and Lapan. In a separate attack, ten contras kidnapped four civilians at Brujil.

* June 10, 1984—Contras attacked a cooperative near Waswalita, Siuna, killing two people and wounding three.

June 11, 1984—Contras attacked the border post at Wasla, Zelaya Norte, and kidnapped a civilian from the INRA farm there.

June 13, 1984—Contras kidnapped CDS leader Florentino Lopez Estrada near Bluefields. He escaped after being taken to a contra camp in the jungle. Another teacher, Florentin Levan, was also kidnapped in the same area but did not return. Errol Dixon, son of a local CDS leader was later kidnapped with his mother in Brown Bank. She was released but he was not.

* June 14, 1984—Contras mutilate and kill Victorino Martinez Urbina in Cuicuinita, Siuna.

June 15, 1984—Approximately 30 contras burned the "Oscar Benavides" Cooperative at El Cacao, near Sebaco; six vehicles were also burned.

June 16, 1984—Contras kidnapped 30 campesinos in the Valle San Juan sector, near San Jose de Bocay.

June 20, 1984—In the district of Aza Central, Zelaya Norte, 12 contras kidnapped eight Nicaraguans.

* June 23, 1984—Contras kidnap Cirillo Jarquin, Delegate of the Word, in Coperna, Siuna. He later escaped.

June 25, 1984—C-4 explosives were placed on two railroad cars coming from Honduras which were transporting agricultural machinery for cotton. The explosives were detonated in the cotton machinery when the cars were, respectively, across from the Somoto granary and the El Espino Park. As a result the machines were partly destroyed and one person was injured.

June 26, 1984—Contras entered Tasbapauni, Zelaya Sur, and kidnapped schoolteacher Florent Leyan Lopez at gunpoint.

June 28, 1984—Contras entered Brown Bank, near Bluefields in Zelaya, looking for the schoolteacher Pedro Sambola Adkinson, 38. When they found his house, they pulled him out into the front yard and began to torture him in front of his wife, their seven children, his step-father, and his wife's grandfather. The contras cut off his ears and tongue, and forced him to chew and swallow them. Then the contras cut off his penis; then they killed him.

June 29, 1984—A group of 100 contras intercepted an INRA truck in Ocote Quipo, kidnapping ten people.

June 30, 1984—Some 90 ARDE contras took over the town of El Tortuguero, killing eight civilians, including an old woman and a child. Seven soldiers were killed, with five wounded and one missing, and the local Health Center and offices of the National Development Bank were destroyed. In a separate attack, contras coming from Chachagua invaded La Bujona, kidnapping 15 people. In addition, 250 contras ambushed a truck in the El Barro sector, near Wiwili, killing three people and wounding five.

July 1, 1984—In the sector of San Martin and San Ramon, a group of approximately 20 contras ambushed a pick-up truck, killing four people. One person was wounded. In separate attacks, contras kidnapped three civilians from the farm of Francisco Herrera, in Cano Tomas, and 30 contras kidnapped six people at Cano El Guayabo. Also, in San Juan de Karahola, a group of contras ambushed a boat which was on a project for INRA. Two people were killed and four were wounded.

July 2, 1984—Some 300 contras ambushed a truck in the El Guale sector, near San Rafael del Norte, killing 13 people and wounding nine.

July 3, 1984—Approximately 250 contras ambushed three MICONS trucks between Kubali and Puente Zinica, killing three people, wounding three and kidnapping six. In separate attacks, contras invaded San Pedro de Asa, kidnapping 19 people; and killed three campesinos in Waslala.

July 5, 1984—Thirty contras kidnapped 40 people in the town of Minisola. In separate attacks, a group of contras kidnapped 65 civilians; and the bodies of four campesinos murdered by contras were found along a river bank in Rio Escondido, Zelaya.

July 6, 1984—Four hundred contras kidnapped nine civilians in Vigia Sur.

July 7, 1984—Seventy contras ambushed a truck at El Porvenir, killing seven people and wounding four. Two were reported missing.

July 8, 1984—Contras invaded Las Conchitas, kidnapping 8 campesinos.

July 10, 1984—Contras ambushed an IRENA truck in El Jocote, kidnapping one civilian and wounding another. In the sector of Los Alpes, the same group kidnapped four campesinos. In a separate attack, contras ambushed a pick-up truck south-east of Nueva Guinea, assassinating four civilians and wounding four others. In another attack, ARDE contras invaded Rama Cay in Bluefields Bay. Before retreating with 15 captives, they destroyed several houses, robbed the store, and damaged the school building. Five hundred of the 700 inhabitants of the island have since gone as refugees to Bluefields.

July 11, 1984—Yali, Matagalpa. FDN contras stopped a truck and kidnapped Oscar Perez, an IRENA worker. They then attacked the village of El Ocote and kidnapped Nidia Torres and Roberto Carcamo, and went on to attack the nearby Los Alpes cooperative where they kidnapped Ernesto and Juan Jose Garcia, Primitivo Nunez, Laureano Flores and Denis Vilchez. During this last attack Perez and Torres, who was wounded, managed to excape.

July 12, 1984—Columbus, Zelaya. MISURA forces attacked this Miskito resettlement area, forcing 52 young students to walk to Honduras. Sixteen excaped but the others were taken to MISURA's military school (CIMM) for training. Those who refused were kept in wooden pens. On August 2, 12 escaped and made contact with the U.N. High Commissioner on Refugees. At the airstrip to go to Tegucigalpa, they were retaken by MISURA which held them and beat them until the UNHCR again interceded. One returnee says there are still 22 Columbus students being held against their will at the CIMM. In a separate attack, contras kidnapped four civilians in the El Jiguero sector. Also, in the El Achiote district, a group of approximately 30 contras kidnapped three civilians. In Sontule, Esteli, the contras attacked the Filemon Rivera cooperative killing two and wounding three including West German technical advisor Thomas Hunt, age 24.

July 13, 1984—Contras kidnapped 11 campesinos from the vicinity San Sebastian de Yali. In a separate attack, 250 contras burned the La Perla cooperative at Miraflor; one person was killed and another was reported missing. In addition, contras kidnapped a number of people from the settlement of Tasba Pri.

July 14, 1984—One hundred contras kidnapped three campesinos in the zone of Fila Teocintal. In a separate attack in Ojo de Agua, Nueva Segovia, Antonio Vasquez, a Delegate of the Word, was kidnapped along with his brothers Juan and Teodoro, but all managed to escape. Eulalio Mendoza, who refused to go with the kidnappers, was killed.

July 17, 1984—Contras kidnapped 17 civilians and a second lieutenant at Helado Hill, near San Sebastian de Yali.

July 18, 1984—In Acoyapa, Chontales, contras ambushed a bus containing some 15 foreign workers. French volunteer Katherine Vince and Nicaraguan communications worker Maria Ester Strever were among the four wounded.

* July 19, 1984—Eighty contras ambushed a truck of the Bernardino Diaz Ocho cooperative in El Guabo, killing three citizens and wounding 14. In a separate attack, contras ambushed several military and civilian vehicles in the Paiwata sector, killing 4 people, including a four year old boy, and wounding five others; and also sabotaged the electric and telephone lines.

July 20, 1984—Approximately 120 contras ambushed an unarmed civilian truck with passengers and a pick-up truck of INRA in the sector of Fila Posolera, near Waslala, killing four people, including a four year old boy, and kidnapping another. In separate attacks, an FDN task force attacked El Cairo, near El Espino, killing a civilian defender and wounding six civilians including three small children; and 60 contras raided the home of a miner in Cinco Pinos, kidnapping three people.

July 21, 1984—In Matiguas, Matagalpa, Noel Rivera Morraz, a coffee grower well known in the region for his cooperative attitude towards the Sandinista government and his commitment to maintaining high levels of productivity, was kidnapped by contras and later beaten and bayoneted to death. He left a wife and five children. In a separate attack, contras ambushed a civilian jeep in the sector of El Toro, Rio Blanco Copalar highway, killing 4 civilians and wounding one. In addition they carried off a large quantity of cattle. Also, 18 contras attacked the district of Guadalupe, kidnapping four people. In addition, contras ambushed a truck at San Pablo de Kubali, killing four civilian defenders and kidnapping three campesinos, including an eight year old boy.

July 23, 1984—Two hundred contras attacked the town of San Martin with mortars and rifle fire, kidnapping two civilian defenders. Six others were missing. The contras also burned the Martha Quezada cooperative.

July 24, 1984—Contras killed a campesina in Salto Verde, Sivna.

July 25, 1984—Contras assassinated six members of the Lopez family in Rio Yaoska. In a separate attack, contras killed one woman and kidnapped another at Salto Grande.

July 26, 1984—On the eve of the national drive to register voters for the November elections, the FDN contras murdered seven unarmed villagers in Tapasle, Matagalpa in an effort to discourage their neighbors from registering. All of the victims were castrated and had their throats slit; some were dismembered and had their body parts scattered. One had the skin scraped off his face. Two other men were kidnapped and have not been returned. In a separate attack, a truck which was distributing fresh produce hit a mine placed by contras at Bismona. Three soldiers were killed and four were wounded.

July 27, 1984—A group of contras ambushed a vehicle in the Wilicon sector, wounding three people, among them the secretary of a local voting precinct. Voter registration workers were killed in Yali and Muelle de los Bueyes.

July 28, 1984—A group of some 15 contras attacked six people who were transporting voter registration documents in the sector of Santa Cruz, carrying off the documents. In a separate attack, 20 contras ambushed seven people who were transporting documents of the voter registration precinct in La Vigia, taking the documents. In addition, approximately 20 contras kidnapped five people in the zone Las Valles.

August 2, 1984—Thirty contras invaded the settlement of Monte Creek, kidnapping three civilians. In a separate attack, 30 to 40 contras kidnapped six people from the INRA encampment at Barra Punta Gorda.

August 3, 1984—Contras kidnapped ten campesinos from El Ojoche. In a separate attack, 30 contras kidnapped five people at Pijibay. Among those kidnapped was Santos Jose Vilchez, President of the voter registration office there.

August 4, 1984—In the Layasiksa sector, some 150 contras kidnapped ten people, including four women.

August 6, 1984—Contras penetrated the town of La Fragua, wounding Siriaco Tercero, a member of the militia, and carrying off 60 of his cattle.

August 7, 1984—Fifty contras invaded El Morado, where they kidnapped ten campesinos. They also took away voter registration cards and threatened to kill those who tried to vote in the elections.

August 12, 1984—Eighty contras kidnapped 12 campesinos from the district of Quebrada de Agua. In a separate attack, 200 contras kidnapped 12 campesinos in California Valley and San Jeronimo.

August 13, 1984—Contras attacked the El Paraiso cooperative, killing two members of the cooperative and kidnapping three others.

* **August 15, 1984**—A group of contras kidnapped 50 people at Waspuko Abajo, Siuna, Zelaya Norte.

August 17, 1984—Contras kidnapped 20 campesinos near Las Minitas, Paiwas.

August 21, 1984—In the sector of Central Waspuk, contras kidnapped nine Nicaraguans.

August 23, 1984—At the Jacinto Baca Cooperative at Santa Elena, 60 contras killed three Nicaraguans and kidnapped four others.

August 24, 1984—Approximately 80 contras ambushed a jeep in the Quebrada sectors, kidnapping six people. In a separate attack, 300 contras kidnapped 15 campesinos in the El Guaya sector.

August 25, 1984—Contras kidnapped 14 merchants at Laguna Verde.

* **August 26, 1984**—Contras hack Aneleto Palacios to death in La Union-Labu, Siuna. The same day, contras kidnapped 20 people from Achote, Buenos Aires and Terrero, Nueva Segovia.

* **September 1, 1984**— Contras ambushed pick-up trucks of CEPAD and TELCOR, killing eight people and wounding four others. They also ambushed trucks from the Army which went to give assistance to the wounded, killing two and wounding two. In a separate attack, eight contras ambushed two unarmed militia

members at the "Camilo Ortega" cooperative, killing one. In a third attack, four airplanes and a helicopter attacked a military training school on family visiting day. Four civilians from nearby Santa Clara, Nueva Segovia, were killed: 12 year old girls, Junana Beltran and Elena Herrera, Alba Luz Hernandez, 13; and Maximo Ponce. The helicopter was shot down, killing all three men aboard, two of whom were American citizens from an Alabama-based anti-communist group.

September 4, 1984—One hundred contras kidnapped five campesinos at El Refugio. The next day the same group kidnapped three campesinos at Buena Vista de Ventillas.

September 5, 1984—Contras intercepted a boat which was in transit from Karawala to Laguna de Perlas, kidnapping Ray Hooker, FSLN candidate for the National Assembly, Patricia Delgado, Zonal Secretary of the FSLN for Laguna de Perlas, and Santiago Mayorga, the boat captain. The three were later released. In separate attacks, in the El Granadino district, contras kidnapped seven civilians, including two members of the civilian defense; and in La Cruz del Rio Grande, 200 contras killed four people.

September 6, 1984—Contras stopped a civilian pick-up truck in the La Laguneta sector, kidnapping seven civilians and burning the vehicle.

September 7, 1984—Twenty contras ambushed a boat with four members of the militia on board at Cano Negro, killing three and injuring one. In a separate attack, 20 contras kidnapped 4 civilians from INRA at Monkey Point, south of Bluefields. Also, 60 contras invaded the Santa Rosa district, kidnapping 19 campesinos. The same day, contras ambushed and killed Jacinto Vargas Estrada and two members of the cooperative he headed in Canonero, South Zelaya.

September 8, 1984—Forty contras kidnapped six campesinos at Mina San Albino, Nueva Segovia.

September 9, 1984—Contras kidnapped 11 civilians from the district of Guayaculy.

September 10, 1984—A group of 80 to 100 contras kidnapped nine people at El Tule.

September 11, 1984—Contras kidnapped seven people from Valle La Esperanza.

September 14, 1984—Contras attacked a sector of the district of San Martin, killing a member of the FSLN and kidnapping two civilians, including the president of the local voting precinct.

*September 15, 1984—Contras assassinated two campesinos in Villagual, Jinotega.

September 22, 1984—Three civilian workers for the State farm in Palo de Arquito were kidnapped by contras along the border as they repaired wires there.

September 23, 1984—In the San Esteban sector, contras ambushed an Army truck in which mothers and family members of soldiers were traveling, killing eight people (including five civilians) and wounding 19 civilians.

September 26, 1984—A group of 120 contras kidnapped three campesinos from the Canta Gallo cooperative.

October 4, 1984—A group of some 250 contras ambushed and burned two trucks between Venencia and Santa Gertrudis. One man was killed, and seven people, including a woman teacher, are missing as a result of the attack. The contras also burned three other vehicles.

October 5, 1984—Contras attacked the Las Llaves cooperative, killing a civilian.

October 6, 1984—Contras stopped a civilian vehicle at Mata de Guineo, near San Rafael del Norte, killing one person and kidnapping them. In another attack, 60 contras kidnapped three campesinos near Valle El Cua, subsequently killing one of them.

October 7, 1984—Ten contras kidnapped five civilians at Truslaya.

* October 9, 1984—Contras slit the throats of five campesinos near Yali, Jinotega, and kidnapped seven others.

October 10, 1984—Contras kidnapped 15 families, consisting of approximately 50-60 persons, in the Bambu sector. Also, contras attacked the Juan Pablo Umanzor Cooperative near San Rafael del Norte, killing five members of the cooperative and wounding two others.

October 11, 1984—Some 300 contras attacked the town of Susucayan, near El Jicaro, killing three civilian defenders and wounding one. The same day, they attacked nearby La Jumuyca, kidnapping three civilians, two of whom escaped.

October 12, 1984—Eighty contras ambushed an INRA truck in Rio Saiz, wounding ten civilians, five of them seriously.

* October 13, 1984—Contras kidnapped 30 campesinos and attacked Siuna.

October 14, 1984—Contras kidnapped 40 campesinos and burned the State farm at Namaji.

October 15, 1984—Contras kidnapped campesinos near Waspuko, Siuna.

October 17, 1984—A group of some 50 MISURA contras kidnapped 17 civilians and two infantry reservists at Campo Uno, near Siuna.

October 18, 1984—A group of 20 contras invaded the Kurinwacito district, killing four campesinos.

October 19, 1984—Contras looted a cooperative in the Poza Redonda district, kidnapping two civilians, including one woman.

October 21, 1984—Contras kidnapped 25 campesinos in the El Jocote Valley sector.

October 22, 1984—A group of 50 contras ambushed three MICONS trucks and a pickup truck from the Ministry of Health in the Las Cruces sector, killing one civilian and wounding three others. Six soldiers were also wounded.

* October 23, 1984—Contras kidnapped numerous campesinos near Uly, Siuna. In a separate attack at 5 A.M., a group of approximately 60 contras attacked the William Baez cooperative at La Paila, killing two civilians and wounding five others.

* **October 24, 1984**—Contras mutilated and killed Luis Cardenas in El Pie de la Cuesta, near El Jicaro. In a separate incident, a group of 150 contras kidnapped 14 campesinos at Siapali, near Quilali, later killing two of them.

* **October 28, 1984**—In several incidents, contras kidnapped 23 campesinos, including Ernesto Pineda, near La Pavona; took 11 campesinos near El Corozo, Siuna; and captured two election workers in El Dorado, Siuna.

* **October 29, 1984**—Contras attacked the Santa Julia cooperative near the town of San Gregorio, 10 kilometers north-east of Jicaro, killing six children and wounding six others. Two people were missing as a result of the attack. In a separate attack, contras ambushed an INRA vehicle in the El Sarayal sector, killing six persons.

October 30, 1984—Contras kidnapped 18 campesinos in the Casa de Tabla sector. In a separate attack, contras killed two persons at Santa Elena.

* **October 1984**—Contras kidnapped Mileydis Salina, 15, and Ermelina Diaz, 14, raping them for 55 days until they escaped.

* **October 1984**—A contra ambush in Frank Tijerino Valley, El Cua, killed one and unjured seven.

November 2, 1984—Approximately 250 contras ambushed a Toyota jeep in the district of El Cedro, killing a woman teacher, a political officer of the El Cedro garrison, a CDS member, and two others.

November 3, 1984—Contras kidnapped young boys from the El Rehen Valley, Esteli.

November 4, 1984—Three hundred contras kidnapped 100 civilians at La Vigia, near Wiwili.

* **November 5, 1984**—Contras attacked the Uly cooperative near Siuna with mortars and heavy machine guns, killing a soldier and four civilians, and kidnapping many.

* **November 7, 1984**—Contras kidnapped 15 campesinos near Yali, Jinotega.

November 7-9, 1984—One hundred contras kidnapped five civilian defenders and a woman from the Las Lajas Cooperative near San Jose de Achuapa. They also looted the nearby El Lagartillo Cooperative.

November 10, 1984—A group of up to 200 contras attacked the Kurinwas district, kidnapping four civilians and killing the local ENABAS manager. In a separate attack, contras kidnapped 17 campesinos at Las Canas, Rio Coco. In a separate attack in Yali, Jinotega, contras ambushed a vehicle carrying seven civilians who were conducting a sports program for children. Five were wounded.

* **November 14, 1984**— Contras attacked the La Sorpresa Coop-

erative, killing seven, injuring four (including two children), and burning the cooperative. In a separate attack, a MICONS truck was ambushed in the district of Planes de Vilan. The vehicle was machine-gunned after it hit a mine; two civilians were killed and three injured.

* **November 15, 1984**—The director of the National Development Bank (BND) for Jinotega and one other civilian was killed and four civilians were wounded in an ambush near La Sorpresa. In a separate attack, contras kidnapped 15 civilians in the district of Asadin, near Siuna.

* **November 18, 1984**—Contras burned the Bernardino Diaz Ochoa cooperative, killing six of its members, including three small children.

November 19, 1984—Four employees of the State electric company were kidnapped by approximately 60 members of MISURA in the community of Tasba-Paunie.

* **November 20, 1984**—Contras maimed and killed five members of a campesino family in Coperna Abajo, Siuna.

November 21, 1984—Contras kidnapped 45 campesinos from the La Pita district.

November 25, 1984—Contras ambushed an agricultural transport truck in the district of Posolera, burning the truck, killing six persons and kidnapping ten others; one other person was missing.

* **November 26, 1984**—Contras attacked a cooperative in Floripon, Siuna, killing one. An unexploded grenade later killed another and injured thirteen.

November 28, 1984—A group of up to 100 contras kidnapped 20 civilians in the El Diamante district.

November 30, 1984—A group of 17 contras kidnapped seven civilians in the district of El Sueno; they also carried off an undetermined number of cattle.

Footnotes

Chapter 1

1. Affidavits of Francisco Lopez Ramirez, Elba Bucardo Blandon and Dina Arcely Padilla, Exhibits 1, 2, and 3.
2. Affidavit of Dina Aracely Padilla, Exhibit 3, para. 5.
3. *id.*, paras. 6-9.
4. Affidavit of Elba Bucardo Blandon, Exhibit 2, paras. 4-8.
5. Affidavit of Francisco Lopez Ramirez, Exhibit 1, para. 7.
6. *id.*, para. 6.
7. *id.*, paras. 9-10.
8. Affidavit of Elba Bucardo Blandon, Exhibit 2, paras. 9-10.

Chapter 2

1. Affidavit of Jorge Luis Briones Valenzuela, Exhibit 2, para. 14.
2. See Affidavit of Jorge Luis Briones Valenzuela, Exhibit 2, para. 13; Affidavit of Santos Roger Briones Valenzuela, Exhibit 7, para. 8; Affidavit of Lucio Rodriguez Gradis, Exhibit 3, para. 7.
3. Affidavit of Santos Roger Briones Valenzuela, Exhibit 1, paras. 9, 18; Affidavit of Jorge Luis Briones Valenzuela, Exhibit 2, paras. 15, 17.
4. Affidavit of Santos Roger Briones Valenzuela, Exhibit 1, paras. 11-12; Affidavit of Jorge Luis Briones Valenzuela, Exhibit 2, para. 18; Affidavit of Lucio Rodriguez Gradis, Exhibit 3, para. 11.
5. Affidavit of Santos Roger Briones Valenzuela, Exhibit 1, para. 13.
6. Affidavit of Lucio Rodriguez Gradis, Exhibit 3, para. 11.
7. Affidavit of Santos Roger Briones Valenzuela, Exhibit 1 paras. 14-15; Affidavit of Jorge Luis Briones Valenzuela, Exhibit 2, paras. 30, 34; Affidavit of Lucio Rodriguez Gradis, Exhibit 3, paras. 11, 13.
8. Affidavit of Santos Roger Briones Valenzuela, Exhibit 1, para. 20.
9. *id.*, para. 16.
10. *id.*, para. 16.
11. *id.*, para. 17; Affidavit of Jorge Luis Briones Valenzuela.

Exhibit 2, para. 32; Affidavit of Lucio Rodriguez Gradis, Exhibit 3, para. 14.

12. Affidavit of Lucio Rodriguez Gradis, Exhibit 2, paras. 1-14; Affidavit of Santos Roger Briones Valenzuela, Exhibit 7, para. 32.

13. Affidavit of Santos Roger Briones Valenzuela, Exhibit 1, para. 18; Affidavit of Jorge Luis Briones Valenzuela, Exhibit 2, para. 31; Affidavit of Lucio Rodriguez Gradis, Exhibit 3, para. 16.

14. Affidavit of Santos Roger Briones Valenzuela, Exhibit 7, para. 22.

15. *id.*, para. 21; Affidavit of Lucio Rodriguez Gradis, Exhibit 3, paras. 20-29.

16. Affidavit of Jorge Luis Briones Valenzuela, Exhibit 2, paras. 34-35.

17. Affidavit of Santos Roger Briones Valenzuela, Exhibit 2, paras. 25-26; Affidavit of Jorge Luis Briones Valenzuela, Exhibit 2, paras. 38-39.

18. Affidavit of Lucio Rodriguez Gradis, Exhibit 3, paras. 23-27.

19. *Nuevo Diario*, December 6, 1984.

Chapter 3

1. Affidavit of Jose Ramon Gallo Bravo, Exhibit 2, para. 17.

2. Quoted in Teofilo Cabestrero, "Dieron La Vida por Su Pueblo," ["They Gave Their Lives for Their People"] *El Tayacan*, Nicaragua (1984), pp. 36-37.

3. Affidavit of Alicia Huete Diaz, Exhibit 2, paras. 2-5; Affidavit of Jose Ramon Gallo Bravo, Exhibit 2, paras. 6-12.

4. Affidavit of Alicia Huete Diaz, Exhibit 2, para. 6.

5. Affidavit of Noel Benavides Herradora, Exhibit 3, para. 2; Affidavit of Jose Ramon Gallo Bravo, Exhibit 2, para. 14.

6. Affidavit of Jose Ramon Gallo Bravo, Exhibit 2, paras. 15-18.

7. *id.*, paras. 18-20.

8. *id.*, para. 20.

9. *id.*, para. 21.

10. Affidavit of Alicia Huete Diaz, Exhibit 1, para. 7.

11. Affidavit of Jose Ramon Gallo Bravo, Exhibit 2, paras. 22-23.

12. *id.*, para. 21.

13. *id.*, paras. 28-30.

14. *id.*, para. 31.

15. Affidavit of Alicia Huete Diaz, Exhibit 1, para. 9.

16. *id.*

17. *id.*

18. Affidavit of Jose Ramon Gallo Bravo, Exhibit 2, para. 39.

19. Affidavit of Noel Benavides Herradora, Exhibit 1, para. 13.

20. *id.*, para. 4.

21. *id.*, para. 5.

22. *id.*, para. 6.
23. *id.*, paras. 7-9.
24. *id.*, paras. 10-12.
25. *id.*, para. 16.
26. *id.*, para. 13.
27. *id.*, para. 16.
28. *id.*, para. 16.
29. *id.*, para. 16-21.
30. Teofilo Cabestrero, "Dieron La Vida por Su Pueblo," *El Tayacan*, Nicaragua (1984), p. 9.
31. *id.*, pp. 10-11.

Chapter 4

1. Affidavit of Salomon Rivera Alaniz, Exhibit 1, para. 3.
2. *id.*, para. 4; Affidavit of Julio Cesar Torres Perez, Exhibit 7, para. 3.
3. *id.*, Affidavit of Salomon Rivera Alaniz, Exhibit 1, para. 12.
4. Affidavit of Julio Cesar Torres Perez, Exhibit 7, para. 10; Affidavit of Jose Ruiz Martinez, Exhibit 6, para. 6.
5. Affidavit of Salomon Rivera Alaniz, Exhibit 1, para. 10; Affidavit of Julio Cesar Torres Perez, Exhibit 7, para. 14.
6. Affidavit of Julia Picado Gonzalez, Exhibit 5, para. 10.
7. *id.*
8. Affidavit of Salomon Rivera Alaniz, Exhibit 1, para. 18.
9. Affidavit of Maria Helena Ferufino, Exhibit 4, para. 5; Affidavit of Julio Cesar Torres Perez, Exhibit 7, para. 15.
10. Affidavit of Julia Picado Gonzalez, Exhibit 5, para. 21; Affidavit of Salomon Rivera Alaniz, Exhibit 1, para. 26; Affidavit of Marta Ruiz Jimenez, Exhibit 2, paras. 4-5.
11. Affidavit of Santos Gonzalez, Exhibit 3, para. 7; see also Affidavit of Salomon Rivera Alaniz, Exhibit 1, para. 19.
12. Affidavit of Santos Gonzalez, Exhibit 3, para. 14; Affidavit of Salomon Rivera Alaniz, Exhibit 1, para. 17.
13. Affidavit of Jose Ruiz Martinez, Exhibit 6, para. 12; Affidavit of Salomon Rivera Alaniz, Exhibit 1, para. 14.
14. Affidavit of Francisco Ernesto Toruno Rodriguez, Exhibit 10, para. 12.
15. Affidavit of Julia Picado Gonzalez, Exhibit 5, para. 23.
16. Affidavit of Julia Picado Gonzalez, Exhibit 5, para. 20.
17. Affidavit of Julio Cesar Torres Perez, Exhibit 7, para. 16.
18. *id.*
19. Affidavit of Julia Picado Gonzalez, Exhibit 5, para. 22.
20. S. Kinzer, "Nicaraguan Rebels Step Up Raids in Coffee Areas as Harvest Nears," *New York Times*, Nov. 23, 1984, p. 1.

Chapter 5

1. Affidavit of Feliciana Rivera Jimenez, Exhibit 3, paras. 2-3.
2. *id.*, paras. 9-11.
3. *id.*, paras. 11-12.
4. Affidavit of Antonia Caceres Centeno, Exhibit 1, paras. 2-3.
5. *id.*, para. 4; Affidavit of Feliciano Rivera Jimenez, Exhibit 2, para. 4.
6. Affidavit of Antonia Caceres Centeno, Exhibit 1, para. 5; Affidavit of Feliciana Rivera Jimenez, Exhibit 3, para. 16; Affidavit of Mercedes Centeno Ramos, Exhibit 2, para. 4.
7. Affidavit of Mercedes Centeno Ramos, Exhibit 2, para. 4.
8. Affidavit of Antonia Caceres Centeno, Exhibit 1, para. 8.
9. Affidavit of Feliciano Rivera Jimenez, Exhibit 3, paras. 18-22.
10. *id.*, para. 23.
11. *id.*, paras. 28-29.

Chapter 6

1. Affidavit of Orlando Wayland Waldiman, Exhibit 1 to Francia Sirpe chapter, paras. 53-54.
2. Affidavit of Raul Davis Arias, Exhibit 1, para. 41; Affidavit of Francisco Calix Romero, Exhibit 8, paras. 6-7; Affidavit of Silvestre Taylor Mendoza, Exhibit 11, para. 4.
3. Affidavit of Cristina Atoya Gonzalez, Exhibit 6, paras. 1-9.
4. Affidavit of Francisco Calix Romero, Exhibit 8, para. 14; Affidavit of Silvestre Taylor Mendoza, Exhibit 11, paras. 5 and 7; Affidavit of Father Antonio Sandoval Herrera, Exhibit 13, para. 7.
5. Affidavit of Francisco Calix Romero, Exhibit 8, para. 14; Affidavit of Silvestre Taylor Mendoza, Exhibit 11, paras. 13-14.
6. Affidavit of Mauricio Gonzales, Exhibit 10, paras. 2-4.
7. Affidavit of Cristina Atoya Gonzalez, Exhibit 6, para. 10.
8. Affidavit of Mauricio Gonzalez, Exhibit 10, paras. 6-8.
9. Affidavit of Rosalia Ralp Obando, Exhibit 3, paras. 2-4.
10. Affidavit of Estela Lacayo Smith, Exhibit 12, para. 6.
11. Affidavit of Avelino Cox Molina, Exhibit 2, paras. 10-11.
12. *id.*, paras. 12-13.
13. Affidavit of Evaristo Waldan Chico, Exhibit 5, paras. 9-10.
14. Affidavit of Raul Davis Arias, Exhibit 1, paras. 9-12.
15. Affidavit of Colombina Lacayo de Sosa, Exhibit 4, paras. 3 and 6; Affidavit of Remigio Manzanares O'Meer, Exhibit 7, para. 16.
16. Affidavit of Avelino Cox Molina, Exhibit 2, para. 16; Affidavit of Evaristo Waldan Chico, Exhibit 5, para. 16.
17. Affidavit of Evaristo Waldan Chico, Exhibit 5, para. 16.
18. See Affidavit of Evaristo Waldan Chico, Exhibit 5, para. 11; Affidavit of Father Antonio Sandoval Herrera, Exhibit 13,

para. 11.

19. Affidavit of Laura Hammer, Exhibit 9, para.8.

20. Affidavit of Avelino Cox Molina, Exhibit 2, para. 23; Affidavit of Raul Davis Arias, Exhibit 1, para. 15.

21. Affidavit of Raul Davis Arias, Exhibit 1, para. 16; Affidavit of Avelino Cox Molina, Exhibit 2, para. 23.

22. Affidavit of Avelino Cox Molina, Exhibit 2, para. 24.

23. *id.*, para. 25.

24. Affidavit of Francisco Calix Romero, Exhibit 8, paras. 8-10; Affidavit of Remigio Manzanares O'Meer, Exhibit 7. para. 16.

25. Affidavit of Remigio Manzanares O'Meer, Exhibit 7, paras. 17-19; Affidavit of Francisco Calix Romero, Exhibit 8, para. 9.

26. Affidivits of Remigio Manzanares O'Meer, Exhibit 7, para. 11; Francisco Calix Romero, Exhibit 8, para. 21; Silvestre Taylor Mendoza, Exhibit 11, para. 19.

27. Affidavit of Silvestre Taylor Mendoza, Exhibit 11, para. 16.

28. Affidavit of Laura Hammer, Exhibit 9, para. 6.

29. *id.*

30. Affidavit of Raul Davis Arias, Exhibit 1, paras. 24-37; Affidavit of Avelino Cox Molina, Exhibit 2, paras. 31-34.

31. Affidavit of Evaristo Waldan Chico, Exhibit 5, para. 16.

32. *id.*, para. 18.

33. *id.*, paras. 23-24.

34. *id.*, para. 25.

Chapter 7

1. Affidavit of Father James Feltz, Exhibit 1, para. 3.

2. *id.*, para. 4.

3. Affidavit of Father Robert Stark, Exhibit 2, paras. 12-13.

4. Affidavit of Father James Feltz, Exhibit 1, paras. 5-6; see also Affidavit of Susana Castro, widow of Perez, Exhibit 6.

5. Affidavit of Felipe Oporta Solano, Exhibit 7, para. 4.

6. *id.*, paras. 5, 7.

7. Affidavit of Father James Feltz, Exhibit 1, para. 8.

8. Affidavit of Valentin Velasquez and Aristina Cerda, Exhibit 3.

9. Affidavit of Augustin Sequeira Rivas, Exhibit 5, paras. 1-5.

10. *id.*, paras. 6-9.

11. Affidavit of Father James Feltz, Exhibit 1, paras. 10-11.

12. *id.*, para. 15.

13. *id.*, para. 16.

14. *id.*, para. 17.

15. Affidavit of Luis Ortiz Martinez, Exhibit 4, paras. 4-5.

16. *id.*, paras. 6-13.

17. *id.*, para. 14.

18. Affidavit of Father James Feltz, Exhibit 1, paras. 18-24.

19. Supplemental Affidavit of Father James Feltz, Exhibit 1, paras. 2-5.

20. *id.*, para. 8.

Chapter 8

1. T. Cabestero, "Dieron la Vida por su Pueblo," *El Tayacan*, Nicaragua (1984), p. 8.

2. Affidavit of Sister Lisa Fitzgerald, Exhibit 5, para. 4.

3. *id.*, para. 6.

4. Fact Sheet Attached to Affidavit of Sister Lisa Fitzgerald, p. 1; See also Chapter 5.

5. *id.*, p. 2.

6. Affidavit of Sister Lisa Fitzgerald, Exhibit 5, para. 7.

7. *id.*, para. 8.

8. *id.*; see also Chapter 1.

9. Affidavit of Wenceslao Ubeda Rivera, Exhibit 4, para. 5.

10. Affidavit of Antonio Valladares Duarte, Exhibit 1, para. 6.

11. *id.*, paras. 5 and 8.

12. *id.*, para. 9.

13. Affidavit of Carmen Gutierrez Castro, Exhibit 2, paras. 3-4.

14. Affidavit of Leonica Corea Canelo, Exhibit 3, paras. 3-5.

15. *id.*, para. 4.

16. Journal attached to Affidavit of Sister Lisa Fitzgerald, Exhibit 5, p. 2.

Chapter 9

1. Their findings are contained in the affadavits of Witness for Peace members Sharon Hostetler and Peter Olson, Exhibits 1 and 2, and in the "Fact Sheet" attached to Peter Olson's affadavit.

2. Affidavit of Maria de los Angeles Montalvan, Exhibit 5, paras. 2-4.

3. *id.*, paras. 6-9.

4. *id.*, paras. 15-17.

5. *id.*, paras. 11-14.

6. Affidavit of Juana Maria Carcamos, Exhibit 3.

7. Fact Sheet attached to the Affidavit of Peter Olson, Exhibit 2.

8. *id.*

9. *id.*, and photographs 1-3 attached to the Affidavit of Sharon Hostetler, Exhibit 1.

10. Fact Sheet attached to the Affidavit of Peter Olson, Exhibit 2.

11. *id.*, and photographs 4-7, attached to the Affidavit of Sharon Hostetler, Exhibit 1.

12. Affidavit of Genaro Paguaga Reyes, Exhibit 7.
13. Affidavit of Ramon Gutierrez, Exhibit 6.
14. Affidavit of Genaro Paguaga Reyes, Exhibit 7, para. 7.
15. *id.*, para. 8.
16. Affidavit of Osmar Amaya Morales, Exhibit 8.
17. Fact Sheet attached to the Affidavit of Peter Olson, Exhibit 2; see also photograph 8, attached to the Affidavit of Sharon Hostetler, Exhibit 1.
18. Fact Sheet attached to the Affidavit of Peter Olson, Exhibit 2.
19. Affidavit of Peter Olson, Exhibit 2, para. 13, and Exhibit B.
20. "CIA Linked to Comic Book for Nicaragua," *New York Times*, Oct. 19, 1984, p. A-8.
21. Affidavit of Reyna Isabel Umanzor, Exhibit 4, para. 5.
22. Fact Sheet attached to the Affidavit of Peter Olson, Exhibit 2.

Chapter 10

1. Affidavit of Zeno Bisoffi, Exhibit 2, incoporating "Pierre Grosjean Medecin au Nicaragua," (Bisoffi, "Grosjean"), p. 22.
2. *id.*, p. 19.
3. Affidavit of Maria Felisa de Solano, Exhibit 1, para. 3.
4. *id.*, para. 6.
5. *id.*, para. 3.
6. *id.*, para. 9.
7. Bisoffi, "Grosjean," Exhibit 2, p. 3.
8. *id.*, and Affidavit of Maria Felisa de Solan, Exhibit 1, paras. 14, 18.
9. *id.*, para. 16.
10. *id.*, para. 17.
11. Bisoffi, "Grosjean," Exhibit 2, p. 6.

Chapter 11

1. Affidavit of Carmela Gutierrez, Exhibit 1, para. 3; Affidavit of Wenceslao Peralta Herrera, Exhibit 2, para. 3.
2. Affidavit of Carmela Gutierrez, Exhibit 1, paras. 2 and 4; Affidavit of Wenceslao Peralta Herrera, Exhibit 2, paras. 2 and 4.
3. Affidavit of Carmela Gutierrez, Exhibit 1, para. 6; Affidavit of Wenceslao Peralta Herrera, Exhibit 2, para. 6.
4. Affidavit of Carmelo Gutierrez, Exhibit 1, para. 5; Affidavit of Wenceslao Peralta Herrera, Exhibit 2, para. 5.
5. Affidavit of Carmela Gutierrez, Exhibit 1, para. 7; Affidavit of Wenceslao Peralta Herrera, Exhibit 2, para. 7.
6. Affidavit of Carmela Gutierrez, Exhibit 1, para. 8; Affidavit of Wenceslao Peralta Herrera, Exhibit 2, para. 8.
7. Affidavit of Carmela Gutierrez, Exhibit 1, para. 9.

8. Affidavit of Wenceslao Peralta Herrera, Exhibit 2, para. 9.

9. Affidavit of Carmela Gutierrez, Exhibit 1, para. 10; Affidavit of Wenceslao Peralta Herrera, Exhibit 2, para. 9.

10. Affidavit of Carmela Gutierrez, Exhibit 1, para. 11; Affidavit of Wenceslao Peralta Herrera, Exhibit 2, para. 10.

11. Affidavit of Carmela Gutierrez, Exhibit 1, para. 12.

12. Affidavit of Carmela Gutierrez, Exhibit 1, para. 14.

13. Affidavit of Wenceslao Peralta Herrera, Exhibit 2, para. 14.

14. Affidavit of Carmela Gutierrez, Exhibit 1, para. 14.

15. Affidavit of Wenceslao Peralta Herrera, Exhibit 2, paras. 12 & 13.

16. *id.*, para. 13.

17. *id.*, para. 19.

18. Affidavit of Carmela Gutierrez, Exhibit 1, para. 17; Affidavit of Wenceslao Peralta Herrera, Exhibit 2, para. 15.

19. Affidavit of Carmela Gutierrez, Exhibit 1, para. 18.

20. Affidavit of Carmela Gutierrez, Exhibit 1, para. 19; Affidavit of Wenceslao Peralta Herrera, Exhibit 2, para. 18.

21. Nesmith, "Contras Bring Terror to Valley in Nicaragua," *Atlanta Constitution*, April 18, 1984, p. 1A.

22. *Id.*, p. 38A.

Chapter 12

1. Affidavit of Father Evaristo Bertrand, Exhibit 2, para. 34.

2. Affidavit of Maria Bustillo Viuda de Blandon, Exhibit 3, paras. 3-5.

3. *id.*, paras. 6-11.

4. *id.*, para. 14.

5. *id.*, para. 16.

6.*id.*

7. Affidavit of Father Evaristo Bertrand, Exhibit 1, paras. 6-12.

8. *id.*

9. Affidavit of Aracelis Torres Aguilar, Exhibit 4, paras. 6-7.

10. *id.*, paras. 9-10.

11. Affidavit of Father Evaristo Bertrand, Exhibit 2, paras. 14-19.

12. Affidavit of Lucio Rodriguez Gradis, Exhibit 3 in Chapter 2, para. 35; Affidavit of Emelina del Carmen Merlo, Exhibit 8, para. 3.

13. Affidavit of Emelina del Carmen Merlo, Exhibit 8, paras. 1-6.

14. *id.*, para. 9; see also Affidavit of Patricio Ruiz Peralta, Exhibit 9.

15. Affidavit of Dora Gutierrez de Altamirano, Exhibit 11, paras. 2-5; Affidavit of Antonio Olivas Zarante, Exhibit 12, para. 2.

16. Affidavit of Dora Gutierrez de Altamirano, Exhibit 11, paras. 2, 7.

17. *id.*, para. 8.

18. Affidavit of Antonio Olivas Zarante, Exhibit 12, paras. 3-5.

19. *id.*, para. 6.

20. *id.*, and Affidavit of of Jose Reynaldo Jiron, Exhibit 10, para. 5.

21. Affidavit of Antonio Olivas Zarante, Exhibit 12, paras. 7-8.

22. *id.*, para. 9-10; Affidavit of Dora Gutierrez de Altamirano, Exhibit 12, para. 12; and Affidavit of of Jose Reynaldo Jiron, Exhibit 10, para. 8.

23. Affidavit of Maria Julia Ortiz, Exhibit 13, paras. 6-7.

24. *id.*, para. 12.

25. *id.*, paras. 9-11.

26. *id.*, para. 12.

27. *id.*, para. 15.

28. Affidavit of Father Evaristo Bertrand, Exhibit 2, para. 24; Affidavit of Maria Soza Valladares, Exhibit 14, para. 2; Affidavit of Aurelia Ortiz Chavarria, Exhibit 15, para. 2; Affidavit of Jose Inez Castellano, Exhibit 17, para. 2; Affidavit of of Presentacion Picardo Garcia, Exhibit 1, para. 2.

29. Affidavit of Maria Soza Valladares, Exhibit 14, paras. 9-16.

30. *id.*, paras. 11-12, 17.

31. Affidavit of Aurelia Ortiz Chavarria, Exhibit 15, para. 5.

32. *id.*, para. 7.

33. Affidavit of Father Evaristo Bertrand, Exhibit 2, para. 34.

34. *id.*, paras. 35-36.

Chapter 13

1. Affidavit of Maria Angela Diaz Montenegro, Exhibit 1, paras. 9-10.

2. *id.*, paras. 4-8.

3. *id.*, paras. 12-16.

4. *id.*, paras. 18, 21.

5. *id.*, paras. 19, 21.

6. *id.*, para. 20.

7. *id.*, para. 27.

8. *id.*, para. 29.

9. *id.*, paras. 30-31.

10. *id.*, para. 37.

11. *id.*, paras. 34-35.

Chapter 14

1. See also Chapters 4, 13, 18, and 21.

2. Affidavit of Inocente Peralta Zamora, Exhibit 1.

3. *id.*, para. 22.
4. *id.*, para. 22.
5. *id.*, paras. 23-24.
6. Affidavit of Terencio de Jesus Flores Hernandez, Exhibit 4, paras. 3-5.
7. *id.*, paras. 7-16.
8. Affidavit of Adrian Ferrufino Siles, Exhibit 2, para. 7.
9. *id.*, para. 3.
10. *id.*, para. 4.
11. *id.*, para. 5.
12. *id.*, para. 6.
13. *id.*, para. 9.
14. *id.*, paras. 10-11.
15. *id.*, paras. 11-12.
16. Affidavit of Terencio de Jesus Flores Hernandez, Exhibit 4, para. 18.
17. *id.*, para. 19.
18. Affidavit of Agusto Cesar Barajona Valladares, Exhibit 3, paras. 6-8.
19. *id.*, paras. 10-11.
20. *id.*, para. 12.
21. *id.*, paras. 14-15.
22. Affidavit of Terencio de Jesus Flores Hernandez, Exhibit 4, paras. 30-32.
23. Affidavit of Doroteo Tinoco Valdivia, Exhibit 5, paras. 4-8.
24. *id.*, para. 11.
25. *id.*, paras. 11-13.
26. *id.*, paras. 13-16.
27. Affidavit of Terencio de Jesus Flores Hernandez, Exhibit 4, para. 26.
28. *id.*, paras. 22-23.
29. *id.*, paras. 24-25.
30. *id.*, para. 28.
31. Affidavit of Terencio de Jesus Flores Hernandez, Exhibit 4, para. 30; Affidavit of Agusto Cesar Barajona Valladares, Exhibit 3, para. 17; Affidavit of Inocente Peralta Zamora, Exhibit 1, para. 4.

Chapter 15

1. Affidavit of Balbino Garcia Lopez, Exhibit 1, paras. 3-10.
2. *id.*, paras. 13, 15.
3. *id.*, paras. 13, 16.
4. *id.*, para. 16.
5. *id.*, paras. 18, 19.
6. *id.*, paras. 21-22.
7. *id.*, para. 25.
8. *id.*, para. 24.

Chapter 16

1. Affidavit of Father Enrique Blandon Vasconcelos, Exhibit 1, para. 2.

2. *id.*, para. 5.

3. *id.*, paras. 6 and 8.

4. *id.*, para. 9.

5. *id.*, para. 10.

6. *id.*, para. 11.

7. *id.*, para. 12.

8. *id.*, para. 13.

9. *id.*, para. 14.

10. *id.*, para. 15.

11. *id.*, para. 16.

12. *id.*

13. *id.*, para. 17.

14. *id.*, para. 20.

15. *id.*

16. *id.*, para. 21.

17. *id.*, para. 23.

18. *id.*, para. 22.

19. *id.*, para. 24.

20. Affidavit of Sister Sandra Price, Exhibit 2, para. 5; Affidavit of Father Enrique Blandon Vasconcelos, Exhibit 1, para. 26.

21. Affidavit of Father Enrique Blandon Vasconcelos, Exhibit 1, para. 26.

22. Affidavit of Father Enrique Blandon Vasconcelos, Exhibit 1, para. 29.

23. *id.*, para. 32.

24. *id.*, para. 30.

25. *id.*, para. 31.

26. *id.*, para. 34.

27. *id.* para. 35.

28. id., para. 36

29. Affidavit of Sister Sandra Price, Exhibit 2, paras. 8, 9.

30. *id.*, paras. 13, 14.

31. *id.*, paras. 15 and 16.

32. *id.*, para. 18.

33. *id.*, para. 20.

34. *id.*, paras. 21 and 24.

35. Affidavit of Florencio Godinez Perez, Exhibit 5, paras. 2-4.

36. *id.*, para. 4.

37. *id.*, para. 5.

38. Affidavit of Cirillo Jarquin Mejia, Exhibit 4, para. 4.

39. *id.*, para. 7.

40. *id.*, para. 15

41. Affidavit of Luz Marina Davila Valle, Exhibit 12, para. 2.

42. *id.*, para 2.

43. *id.*, para. 3. See also Affidavit of Father Enrique Blandon Vasconcelos, Exhibit 1, para. 25.

44. Affidavit of Valeriano Polanco Lopez, Exhibit 6.

45. *id.*

46. Affidavit of Douglas Spence, Exhibit 3.

47. *id.*

48. Affidavit of Pablo Perez Landeros, Exhibit 8.

49. *id.*

50. Affidavit of Pablo Perez Tercero, Exhibit 9.

51. *id.*

52. Affidavit of Eladio Rodriguez Flores, Exhibit 10, para. 2.

53. Affidavit of Cristobal Granado Perez, Exhibit 11.

54. Affidavit of Felix Arauz Mendoza, Exhibit 7.

Chapter 17

1. Affidavit of Ismael Cordoba Centeno, Exhibit 12, para. 2.

2. Affidavit of Angela Zamora Aguirres, Exhibit 13, paras. 2-3.

3. *El Nuevo Diario*, May 23, 1984.

4. Affidavit of Filemon Zavala Cruz, Exhibit 3.

5. Affidavits of Filemon Zavala Cruz, Maria Sabina Galeano, and Maria Anita Hernandez de Martinez, Exhibits 3, 7 and 11.

6. *El Nuevo Diario*, May 23, 1984.

7. Affidavit of Father Enrique Alberto Oggier Rufiner, Exhibit 10, para. 9.

8. Affidavits of Jose Ramon Castillo, Filemon Zavala Cruz and Eusebia Matey Lopez, Exhibits 2, 3, and 5.

9. Affidavit of Jose Ramon Castillo, Exhibit 2, para. 9.

10. *El Nuevo Diario*, May 23, 1984.

11. Affidavit of Father Enrique Alberto Oggier Rufiner, Exhibit 10, para. 10.

12. *id.*, paras. 5-7; Affidavit of Angela Zamora Aguirres, Exhibit 15, para. 4; Affidavit of Maria Sabina Galeano, Exhibit 7, para. 6; Affidavit of Maria Anita Hernandez de Martinez, Exhibit 11, paras. 4-5.

13. Affidavit of Angela Zamora Aguirres, Exhibit 15, para. 6.

14. Affidavit of Ismael Cordoba Centeno, Exhibit 12, paras. 1, 5.

15. Affidavit of Maria Espinoza Zavala, Exhibit 14, paras. 2, 6.

16. Affidavit of Flora Cordoba Centeno, Exhibit 13, para. 4.

17. Affidavit of Maria Anita Hernandez, Exhibit 11, paras. 3, 6.

18. Affidavits of Etemina Rodriguez, Exhibit 4, and Maria Guadalupe Rodriguez, Exhibit 1.

19. Affidavit of Father Enrique Alberto Oggier Rufiner, Exhibit 10, para. 12.

20. *Barricada*, September 24, 1984.

21. Affidavit of Father Enrique Alberto Oggier Rufiner, Exhibit 10, para. 13.

22. *id.*, para. 3.

23. *id.*, para. 14.

Chapter 18

1. Affidavit of Lucilia Chavarria Lanza, Exhibit 7, para. 5; Affidavit of Olivia Benavides Meza, Exhibit 2, para. 2.

2. Affidavit of Cristovalino Sovalbarro, Exhibit 4, para. 5; see also Affidavit of Olivia Benavides Meza, Exhibit 2, para. 3.

3. Affidavit of Lucilia Chavarria Lanza, Exhibit 1, para. 6.

4. *id.*, para. 7.

5. *id.*, para. 8.

6. *id.*, and Affidavit of Abrahan Castro, Exhibit 3, para. 6.

7. Affidavit of Olivia Benavides Meza, Exhibit 2, para. 3.

8. Affidavit of Lucilia Chavarria Lanza, Exhibit 1, para. 9.

9. *id.*, para. 12.

10. *id.*

11. Affidavit of Abrahan Castro, Exhibit 3, para. 9.

12. See *id.* and Affidavit of Lucilia Chavarria Lanza, Exhibit 1, para. 16.

13. *id.*, paras. 17-18.

14. *id.*, para. 19.

15. Affidavit of Maria Castro, Exhibit 6, paras. 3-4; Affidavit of Carmen Castro, Exhibit 5, para. 4.

16. Affidavit of Maria Castro, Exhibit 6, para. 4.

Chapter 19

1. Statement of Sister Nancy Donovan, attached to her affidavit, Exhibit 1, p. 5.

2. *id.*, p. 1.

3. *id.*

4. *id.*, p. 2.

5. *id.*, p. 3.

6. *id.*, p. 4.

7. *id.*

8. *id.*, pp. 4-5.

Chapter 20

1. Affidavit of Federica Alvarez Johnary, Exhibit 1, para. 5; Affidavit of Jorge Barrow Vicente, Exhibit 2, para. 3.

2. Affidavit of Federica Alvarez Johnary, Exhibit 1, paras. 4-5; Affidavit of Jorge Barrow Vicente, Exhibit 2, para. 4.

3. Affidavit of Federica Alvarez Johnary, Exhibit 1, para. 5.

4. *id.*, para. 10.

5. Affidavit of Jorge Barrow Vicente, Exhibit 2, para. 6.

6. *id.*, paras. 8-9.

7. *id.*, para. 8.

8. Affidavit of Federica Alvarez Johnary, Exhibit 1, para. 11; Affidavit of Jorge Barrow Vicente, Exhibit 2, para. 10.

9. Affidavit of Jorge Barrow Vicente, Exhibit 2, para. 11.

10. *id.*, para. 12.

11. Affidavit of Federica Alvarez Johnary, Exhibit 1, para. 12.

12. *id.*, para. 15.

13. *id.*, para. 16.

14. *id.*, para. 17.

15. Affidavit of Federica Alvarez Johnary, Exhibit 1, para. 13, (6 dead); Affidavit of Jorge Barrow Vicente, Exhibit 2, para. 17, ("about 7").

16. Affidavit of Jorge Barrow Vicente, Exhibit 2, para. 17.

Chapter 21

1. Affidavit of Jose Anibal Gonzalez Lopez, Exhibit 2, paras. 5-9.

2. *id.*, para. 11.

3. *id.*, para. 20.

4. *id.*, para. 12.

5. *id.*, para. 13.

6. *id.*, para. 19.

7. *id.*, paras. 15, 18.

8. *id.*, para. 19.

Chapter 22

1. Affidavit of Jose Anibal Gonzalez Lopez, Exhibit 1, paras.

2. *id.*

3. *id.*, paras. 8-9.

4. *id.*, paras. 10-13.

5. *id.*, paras. 14-18.

6. Affidavit of Antonio Espinoza Morales, Exhibit 2, para. 5.

7. *id.*, paras. 6-7.

8. *id.*, paras. 10-11.

9. *id.*, para. 12.

10. *id.*, paras. 15-17.

11. *id.*, paras. 23-24.

12. *id.*, para. 26.

13. *id.*, para. 30.

14. Affidavit of Ernesto Pineda Gutierrez, Exhibit 3, paras. 4-6.

15. *id.*, paras. 7-8.
16. *id.*, paras. 9-13.
17. *id.*, para. 14.
18. *id.*, paras. 15-18.
19. *id.*, paras. 20-22.
20. *id.*, paras. 23-28.
21. *id.*, paras. 29-31.
22. *id.*, para. 32.
23. *id.*, paras. 33-34.
24. Affidavit of Moise Fajardo Sambrana, Exhibit 4, para. 3.
25. *id.*, paras. 4-12.
26. *id.*, paras. 13-15.
27. *id.*, para. 16.
28. Affidavit of Jose de la Luz Padilla Rojas, Exhibit 5, para. 3.
29. *id.*, para. 6.
30. *id.*, para. 9.
31. *id.*, para. 15.
32. *id.*, paras. 16-17.
33. Affidavit of Amado Gutierrez Diaz, Exhibit 6, para. 2.
34. *id.*
35. *id.*, para. 3.

B. Mass Kidnappings

1. Affidavit of Baudilio Rivera, Exhibit 1 to Sukatpin chapter, para. 17.

Chapter 23

1. Affidavit of Rosalia Gutierrez Lopez, Exhibit 1, para. 3.
2. Affidavit of Juan Bustillo Mendoza, Exhibit 5, para. 8.
3. *id.*, paras. 5-7.
4. *id.*, paras. 9-13.
5. Affidavit of Hereberto Siles Martinez, Exhibit 6, paras. 5-6.
6. Affidavit of Nicolas Chan Irias, Exhibit 4, paras. 4-9.
7. Affidavit of Rosalia Gutierrez Lopez, Exhibit 1, para. 12; Affidavit of Nicolas Chan Irias, Exhibit 4, para. 14. In its report "Trabil Nani", at p. 37, the Centro de Investigaciones y Documentacion Sobre la Costa Atlantica, a government-funded research institute, gives an estimate of 1,250.
8. Affidavit of Nicolas Chan Irias, Exhibit 4, para. 14.
9. *id.*
10. Affidavit of Nicolas Chan Irias, Exhibit 4, para. 12; Affidavit of Hereberto Siles Martinez, Exhibit 6, para. 8.
11. Affidavit of Rosalia Gutierrez Lopez, Exhibit 1, para. 11; Affidavit of Nicolas Chan Irias, Exhibit 4, para. 15.
12. Affidavit of Rosalia Gutierrez Lopez, Exhibit 1, paras. 12-16; Affidavit of Nicolas Chan Irias, Exhibit 4, paras. 6-15.

13. Affidavit of Inocente Tinoco Diaz, Exhibit 3, paras. 11-13.
14. Affidavit of Juan Bustillo Mendoza, Exhibit 5, paras. 17-18.
15. Affidavit of Rosalia Gutierrez Lopez, Exhibit 1, para. 18.
16. *id.*, paras. 20-24.
17. Affidavit of Juan Bustillo Mendoza, Exhibit 5, para. 24.
18. Affidavit of Rosalia Gutierrez Lopez, Exhibit 1, para. 25.
19. *id.*, para. 28.
20. *id.*, para. 30.
21. Affidavit of Gregorio Winter, Exhibit 2, para. 4.
22. Affidavit of Rosalia Gutierrez Lopez, Exhibit 1, para. 31.
23. *id.*, para. 33.
24. *id.*, paras. 34-37.
25. *id.*, paras. 40-43.
26. *id.*, paras. 41-43.
27. Affidavit of Juan Bustillo Mendoza, Exhibit 5, paras. 28-29.
28. *id.*, para. 30.
29. *id.*, paras. 31-32.
30. Affidavit of Juan Bustillo Mendoza, Exhibit 5, paras. 33-43.
31. Affidavit of Rosalia Gutierrez Lopez, Exhibit 1, paras. 47-49.
32. *id.*, para. 50.
33. *id.*
34. Affidavit of Nicolas Chan Irias, Exhibit 4, para. 18.
35. Affidavit of Rosalia Gutierrez Lopez, Exhibit 1, para. 54.
36. *id.*, para. 51.
37. *id.*, para. 56; Supplemental Affidavit of Nicolas Chan Irias, Exhibit 4, para. 7.
38. Affidavit of Rosalia Gutierrez Lopez, Exhibit 1, para. 56.
39. *id.*, paras. 57-59.
40. *id.*, para. 61.
41. Supplemental Affidavit of Nicolas Chan Irias, Exhibit 4, para 6.
42. *id.*, paras. 10-14.
43. Affidavit of Nicolas Chan Irias, Exhibit 4, paras. 19-28.
44. Affidavit of Rosalia Gutierrez Lopez, Exhibit 1, paras. 62-72.

Chapter 24

1. Affidavit of Orlando Wayland Waldiman, Exhibit 1, para. 11; Affidavit of Otto Borst Conrado, Exhibit 2, para. 12.
2. Affidavit of Orlando Wayland Waldiman, Exhibit 2, para. 7.
3. *id.*, para. 8.
4. Affidavit of Lucio Vargas Hooker, Exhibit 3, para. 5.
5. *id.*

6. *id.*, para. 9.

7. *id.*

8. Affidavit of Otto Borst Conrado, Exhibit 2, paras. 16-17.

9. *id.*, paras. 17-18.

10. *id.*, paras. 20-21.

11. Affidavit of Orlando Wayland Waldiman, Exhibit 1, para. 9; Affidavit of Otto Borst Conrado, Exhibit 2, para. 19.

12. Affidavit of Orlando Wayland Waldiman, Exhibit 1, para. 9; Affidavit of Otto Borst Conrado, Exhibit 2, para. 14.

13. Affidavit of Orlando Wayland Waldiman, Exhibit 2, para. 13.

14. *id.*, paras. 20-21.

15. *id.*, paras. 21-23.

16. Affidavit of Otto Borst Conrado, Exhibit 2, para. 29.

17. Affidavit of Orlando Wayland Waldiman, Exhibit 1, para. 14.

18. Affidavit of Orlando Wayland Waldiman, Exhibit 7, para. 10.

19. *id.*, para. 15.

20. Affidavit of Otto Borst Conrado, Exhibit 2, para. 27; Affidavit of Lucio Vargas Hooker, Exhibit 3, paras. 10-15.

21. Affidavit of Otto Borst Conrado, Exhibit 2, para. 28.

22. *id.*

23. *id.*, para. 31.

24. Affidavit of Orlando Wayland Waldiman, Exhibit 1, para. 17.

25. *id.*, para. 20.

26. *id.*, para. 11.

27. *id.*, para. 22.

28. *id.*, paras. 23-24.

29. *id.*, paras. 25-26.

30. *id.*, para. 26.

31. *id.*, para. 28.

32. *id.*, para. 30-31.

33. *id.*, paras. 32-33.

34. *id.*, paras. 33-35.

35. *id.*, paras. 36-42.

36. *id.*, para. 43.

37. *id.*, paras. 44-48.

38. *id.*, para. 49.

39. *id.*

40. *id.*, paras. 49-50.

41. *id.*, para. 51.

42. *id.*, para. 52.

43. *id.*, paras. 53-54.

44. *id.*, para. 55.

45. *id.*

46. *id.*, para. 56.

47. *id.*, paras. 57-61.

48. Affidavit of Otto Borst Conrado Exhibit 2, para. 38.
49. *id.*
50. *id.*, para. 35.
51. Affidavit of Lucio Vargas Hooker, Exhibit 3, paras. 11-12, 20.
52. *id.*, para 17.
53. *id.*
54. *id.*, para. 19; Affidavit of Otto Borst Conrado, Exhibit 2, para. 39.

Chapter 25

1. Affidavit of Father Martin Piner Miranda, Exhibit 1, paras. 1-4, 10.
2. *id.*, paras. 5, 10.
3. *id.*, para. 8.
4. *id.*, para. 9.
5. *id.*, paras. 6, 10.
6. *id.*, paras. 12-15.
7. *id.*, paras. 12-15.
8. *id.*, paras. 16-17.
9. *id.*, para. 18.
10. *id.*, para. 19.
11. *id.*, paras. 20-25.
12. *id.*, paras. 24-26.
13. *id.*, paras. 27-32.
14. *id.*, paras. 33-35.
15. *id.*, paras. 36-39.
16. *id.*, paras. 40-41.
17. *id.*, paras. 42-43.
18. *id.*, paras. 44-45.
19. *id.*, para. 47.
20. *id.*, paras. 49-51.
21. *id.*, paras. 59-60.
22. *id.*, paras. 61-62.

Chapter 26

1. Affidavit of Baudilio Rivera Perrera, Exhibit 1, paras. 3-4.
2. *id.*, para. 6.
3. *id.*, para. 5.
4. *id.*, paras. 9-12.
5. *id.*, paras. 12-14.
6. *id.*, paras. 15-16.
7. *id.*, para. 18.
8. *id.*, para. 19.
9. *id.*, para. 22.

10. *id.*, para. 24.
11. *id.*, paras. 2, 26.

Chapter 27

1. Affidavit of Johnny Briman Lopez, Exhibit 1, para. 6.
2. *id.*, para. 9.
3. *id.*, para. 8-10.
4. *id.*, para. 11.
5. *id.*, para. 15-16.
6. *id.*, paras. 17-19.
7. *id.*, para. 22-23.

Chapter 28

1. Affidavit of Digna Barreda de Ubeda, Exhibit 1, paras. 1-2.
2. *id.*, paras. 6-11.
3. *id.*, para. 12.
4. *id.*, para. 14.
5. *id.*, paras. 15-18.
6. *id.*, para. 20.
7. *id.*, para. 20.
8. *id.*, paras. 21-22.
9. *id.*, para. 23.
10. *id.*, paras. 25-32.
11. *id.*, paras. 33-34.
12. *id.*, para. 35.
13. *id.*, paras. 37-38.
14. *id.*, para. 43.
15. *id.*, paras. 39-40.
16. *id.*, paras. 44-47.
17. *id.*, paras. 48 and 51.
18. *id.*, para. 52.
19. *id.*, paras. 53-56.
20. Affidavit of Marta Arauz de Ubeda, Exhibit 2, paras. 1 and 3.
21. *id.*, paras. 4-9.
22. *id.*, para. 11.
23. *id.*, paras. 12-15.
24. *id.*, paras. 15-17.
25. *id.*, para. 18.
26. *id.*, paras. 19-22.
27. *id.*, paras. 23-27.
28. Interview attached to Affidavit of Mirna Cunningham, Exhibit 3, pp. 19-20.
29. *id.*, p. 20.
30. *id.*, p. 20.

31. *id.*, pp. 20-21.

32. *id.*, p. 21.

33. *id.*, p. 22.

34. *id.*, p. 23.

35. *id.*, p. 23.

36. Affidavit of Mileydis Salina Azevedo, Exhibit 4, paras. 3 and 4.

37. Affidavit of Ermelina Diaz Talavera, Exhibit 5, para. 4.

38. Affidavit of Mileydis Salina Azevedo, Exhibit 4, para. 3; Affidavit of Ermelina Diaz Talavera, Exhibit 5, para. 6.

39. Affidavit of Mileydis Salina Azevedo, Exhibit 4, para. 6 and Affidavit of Ermelina Diaz Talavera, Exhibit 5, para. 7.

40. Affidavit of Ermelina Diaz Talavera, Exhibit 5, para. 8.

41. *id.*, para. 12.

42. Affidavit of Mileydis Salina Azevedo, Exhibit 4, paras. 10, 20; Affidavit of Ermelina Diaz Talavera, Exhibit 5, paras. 10, 11.

43. Affidavit of Mileydis Salina Azevedo, Exhibit 4, para. 20; Affidavit of Ermelina Diaz Talavera, Exhibit 5, para. 10.

44. Affidavit of Mileydis Salina Azevedo, Exhibit 4, para. 20.

45. *id.*, paras. 21 and 22; Affidavit of Ermelina Diaz Talavera, Exhibit 5, paras. 13 and 14.

46. Affidavit of Mileydis Salina Azevedo, Exhibit 4, para. 23; and Affidavit of Ermelina Diaz Talavera, Exhibit 5, para. 15.

47. Affidavit of Abelina Inestroza, Exhibit 7, para 6; see also Affidavit of Josefina Inestoza de Reyes, Exhibit 6, para. 6.

48. Affidavit of Josefina Inestroza de Reyes, Exhibit 6, para. 7.

49. *id.*, para. 8; Affidavit of Abelina Inestroza, Exhibit 7, paras. 8-9.

BIBLIOGRAPHY

Americas Watch. *Violations of the Laws of War by Both Sides in Nicaragua 1981-85*. New York, 1985.

____*Human Rights in Nicaragua: Rhetoric and Reality*. July 1985.

____*The Miskitos in Nicaragua 1981-84*. 1984.

Berryman, Phillip. *Inside Central America*. New York: Pantheon, 1985.

Black, George. *Triumph of the People: The Sandinista Revolution in Nicaragua*. London: Zed Press, 1981.

Brown, Cynthia, ed. *With Friends Like These: The Americas Watch Report on Human Rights and U.S. Policy in Latin America*. New York: Pantheon, 1985.

Cabestrero, Teofilo. *Blood of the Innocent: Victims of the Contras' War in Nicaragua*. New York: Orbis Books, 1985.

Center for International Policy. "Contadora: A Text for Peace," *International Policy Report*, November 1984.

Collins, Joseph with Frances Moore Lappe, Nick Allen and Paul Rice. *Nicaragua: What Difference Could a Revolution Make?*. San Francisco: Food First/Institute for Food and Development Policy, revised edition, 1985.

Garfield Richard and David Siegel. *Health and the War Against Nicaragua 1981-1984*. New York: The Central America Health Rights Network/LINKS, 1985.

Grossman, Karl. *Nicaragua: America's New Vietnam*. Sag harbor, New York: The Permanent Press, 1984.

International Human Rights Law Group and Washington Office on Latin America. *A Political Opening in Nicaragua: Report on the Nicaraguan Elections, November 4, 1984*. Washington, D.C.: Washington Office on Latin America, 1984.

Latin American Studies Association. *The Electoral Process in Nicaragua: Domestic and International Influences*. Austin, Texas: Central America Resource Center, 1984.

Lawyers Committee for International Human Rights. *Nicaragua, Revolutionary Justice: A Report on Human Rights and the Judicial System*. April 1985.

Miller, Valerie. *Between Struggle and Hope: The Nicaraguan Literacy Crusade*. Westview, Connecticut: Westview Press, 1985.

Nairn, Allan. "Endgame: A Special Report on U.S. Military Strategy in Central America," *NACLA: Report on the Americas*. May/June 1984.

National Action Research on the Military Industrial Complex. *Invasion: A Guide to the U.S. Military Presence in Nicaragua*. Philadelphia: American Friends Service Committee, 1985.

Policy Alternatives for the Caribbean and Central America (PACCA). *Changing Course: Blueprint for Peace in Central America and the Caribbean*. Washington, D.C.: Institute for Policy Studies, 1984.

Rosset, Peter and John Vandermeer. *The Nicaragua Reader: Documents of a Revolution Under Fire*. New York: Grove Press, 1983.

U.S. Central Intelligence Agency. *Psychological Operations in Guerilla Warfare*. New York: Vintage, 1985.

Witness for Peace. *What We Have Seen and Heard: The Effect of Contra Attacks Against Nicaragua*. Washington, D.C., 1985.